PLAYING WITH TIGERS

PLAYING
WITH
TIGERS

A Minor League Chronicle of the Sixties

George Gmelch

UNIVERSITY OF NEBRASKA PRESS

Lincoln and London

© 2016 by George Gmelch

A version of chapter 3 previously appeared as "Rookie Ball, 1965," *NINE* (2012). A version of chapter 5 previously appeared as "Tiger Town: Spring Training, 1966," *NINE* (2013).

Library of Congress Cataloging-in-Publication Data

Names: Gmelch, George, author.
Title: Playing with Tigers: a Minor League chronicle of the Sixties / George Gmelch.
Description: Lincoln: University of Nebraska Press, [2015] | Includes bibliographical references.
Identifiers: LCCN 2015032704
ISBN 9780803276819 (cloth: alk. paper)
ISBN 9780803284852 (epub)
ISBN 9780803284869 (mobi)
ISBN 9780803284876 (pdf)
Subjects: LCSH: Minor league baseball—United States—Anecdotes. | Baseball players—United States—Anecdotes. | Gmelch, George. | Baseball—United States—History—20th century. | Detroit Tigers (Baseball team)—History—20th century.
Classification: LCC GV875.A1 G58 2015 | DDC 796.357/640977434—dc23 LC record available at http://lccn.loc.gov/2015032704

Set in Lyon by M. Scheer.
Designed by Rachel Gould.

For my teammates

Alex, Hook, Shifty, Pig, Polak,

Felber, Fitz, Granny, Humper,

and others who shared their stories of our

baseball times together

CONTENTS

ILLUSTRATIONS

ACKNOWLEDGMENTS

This book did not spring full-blown from my head or from my 1960s journals and letters. It grew out of many conversations with colleagues, friends, and former teammates to whom I am greatly indebted. Jean Ardell, Howard DeNike, Rob Elias, Sharon Gmelch, Dan Gordon, and Mary Mar were superstar editors. Jack Fitzpatrick, Bob Gear, Morgan Gmelch, Walt Gmelch, David Jaeger, Craig Root, Diane Royal, Peter Rutkoff, and Tim Wiles made valuable suggestions. My editor at the University of Nebraska Press, Rob Taylor, and my agent, Rob Wilson, were a sounding board and provided wise counsel. Jean Ardell, Rob Elias, Liz McKenzie, and Dan Nathan urged me to tell the inner story and helped me to understand what a memoir must do to invite readers into another person's world. Others, when invited to read some of the manuscript, were too kind to say no, even when they had much better things to do. Champions in this much-underestimated art were Larry Hill, Joanna LaFrancesca, Franklin Otto, Joan Piasta, Barnett Richling, Bill Tierney, and Bob Wheelock. Annette Wenda was a champion copy editor.

I am also grateful to the following former teammates, managers, and sportswriters who read specific chapters relating to seasons we shared together: Dave Bike, Les Cain, Larry Calton, Claude Coté, Bob Felber, Dennis Grossini, Gail Henley, Greg Kuhl, John Noce, Frank Pignataro, Jim Riggs, Pierre Roux, Carl Solarek, and Jon Warden. They served as fact-checkers along with providing fresh anecdotes. I have depended on all of these readers to know what to keep and what to excise.

I am also indebted to my former girlfriends Claire and Audrey, both pseudonyms, for digging into their memories to help me reconstruct our times together. Dan Nathan and Kenji Tierney recommended more good books and articles on memory and sport than my slow reading could ever digest. Thanks also to Judith Hoch, Amy Joseph, and Audrey Zielinski for their assistance in miscellaneous ways.

For photographs I thank Randall Anderson of the Chautauqua Sports Hall of Fame, New York; Traci Thompson of the Braswell Library, Rocky Mount, North Carolina; Marlee Teadt of the Detroit Tigers; Kevin Logan at the Lakeland Public Library, Florida; Jim Riggs of the *Jamestown (NY) Morning Journal*; Claude Coté; and Joanne Lincoln.

I owe my colleagues at the annual "Baseball and American Culture" symposia in Cooperstown, New York, and the journal *NINE*'s annual spring-training conference in Phoenix for providing a nurturing atmosphere for baseball scholarship of all stripes. The University of San Francisco's Faculty Development Fund generously supported the research and provided funds for several creative and diligent student research assistants in Joanna LaFrancesca, Joan Piasta, and Diane Royal. At the National Baseball Hall of Fame, Freddy Berowski, Bill Francis, and Tim Wiles were always ready to lend a hand. Town librarians and historians, including Timothy Johnson in Rocky Mount, North Carolina, and Carrie Radam in Daytona Beach, Florida, tracked down local news coverage of teams I played for. I thank my late mother, Edna Gmelch, for having saved my letters and clippings and for being an exemplary parent and role model. I learned more from her than I could ever acknowledge. I thank my son, Morgan, for not being too freaked out by details of his father's early sex life and reckless youth. Finally, I owe my wife and fellow anthropologist, Sharon Gmelch, an enormous debt. She was a sounding board throughout and encouraged me to stick with it when I had doubts.

INTRODUCTION

Nearly twenty-five years after my career ended ignominiously, with no chance of redemption, I came back to baseball. My wife, Sharon, who like me had become a professor of anthropology, suggested the idea. It was the early 1990s, and with the boom in popularity of baseball a few social scientists had begun to study the game. Sharon thought it would be interesting for me to look at how the culture of professional baseball had changed since the 1960s, when I had last played in the Detroit Tigers organization.

I hadn't paid much attention to the game since, except when asked to explain something—like why left-handed batters are better lowball hitters—by someone who knew I had played pro ball. During the summers we were usually abroad doing fieldwork in places where the American game was out of sight and without media coverage. And I also may have ignored it because I didn't want to be reminded of the mess I had made of my career due to the awakening of my social conscience. But as our son, Morgan, began playing Little League and I agreed to coach, my interest in the game started to return. Then one day as I walked through the parlor while Morgan was watching a game on TV, I noticed a familiar face on the screen—Jim Leyland, my old teammate, who was then managing the Pittsburgh Pirates. Another former teammate, Gene Lamont, stood in the coaching box at third base, fifty pounds heavier but still recognizable. With two former teammates still in baseball, my going back to study the game entered the realm of possibility. I sat down with Morgan and watched the rest of the game, eager to see more of Leyland and Lamont. Before long I was planning my return.

My initial thought was to relate the changes in baseball to the changes in American society over the past thirty years, to look at baseball as social history. Did the increase in international players, specialization on the field (such as the designated hitter [DH] and closers), and growing income inequality between elite players and all others reflect similar changes in American society? Put differently, was baseball really a microcosm of the larger society? This idea fizzled after I attended a well-known symposium, "Baseball and American Culture," held annually at the Baseball Hall of Fame in Cooperstown, New York. The symposium draws baseball scholars, especially historians, from around the country. After listening to their papers and discussions about the game and its place in American society, I realized I was out of my league. As an anthropologist devoted to the study of other cultures, I knew comparatively little about historical trends in my own society. It was presumptuous to think I would have something new to add.

But the symposium did point me in a new direction. During the discussion of a paper on professional baseball in Canada, the speaker mentioned to the audience that I had once played in the Québec Provincial League (QPL) and might be able to shed some light on the topic. Cast in the role of insider, I did have something to contribute. After the session several participants came up to me with further questions. The advantage of once having been a player became apparent, as were my own discipline's methodology and perspective. I redefined my inquiry: I would do an *ethnography* of professional baseball in the same fashion as I had previously studied Irish Travellers, English Gypsies, Alaskan Natives, and Barbadian villagers. I would seek an insider's perspective and render explicit what is often unseen or obscure to fans, such as why superstitions and pranks are such a big part of the life.

When I returned home I retrieved the journals I had kept during my playing days from our attic. I was stunned to find this entry from Rocky Mount, dated July 1, 1967: *If I play minor league baseball long enough, I would like to write a book about the rigors of the life.* I had no recollection of ever wanting to write a book about baseball. I also wondered why I mentioned only the Minor Leagues. Had I already concluded I wasn't going to make it to the big leagues?

Long accustomed to doing fieldwork by taking up residence with the people I wished to study and immersing myself in their lives, I wondered how I might do this with ballplayers. Perhaps accompanying teams on road trips was the answer: it would allow me to be in close quarters with the players and coaches on the bus and in hotels, restaurants, and clubhouses. But when I first proposed traveling with the AA Birmingham Barons—a team co-owned by my college friend Marty Kuehnert—no one in the parent Chicago White Sox organization would approve my request. Marty discovered that they were concerned about what I might write. As Marty persisted, my bid to shadow the Barons on a road trip passed up and down the organizational chain until it reached the desk of White Sox president Jerry Reinsdorf. He took a chance, and I began traveling with the Barons.

As the Barons' bus pulled out of the stadium parking lot on a hot, sticky day in mid-June 1992—destination Jacksonville, Florida—the manager, Tony Franklin, stood up to introduce me: "I'd like you to meet George Gmelch. He's an anthropologist studying your lives as ballplayers. I don't know why anyone would find what you do interesting, but that's his business and he's a whole lot smarter than me [laughter]. Anyway, he was a player in the Tigers organization in the sixties, so he knows his way around. I want you to help him any way you can." The players turned in their seats, craning to get a good look at me. I smiled a lot, trying not to show my nervousness.

I realized quickly how different the world of pro ball had become.

We'd gone only a mile from the ballpark when the team bus pulled into a Blockbuster video store. A half-dozen players piled off and returned with a stack of videos. Around four in the morning, during the fifth consecutive film, *Robo Cop 2*, I finally wadded up bits of paper napkin, stuffed them in my ears, and thought back to the cramped team buses of the sixties when players passed the time playing cards and trivia games, looking out the window, and talking. Back then, someone often had a guitar, and a few would join in singing, or we'd listen to the music from Shifty Gear's ruby-red record player in the back of the bus. On the Barons' bus the banter and fellowship I fondly remembered were missing. After one player's Walkman broke, he told me he didn't know how he was going to survive the trip. I began to think of myself as a baseball Rip Van Winkle waking up after a twenty-year sleep in academia.

In the coming days there were times when I also doubted my abilities to do the research. In my playing days few players had been to college, and there was wariness about things intellectual. I had been nicknamed "Moonbeam," largely because I read books and sometimes visited libraries. Some of this atmosphere still existed. When I met Jamestown Expos manager Eddie Creech for the first time and used the term *occupational subculture* in explaining my research, he said, "Whoa, slow down with them big words. You're talking to an uneducated southern boy." Creech turned out to be bright, articulate, and helpful, but his response made me wonder how his players would react to my scholarly queries and whether I could even relate to the guys. Would they accept a bearded, graying, middle-aged professor hanging out with them?

My concerns, though, proved baseless. On the night of that first road trip with the Barons, as I made my way to the back of the bus to use the toilet, the players I passed, some half asleep in the darkened bus, briskly moved their outstretched legs from the aisle to let me by. It was a small gesture but done in a way that suggested I was welcome. Once I got the hang of traveling with Minor League teams and got to know the players better, my insecurity disappeared and I shed the baggage of my past.

One of the great pleasures of returning to baseball was being back in ballparks. Ballparks are magical places—emerald-green fields crisply outlined in chalk, the sweep of the grandstands stacked in tiers, and the silhouette of the light towers with their bright lights against the dark night sky. Phillip Lowry titled his book *Green Cathedrals* because the more he studied ballparks, the more he thought they resembled places of worship. Ballparks are also exciting for their activity—batting practice (BP), fielders taking infield, outfielders shagging fungos, fans pleading for autographs, players being interviewed by the media, others sprawled on the grass stretching or playing pepper, groundskeepers watering the deep-brown infield dirt or renewing the foul lines with fresh chalk. For me no research setting will ever match the ballpark.

A few years later, when I submitted the book manuscript that emerged from the research for publication, a Simon and Schuster editor suggested that I scrap the ethnography and write a memoir. I dismissed the idea then, having no interest in writing about my own experiences and clueless how I would go about it even if I wanted to. Instead, I submitted my manuscript elsewhere; it was published by the Smithsonian Institution Press as *Inside Pitch: Life in Professional Baseball*. Apparently, though, I never completely forgot the editor's suggestion. In 2010, while reading a new Minor League memoir, the idea sprang back full force. For three nights I laid awake recalling teammates, experiences, and stories from my playing days. The images were so vivid that I put a tape recorder beside my bed so I could dictate notes and soon decided I'd give memoir a try while retaining my anthropological lens and using some of my previous research to reconstruct the culture and times of Minor League ball in my day—the 1960s.

The material in this memoir draws on the journals I kept while a player, letters I wrote home, and recent interviews with thirty former teammates, coaches, club officials, and girlfriends, the vast majority with whom I'd had no contact since 1970. The Internet made it possible to track them down. I probably could not have written this book without it. Nor could I without my journals and letters (which my mother had stored away in an old file cabinet), whose entries tracked my ups and downs, revealed my insecurities, provided long-forgotten details, and documented a political awakening. Some passages elicited entirely new recollections. Each remembrance was like another piece in a puzzle. Excerpts from my journals and letters are *italicized* in the text. Also useful were the notes I made at the time for the features I wrote for a San Francisco Bay Area newspaper about Minor League life.[1]

After a while I came to think of the research as an *archaeology* of memory—excavating scraps of recollections from all these sources and then assembling them into a picture of the past. I also combed through the old sport sections of the local newspapers from the half-dozen towns I played in. As I cranked the microfilm reader, the days of seemingly endless baseball seasons rolled by, fleshing out what had happened and sometimes contradicting my own memories. On the front pages, which I found hard to skip, I reencountered the harsh reports of the Vietnam War, the ghastly assassinations of Robert Kennedy and Martin Luther King, deteriorating race relations, riots in Chicago and Los Angeles, the civil rights movement, and the beginnings of the countercultural revolution. I was taken aback by how much had happened during the years I was a ballplayer—and disappointed at how long it took me to notice.

But perhaps it shouldn't have been surprising, for when I went off that first season in 1965 to play rookie ball in Duluth, Minnesota, I knew little of the world, or about life, for that matter. I'd barely ventured outside of the all-white, middle-class Bay Area suburb of my childhood. Over the next four seasons, however, I would come of age in baseball's Minor Leagues. It was an education unlike any other, from learning the craft of the professional game to becoming conscious of race and class for the first time. In the course of doing so, I threw off religion and acquired politics. While playing in the Midwest, Northeast, mid-Atlantic, and Florida, I got to know small-town America—all against the backdrop of the Vietnam War and civil rights protests and the emerging counterculture. The social and political turmoil of the times spilled over into the world of baseball with personal consequences, especially after my immersion in the Jim Crow South.

While *Playing with Tigers: A Minor League Chronicle of the Sixties* recounts the struggle of young athletes trying to make their way in the Minor Leagues in that era, its significance goes beyond baseball's farm system. Fans can never fully understand Major League ballplayers without understanding the Minor League system that produced them. The Minors are where future big leaguers learn the *culture* of pro ball—the professional brand of the game along with its codes or unwritten rules. It is also where they learn to cope with the physical and psychological demands of playing every day, where they acquire a nickname, discover groupies, learn the importance of staying on an "even keel," and develop their identities as professional athletes. Unlike players in the National Football League (NFL) and National Basketball Association (NBA), Major League Baseball (MLB) players serve a long apprenticeship—an average of four years before the lucky few get called up. Only 8 percent of Minor League players starting out in rookie ball ever make it to the big leagues—a success rate so low that it says much about the powerful allure of pro ball that keeps young men in its grasp.

Far more professional baseball in America is actually played in the Minor Leagues than in the Majors. While there are only two big leagues, the American (AL) and the National (NL), the Minors have sixteen leagues—the International League, Pacific Coast League, Southern League, Northwest League, California League, and Carolina League, to name just a few—encompassing more than 180 teams. For the countless fans in the towns they play in, whether tiny Pulaski, Virginia, or metropolitan Buffalo and New Orleans, Minor League Baseball is the game in town.

Memoir is less the sequence of one's life than the *stories* that have given that life its shape and make the past come alive. To write a memoir is to repossess those stories. For me, looking back to the sixties as I attempted to put my and my teammates' baseball experiences into words has restored a vanished world.

PLAYING WITH TIGERS

1

AMBITION FOR THE GAME

While I don't remember exactly when baseball first gripped me, I did find some clues in letters my mother wrote to my father while he was on a business trip in Asia. "George is still very interested in baseball and plays every afternoon," she wrote in May 1954, when I was nine. Another day she noted, "It's drizzling, and the boys are still outside playing baseball and haven't come home. I hope they're not too wet." Her letters merely indicate that I, like so many American boys in the 1950s, with far fewer alternative games and pastimes than today, had a passion for baseball. At that time I only knew the sandlot variety.

Our field, one block away, was an uneven and rocky stretch of undeveloped land beneath a steep hillside in suburban San Mateo, California. It was slated to be bulldozed for new housing. Contrary to the adult-supervised Little League, we never had more than four or five players on a side. We were of mixed ages, and we made up the rules—hits only to one side of the field, two fouls and you're out!—we umpired our own games, and we resolved our own disputes. Finally, we set the sides as even as we could to keep the games close. The action was swift and continuous; we each got a dozen or more at bats and many chances in the field in a single afternoon. And we didn't pay much mind to winning or losing. I doubt that Little League could have given me the same passion for baseball. Sandlot ball was so much fun that I could hardly wait to get home from school to play. But wanting to pursue baseball as a career was a different matter. For that three vivid memories stand out.

1. My first uniform, age seven.

ZION NATIONAL PARK, 1955

The first is from a family camping trip to Zion when I was eleven. I am pitching to my father, who is smoking a cigar, wearing a catcher's mitt, and squatting behind a square of cardboard serving as home plate. I'm throwing pretty hard, and the ball makes a loud pop as it strikes the

2. Warming up for a game in the San Mateo rec league, age ten, with brother Walt (striped shirt).

leather, the sound amplified by the nearby canyon wall. Several Cub Scouts stop to watch. I overhear one of them comment on how hard I throw. I like the attention; it makes me feel special.

YANKEE STADIUM, 1956 WORLD SERIES

The second memory is of attending my first Major League game when I was twelve. This isn't any ordinary regular-season game; it is Game Four of the 1956 World Series. The mythic New York Yankees, my team, are playing their cross-town archrivals, the Brooklyn Dodgers. My father, an executive in a San Francisco shipping company, was planning an East Coast business trip and had asked if I'd like to come along and see a World Series game. "Wow, can I?!" I asked. I remember my first glimpse, from a few blocks away, of Yankee Stadium, draped in World Series bunting, and then our emerging from the tunnel into the bright bowl of the "House That Ruth Built," with its vast expanse of green grass lined in white chalk and the huge wall of noisy fans. My dad holds my hand as we make our way through the crowd. There are sixty-nine thousand people in the stadium, and the atmosphere is electric. I am in awe. That awe is reinforced the next day as I watch alone—my dad is at a business meeting—Game Five on TV in our hotel room and see Don Larsen throw a perfect game, the only one in World Series history.

FITZGERALD FIELD, 1958

My third childhood memory is from two years later. I am in the eighth grade and have gone to Fitzgerald Field in my hometown of San Mateo, California, to watch the Baltimore Orioles play. They are not the real Baltimore Orioles. Like the other teams in the Peninsula Winter League, they carry the name and wear the uniforms of the Major League clubs that sponsor them. A few of the players, however, are Minor Leaguers. The grass is lush, and there is a stand of redwoods in right field, forcing the outfielders to chase down extra-base hits in the trees. The players are resplendent in the black-and-orange piping of their Orioles uniforms. I sit in the front row, right behind home plate. A tall player is standing in the batter's box, firmly dug in, his gaze fixed on the pitcher; a fastball whizzes inches from his chest, but he does not flinch. I wonder how he can be so sure the ball won't hit him. He seems brave, I think. On the bus ride home, an idea forms: *I want to be a professional baseball player.* Such an ambition must have seemed foolish at the time. I was a fair athlete but not a great baseball player. What talent I had was in pitching, yet I was now aspiring to be a great hitter. At thirteen, though, all things seem possible, at least to middle-class white kids. The affluent, hillside suburb of my youth was a world without limitations, one in which I could easily imagine myself playing first base for the New York Yankees.

Like most sons, I valued the same things as my dad, George Sr., a handsome man with blue eyes, a cleft chin, perfect teeth, and dark wavy hair who liked to fish, hunt, and talk baseball. So did I. I even liked his favorite foods: liverwurst, pickles, blue cheese, sourdough bread, and cracked crab. My father's baseball hero was Lou Gehrig, and even though the "Iron Horse" was long dead, I also revered him. My father, who had moved our family to the West Coast when I was two, told me that Lou Gehrig and Babe Ruth had once gone out on my grandfather's fishing boat off Long Island and that there was a picture of them on the boat hanging in the Hall of Fame in Cooperstown. I was doubtful until years later, when visiting Cooperstown, I unexpectedly came upon the picture in the Babe Ruth exhibit on the second floor of the museum. But then a decade later when I tried to show it to my son, it was gone . . . moved to basement storage.

My father was a self-made man, a plumber's son. Through hard work and intelligence—and without having set foot in a college classroom—he became the executive vice president of a large West Coast shipping line. His personal success made him a Republican and a big believer in the American Dream, whose material aspects could be seen in our comfortable house with a view of the bay, a two-car garage, a thirty-five-foot cruiser berthed at the St. Francis Yacht Club, and his memberships in golf, hunting, and men's clubs. The Bay Area's affluent suburbs were to him a Garden of Eden.

Although he listened to the Giants broadcast on radio, usually with an unlit cigar in the side of his mouth, he was also a passionate Yankees fan from his upbringing in Queens. He had once been a ballplayer, local semipro, so it was not surprising that he would encourage my new ambition, saying that I could be whatever I wanted if I was willing to work hard at it.

And that's what I did. With single-minded determination I practiced and practiced to develop my skills. A childhood friend, Chris Nelson, shared my dream. Together we went to the ballpark every chance we had—throwing BP to one another, hitting grounders and fungos, and playing games like workup, over the line, and home run derby. If the

3. My dad, George Sr., teaching me how to shoot skeet. Photo by Edna Gmelch.

weather was inclement or the grass wet from the sprinklers, we'd play stickball. When there was no one to play with, I would throw a rubber-coated baseball, or *semi*, against our garage or swing a weighted bat. To strengthen my forearms, I carried a rubber ball to school and squeezed it secretly during class. At home I skipped rope and did chin-ups and sit-ups to strengthen other muscles. To increase my foot speed, I joined my Hillsdale High School cross-country team, declining invitations to play football from our young coach Dick Vermeil (who later led two NFL teams—the Eagles and Rams—to the Super Bowl). In summer I joined as many baseball leagues as I could, playing in as many as three at a time. I kept detailed records, entering my stats on a sheet after each game. I could always tell you my batting average in each league. I read books about baseball, both player biographies and the how-to-improve-your-game genre by big leaguers such as Harvey Kuenn and Ted Williams. I subscribed to *Baseball Digest*, the monthly magazine of baseball history and current doings. By age thirteen baseball had become the organizing principle of my life.

Although tens of thousands of youngsters across the country held the same dream of becoming a big leaguer, I doubt that many were as single-minded. Once, for example, I rode by bus with my brother, Walt, to a Giants game at Candlestick Park and then left in the sixth inning when I got the urge to go home and practice (a chilly fog rolling in probably contributed to my decision). That the horizons of my existence did not extend far beyond the baseball diamond became a concern of my high school English teacher Mr. Beltrame, who called my mother in for a conference to discuss how the school might broaden my interests. At the ceremony during which I was to be confirmed in the Lutheran Church, my pastor told the assembled parents and guests, after I badly fumbled the Twenty-Third Psalm, "George puts baseball before God." Surprisingly, when we got home after the ceremony, my parents didn't seem upset by my public humiliation. I got the feeling my dad was amused. My mother was just glad that I had a passion for something, anything, unlike most of my school friends.

About the only time my thoughts for the future turned from baseball occurred in mid-October 1962, when my family stockpiled food and water in our cellar and anxiously waited to find out if the "Cuban missile crisis" would end in mutual nuclear annihilation.

As a high school sophomore I asked my parents if I could go away to a summer baseball camp. My father, always frugal and practical, traits we attributed to his Depression-era upbringing, suggested that I put the money toward a pitching machine instead, which over the long haul might prove more beneficial than a few weeks of instruction. I opted for technology. We set aside a patch of our backyard for a batting cage. The area was on a steep incline and required building a retaining wall and then adding many yards of dirt fill to create a level surface. My father said I could have the space if I did the work. I excavated an area under our house for the earth fill, creating room for a basement workshop, while hauling hundreds of wheelbarrow loads down the hill. Not until the fill nearly reached the top of the wall did my dad order the $325 Dudley pitching machine. We covered the cage in chicken wire and put up lights so that I could hit at night. I found time every day to hit and would have put in even more hours had not the noise—the crack of bat striking ball—caused our neighbors to suggest a curfew: no hitting after nine o'clock.

The discipline paid off. By junior year in high school I led the team in hitting and had become a steady fielder (first base and outfield). **"GMELCH BOYS BENEFIT FROM MACHINE AGE"** ran a headline in the *San Mateo Times* sports section. My father built dugouts for the team, appearing before the school board to request permission and then getting local firms to donate the materials. The school board members approved, but only on condition that the dugouts were "secure," that is, had lockable doors at both ends to keep amorous couples out. Sadly, the tryst-proof design limited the interior space and legroom, making our new dugouts even less comfortable than what we had before when we sat outside on a wind-exposed bench. It left such a sour taste that my father never again got involved in local philanthropy.

4. Hitting a backyard batting cage pitch, age fifteen. Photo by Edna Gmelch.

Senior year I won all the honors—team captain, all-league, and most valuable player (MVP). I loved seeing my name in the *Times* sports section headlines: "GMELCH LEADS KNIGHTS TO VICTORY," "GMELCH HOMER FOR WIN," "GMELCH TIPS MILLS NINE," and, best of all, "GMELCH AGAIN." With each success on the field, baseball assumed a still larger role in my

5. My mother's photo of me at Hillsdale High School graduation. Photo by Edna Gmelch.

life, boosting my confidence and giving me an identity. Baseball was the first thing in life that I could do well. Sure, I'd become an Eagle Scout in record time, but in my mind that didn't hold a candle to baseball. Nor was it something that impressed teenage girls.

But as I graduated from high school in 1963 there were no offers to sign a professional contract. There had been scouts at my ball games. Deeply tanned, they were unmistakable in their slacks and alpaca sweaters, notebook and stopwatch in hand. But I hadn't caught their eye. They were there to watch other young stars, such as Wally Bunker, who just a few months out of Capuchino High would be pitching for the Baltimore Orioles, and Jan Dukes, Danny Frisella, Ron Law, and Norm Angelini, all of whom would someday also pitch in the big leagues.[1] That summer as I led a strong American Legion League in hitting at a whopping .473, there was still no evidence of scouts following me. Near desperation, I phoned the local Baltimore Orioles bird dog, Paul Thibodeau, and, lowering my voice to pretend I was someone else, I asked him what he thought of "that Hillsdale kid, George Gmelch." His review was mixed, concluding that I was a "watch and follow." Thankfully, he never caught on that it was me on the other end.

In the fall I enrolled in nearby College of San Mateo, mostly for its excellent baseball program headed by a smart and dedicated coach, John Noce. I hoped to put up good numbers at CSM, attract the attention of scouts, and "sign." My ambition was also fueled, I now know, to attract the attention of pretty girls. My father also viewed college primarily as a place for me to play ball. Only my mother, a photographer and lifelong learner who was always enrolled in classes at the community college, appreciated college for the education it provided. My freshman year was a huge disappointment on the diamond, as I hit just .242. Discouraged and burned out, I took a break from baseball that summer to join friends on a two-month road trip. We towed a small boat and camped and fished our way through the Northwest and western Canada.

At the start of the new baseball season, after taking the summer off, I felt refreshed. Voted team captain, I got off to a good start in preseason games. I was back on track. But when league play began, I went into a dismal prolonged slump, collecting just one hit in twenty-seven at bats. Coach Noce called me aside and said he'd have to bench me if I didn't start producing, despite my being captain. I changed my uniform number from 7 to 8, hoping to find some luck, and that day I busted out, hitting a clutch home run in each end of a doubleheader. After that my bat never cooled off, as I hit .458 the rest of the season. I soon noticed that Detroit Tigers scout Bernie DeViveiros was following me. After a game in San José, he finally introduced himself, complimented my play, and asked some questions about my interest in playing pro ball versus staying in college. I was elated and eager to get home to tell my mother and father.

On April 29, 1965, our team was playing a doubleheader against Contra Costa College. Bernie DeViveiros was there at Fitzgerald Field, sitting high in the stands above third base. In the first inning I hit an opposite-field triple to deep left-center but then got picked off at third base. As I walked back to the dugout, I saw Bernie get up and leave the ballpark. I was certain he was leaving because I had been carelessly picked off. What followed was the best day in baseball I ever had, as I drove in eleven runs with seven hits, including two triples and three home runs. The last home run cleared the redwood trees in right-center and four lanes of El Camino Real before hitting a building on the far side. It was a monster shot. The image of the baseball clearing the redwood trees is still fixed in my mind's eye. A local sportswriter wrote about my "booming bat" and nicknamed me "Long Gone." This was the wood-bat era, when home runs were not common in amateur baseball. My three home runs that day were more than most of my teammates hit the entire season.

But Bernie hadn't been there to see it. I couldn't believe my bad luck. When I got home I was both elated and depressed. The next day I called the New York Yankee area scout, Dolph Camilli, who had once been my coach and was Bernie's friend. I told Dolph what had happened. The implied message of my telephone call was that I was eager to sign with the Tigers. Bernie was at my next game and afterward asked if he could come around to my home to meet my parents and talk about my signing with the Tigers. This was just two weeks before the first-ever free-agent draft.

When Bernie arrived at the front door a few days later, he wasn't wearing his Detroit Tigers cap. I had never seen him without it, and obviously he seldom took it off, since there was a sharp line between his deeply tanned face and his white dome, which must have never seen the light of day. He looked almost comical for a man of his stature, a former Major Leaguer and well-respected scout. In the living room Bernie talked up the Tigers, saying that it was a great organization, that I would be well taken care of, and that if I played well there would be ample opportunities to move up the Minor League ladder. He reviewed my strengths with my father—my hitting, power, and attitude, by which he meant work ethic and determination to succeed. Bernie, who was also the Tigers' infield and sliding instructor, even got down on our living room carpet to demonstrate the benefits and drawbacks of the hook and bent leg slides.

Finally, after all the talk, he mentioned a bonus of one thousand dollars. It was disappointing, although after having revealed my hand in the phone call to Dolph Camilli, I knew not to expect too much. My father and I consulted, and we countered with a request for twenty-five hundred, which would cover the cost of two years at Stanford University, where I had just been accepted. Bernie readily agreed and wrote out a Detroit Tigers check. After I signed the contract, he said that he hadn't left the Contra Costa game because I had gotten myself picked off and that it was silly of me to think so. Rather, he'd been scheduled to be at another game and had already made up his mind about me. So there it was—my impatience and impulsiveness in calling Camilli had cost me a larger bonus. I cared less about the money than the status attached to it. When the newspapers called the next day to ask about my signing, I would not reveal the dollar amount, saying only that it was a "modest bonus."

Although it was late when Bernie left our house, I celebrated with my parents and brother, Walt. My two sisters were too young to understand the significance of it all. My father, always a quiet man, never told me so in words, but I could tell that he was enormously proud. My mother,

Edna, who didn't care much about baseball, was happy that my hard work had paid off.

In August 2015, just as this book was about to go to press, I received from the archivist at the National Baseball Hall of Fame, a copy of the April 1965 letter that Bernie had written to the Detroit Tigers front office and enclosed with my signed contract. It described, perhaps with the hyperbole of a scout touting his new signee, my home and family ("conditions are great . . . these are fine people . . . the father is a vice president of a steamship line."); my ambition ("the boy wants to play so bad it hurts"); my ability ("the boy has real nice action and looks like a ballplayer. He can hit the ball to all fields with power. . . . Tremendous power . . . wait till you see him swing the bat"); my character, the so-called intangibles, ("great attitude and a gentleman. Does not drink or smoke and all man"); and one liability ("The only thing against him is his wearing glasses."). Bernie's letter confirmed my suspicion about receiving a smaller signing bonus than I deserved: "The boy is worth more than I gave him." The letter closed with a request that the Tigers bring me to Detroit on the way to my Minor League assignment: "Bring him in and let him meet Pat and all the boys; they will make him feel great and me too." It never happened.

In the last few weeks of classes before reporting to the Duluth-Superior Dukes of the Northern League, I spent my time daydreaming about what was to come. There were nice articles in the college and local newspapers about my signing. *San Mateo Times* sports columnist Jack Bluth predicted that I would make it to the big leagues because of "ambition, dedication, and love of labor" more than my talent. Whenever I passed an attractive girl on campus, I wondered if she knew that I was now a professional ballplayer, under contract to the Detroit Tigers. Looking back on it today, it's hard to separate how much my ambition sprang from a love for the game, how much to please my father, and how much from a desire to be somebody.

2

BREAKING IN

Duluth-Superior Dukes

Two weeks had passed since I signed my contract with the Tigers. Finally, I was on my way—to Minnesota to play for the Duluth-Superior Dukes of the Northern League, Detroit's bottom-rung farm club. As I boarded the United flight in San Francisco, I noticed an attractive flight attendant, half hoping she might take an interest in me. After all, wasn't I now a professional athlete? But when I greeted her in the aisle, she merely responded, with a southern accent, "Hello, sonny." I dropped into my seat and waved good-bye to my dad, who was still visible through the concourse window.

Although I didn't know it at that time, I was starting my career at the nadir of Minor League Baseball's popularity. In 1965 the number of leagues (fifteen) and the number of teams (118) had reached an all-time low. Only fifteen years earlier there had been four times that many leagues and franchises—in fact, a whopping 438 teams. With just as many American boys wanting to become professional baseball players as ever, the shrunken number of leagues and teams intensified the competition for the available roster openings. The decline in Minor League Baseball was attributed to the increasing number of Americans moving to the suburbs, away from downtown ballparks, and to the advent of window air-conditioners. The latter brought indoor relief in the summer and encouraged families to stay at home to watch Major League Baseball on television rather than go out to a Minor League ballpark. Also, it didn't help that football had just surpassed baseball as America's favorite sport.

The Duluth-Superior Dukes were an oddity, a farm team jointly owned by the Detroit Tigers and Chicago Cubs, with each organization contributing half the team's players. The Northern League was also unusual in having just four teams (Duluth and St. Cloud in Minnesota and Aberdeen and Huron in South Dakota). And unlike the other Class A leagues, it didn't start play until late June and had a sixty-eight-game schedule, about half the usual number.

It sure didn't feel like mid-June when I stepped off the plane in Duluth. A cold wind was blowing off Lake Superior, and the temperature was in the forties. I was sorry I'd left my jacket at home. On the way to the YMCA, where the ball club instructed players should stay until we could find our own accommodations, the shuttle blew a tire, and it took forever to get back on the road. It was dark when I arrived, and the Y looked old and run down. The desk clerk gave me a key and directions to a room on the third floor. The dresser had four drawers but only two knobs; I made sure not to close them all the way. A bare bulb hung from the ceiling. There was no decoration, unless you counted the abstract cracks on the walls. I located the bathroom down the hall by smell.

Wanting to get my baseball career off on the right foot, I had arrived a day early to be rested and fresh for our first workouts. My teammates were not due until the next day, and I was lonely. Nevertheless, as I wrote in my journal that night, I could hardly believe that I was soon to be a "Duluth Duke." On a cross-country family car trip two summers before, we had stayed overnight in Duluth. I had seen the ballpark, whose massive brick walls looked more like a fortress than a stadium, and I had quizzed the waitress at dinner about the team. It turned out to be the only team and Minor League park I would visit on the entire trip from San Francisco to New York—and now I was going to be a Duke.

When I awoke midmorning, it was still gray and cold. I could see whitecaps on Lake Superior. Putting on several layers of clothing, I left the Y to find breakfast. Afterward I bought a world map and thumbtacks to cheer up my room. Then I spent the day exploring the town, hoping to meet some girls, still under the assumption that meeting attractive girls was one of the perks of being a professional athlete. I observed a group of high school girls during lunch, later noting in my journal, *They all had pale skin and looked cadaverous . . . and their clothing was primordial.*[1] Today, I cringe when I read these words and the many other trite and overblown descriptions in my journal. I was into self-improvement and had recently read a book on how to expand your vocabulary, and I also regularly consumed the "Word Power" section in my mother's *Reader's Digest.*

The next day my teammates arrived. To the other denizens of the Y, we were easily recognizable as ballplayers. Our short hair either stood straight up with the help of Butch wax or lay flat and neatly parted with a little dab of Brylcreem. We mostly dressed in chinos, Ban Lon shirts, cardigan sweaters, and wing-tip shoes. We had no facial hair, wore no jewelry, and certainly had no tattoos. Even if we had wanted to mimic the hair and dress styles of college-campus counterculture, such as bell-bottoms and tie-dyes, I'm certain our coaches and managers would not have tolerated it. In culture as well as politics, we were a pretty conservative lot. Throughout the 1960s baseball coaches had no difficulty insisting upon short hair and conformity in dress. We were not unlike soldiers in the military in giving in to rules, discipline, and training.

Some of my newly arrived teammates gathered in my room to shoot the breeze and get acquainted. We talked awkwardly about our journeys, the places we had come from, and where we had played ball. That evening I discovered that three of us—Rick Wagner (soon nicknamed

Wags), Gary Renkenberger, and I—were all first basemen and all left-handed. *Ludicrous*, I wrote, using one of my new words, assuming I would not get much playing time. I was too green to understand how the Minor Leagues worked—that we were all at a minicamp, which is an abbreviated spring training, and not all of us would spend the season in Duluth. It would have made things a lot easier had someone from the ball club or Detroit's front office simply explained this, but such was not the policy back then.

At the ballpark the following day we met Doc Daugherty, our manager, and George Spencer, the roving pitching coach. The low Minors then had no permanent hitting or pitching coaches. Instead, instructors moved from team to team, spending a few weeks with each. Doc was square jawed and muscular, unlike most coaches, who stopped working out once their playing days were over. He had played briefly for the Detroit Tigers in 1951, and although he had only one Major League at bat and a lifetime batting average of .000, he had made it all the way to Tiger Stadium, which to my way of thinking counted for something. He'd also been an All-American running back at Ohio State. Like many baseball managers of that era, Doc was taciturn. He didn't think it important to talk to his players or get to know them. He was not a communicator. George Spencer, by comparison, was garrulous. But his interest was in the pitchers, so we rarely spoke. He had spent nearly a decade in the big leagues, putting up good numbers with the New York Giants before finishing up with Detroit.

I was impressed by Duluth's imposing stadium, with its high brick walls. Known as the Wade by local fans, it was one of hundreds of ballparks and stadiums (along with bridges, civic centers, and other public buildings) built in the thirties by the Works Progress Administration to provide jobs and financial relief during the Great Depression.

The Dukes had played there continuously since it opened in 1941, except for two years during World War II when play was suspended as players responded to the nation's call to arms and the ranks of pro ball were depleted. My new teammate Chris Barkulis, who had played in Duluth the year before, characterized the Wade well: "It's a pretty neat park, but it's colder than a witch's tit in a brass bra."

At dinner that second day a half dozen of us gathered at a corner table in a shiny roadside diner reminiscent of Mel's Drive-in in *American Graffiti*. We all ordered burgers and fries. Between mouthfuls I asked if anyone knew when we'd be getting our first paycheck. Doc had told us earlier that we'd be working out from ten o'clock to three every day except Sunday until the season opener in ten days. In a tone suggesting that I should know better, Larry Calton, who would later reach the big leagues as a broadcaster for the Minnesota Twins, told me that in pro ball no one gets any salary until the season starts. "What?" I exclaimed. "We're working our butts off every day for two weeks without any pay? That's exploitation." On the telephone I asked my businessman father if that was legal. He said not to make waves.

After dinner we walked around town to kill time, not easy to do in a big group, especially when you're just getting to know one another and no one wants to take the lead. Fortunately, Duluth was a port city with a sizable downtown and a population of more than one hundred thousand. It wasn't the small backwater that most rookie Minor Leaguers found themselves in.

We had a little excitement when we were stopped by a police car and two patrolmen accused us of tampering with parking meters. One of our group had shaken a few meter heads to see if any coins would come out, but that was all. After running out of places to explore and store windows to look into, my new teammates went into a bar—the default refuge of ballplayers in strange towns. Never much of a drinker, I continued walking on my own and struck up a conversation with a young woman, wearing red pedal pushers and a navy peacoat, who showed me around the waterfront and Duluth's prized landmark, the Aerial Lift Bridge, which spanned the port.

She was a good guide, but I see from my journal that our time together *came to nothing*. What had I expected? Did I think that she was going to take me back to her place just because I was a Duluth Duke? As I wrote in a letter to my parents a few days later, *You just tell the girls that you play for the Dukes, and they'll do anything for you.* Except for a few groupies, this wasn't true, but that's not what we ballplayers wanted to believe.

The next day we again practiced from ten to three. Exhausted from the workout, I returned to the Y and napped until evening, when I went to the movies with Wags and Charlie Smith. Charlie, a stocky pitcher with a butch haircut from Washington DC, and Wags, a ruggedly handsome, sandy-blonde three-sport all-star from Marysville, California, were fast becoming my new buddies. We all liked *The Amorous Adventures of Moll Flanders*, a recent film adaptation of a novel about an eighteenth-century servant girl who has a string of affairs with rich gentlemen before finding true love with a dashing outlaw. Inspired by the movie, we went to a bar seeking our own adventures. We met three switchboard operators who had a car, and they drove us all over Duluth and its twin city, Superior, to show us the sights. Their tour included a lumberyard by the docks, where they shone the car headlights on a hole in the ground where a homeless man lived under a pile of scrap lumber and debris. Two other cars of teenagers arrived to gawk as well, but at least one of them had brought him food. I had never seen a homeless man up close before, and that night I awoke thinking how hard it must be for him to live outside in Duluth's unfriendly climate.

The next day a group of us went out looking for an affordable used car that would last us through the summer. We ended up with a package deal, two cars for $225—a '55 Buick and a '57 Ford. Each player's share came to $32.71. Charlie, Wags, and I took the Ford; the others settled for the Buick, which, although older, had less rust. It felt great to finally have our own wheels and some independence, and we immediately set about trying to find an apartment or house to rent.

That night there was talk about the Astrodome, the world's new and first indoor baseball park. Its grass was dying from lack of sunlight, as many of the dome's semitransparent Lucite ceiling tiles had been painted over after outfielders complained of glare. The failing grass was painted green to make it look natural, but before long the Astros were playing on green painted dirt.[2]

JUNE 20 . . . Because it was Sunday and there was no practice, Charlie, Wags, a lanky southpaw named Dave Langrock, and I took our '57 Ford on the road. We covered a big chunk of northeastern Minnesota, traveling up the northern shoreline of Lake Superior, turning inland to Ely in the Vermillion Iron Range, then south to the town of Virginia in the Mesabi Iron Range, before completing our 250-mile circuit by going west back to Duluth, where all the iron ore was loaded onto boats. We were relieved our car held up and impressed with the many lakes, forests, and small towns we had seen. *Wow*, I wrote. *Minnesota is beautiful.* It seems my efforts to expand my vocabulary did not include descriptions of place.

JUNE 21 . . . Another long workout today, but I didn't mind because I was hitting the ball well. In our intrasquad game I started at first base for the A team and batted fifth. When we came out of the ballpark, the battery of our Ford was dead, which seemed impossible considering all the driving we'd done. None of us wanted to buy a new battery, so we pushed the car to jump-start the engine and thereafter always parked on an incline, which wasn't always easy, since not every part of Duluth has hills or downhill parking spots. That evening we went out on the town to look for girls again and met three students from the University of Minnesota-Duluth. They showed us the campus, including the science labs and a taxidermy display. My teammates were hunters, and I had done an independent study in college collecting and stuffing animals for my school's natural history museum.

JUNE 22 . . . Another intrasquad game. I had two doubles as we won,

4–1. A local television station interviewed each of the starters. I asked if we could see the interviews, so after the game a few of us went to the TV studio and viewed the film. None of us had ever seen ourselves on a TV screen before. The first consumer video or camcorder was still two decades off. Today, most American kids have watched countless hours of themselves playing ball, from Little League on up, recorded by parents and coaches. But we hadn't, and we were thrilled to see ourselves on the monitor. I was disappointed, however, that my voice wasn't deeper. The next day Charlie, Wags, and I found a two-bedroom white clapboard bungalow to rent for $125 per month; with the car and a place of our own, we were beginning to feel settled.

JUNE 24 . . . We played our second practice game, this time against a local semipro team called the Solons, and beat them badly, 23–0. I thought the score revealed something about the considerable difference between semipro and professional ball. Incidentally, Minor Leaguers hate when people mistakenly refer to them as being or playing "semipro." Minor Leaguers make much less money than big leaguers, but they are professionals just the same. I collected two singles and seemed to have sewn up the starting first base job. I was feeling pretty good about myself.

The local newspaper—the *Duluth News Tribune*—was running short articles about the Dukes players. That day was my turn. In addition to the standard bio (hometown, schooling, sports honors, height, and weight), the article about me said, "Most professional rookies are intent only on making it to the Major Leagues . . . but the 6'2", 190 pound Gmelch hopes someday to manage professional ball. . . . [H]e also wants to pursue a PhD in Marine Biology." I had only just graduated from a community college, and here I was telling a reporter I intended to go for a doctorate. I wonder what Doc and my teammates thought when they read that. I had fully and uncritically bought into my father's mantra and one of America's foundational myths: you can be anything you want if you are willing to really work at it.

JUNE 25 . . . Doc gave us a brief talk before practice and advised position players like myself to stop swinging for the fences. The Wade is a pitcher's park, 340 feet down each foul line with 18-foot fences in all fields. "In this big ballpark," Doc said, "you're not going to hit many home runs, so get that out of your heads right now." In batting practice that day, I belted two out. No one else came close. "What do you think of that, Doc Daugherty," I mused. That night Wags, Charlie, Dave, and I drove 150 miles to Bloomington to watch our parent Detroit Tigers play the Minnesota Twins. Next to us in the mezzanine was Detroit outfielder George Thomas's wife, looking like a fashion model. She was unhappy when the Tigers blew a lead in the ninth and lost 4–3. But perhaps it wasn't the loss as much as that her husband was in a slump and riding the bench. He hit only .213 that year and was traded to Boston in the off-season.

Although we were members of the Detroit Tigers organization—which had scouted us, signed us, paid our salaries, and tracked our progress every day—whether the big club won was of little consequence to us. The big leagues were a world away, five levels above us: three teams at Class A and one each at Double and Triple A. If you were a really talented player who had all the tools, it would still take four or five years before you could hope to reach the bigs. I figured it could take me even longer, and some luck, because playing first base for the Detroit Tigers was an All-Star, Norm Cash. He led the American League in hitting and home runs, and just beneath him were several other big, talented first sackers.

I soon learned that players did not identify with the big club until they reached Double A, at which stage some of their former teammates would be on the Major League roster and they themselves were just one good year, or an injury to the player above them, away from being called up. For now I was happy just to be a Duluth Duke and to be the starting first sacker.

JUNE 26 . . . Our last practice game. I went hitless—two dribblers and a lazy fly ball, all on outside pitches that I had tried to pull. Whenever I did that, I'd remind myself to wait longer, let the pitch get deeper in the box, and drive it back through the middle or to the opposite field. But that was easier said than done. That night I wrote: *Suffering from a bad cold, I need to stay in and get well as the season opens tomorrow.* A Californian, I had never before had a cold in summer.

JUNE 27 . . . Our season opener was rained out. Worse, we had to wait around the ballpark for three hours before the game was called. Some of us then went to the movies, a double feature. Nearly all movies back then were double features. The second film was *Baby the Rain Must Fall*, which we remarked was fitting considering the torrents outside. Because of the rainout, we all had pent-up energy, and once back at the Y Charlie and Wags discharged a fire extinguisher. A few of us retaliated by unraveling the hallway fire hose and turning it on them. Things got wet, and the manager of the Y threatened to boot us out.

JUNE 28 . . . The New York Mets signed an eighteen-year-old right-handed pitcher named Nolan Ryan, having drafted him in the twelfth round. It was our season opener and my first professional ball game. I had never played a night game and had difficulty seeing the ball well. I went hitless and made an error. In the ninth inning with the score tied, I was on third with a chance to score the winning run. Doc put on a suicide squeeze. I broke for the plate with the pitch, but the batter had missed the sign and the catcher tagged me out. It wasn't my fault, but I was still bummed. That night I wrote: *If tonight's performance is any indication of my future in baseball, I might as well retire now.* It's obvious looking back that I had much to learn about playing pro ball.

JUNE 29 . . . First road trip. We had to be at the ballpark at nine thirty to pack our gear and get on the bus before its ten o'clock departure. Doc had warned that anyone who wasn't on board would be left behind and fined twenty-five dollars. We were all ready to go well before ten. I'd heard the story of a Cubs farmhand who was forever nicknamed "Bus" after he had arrived late and missed his first road trip. Just as in high school and college, the coaches and trainer sat up front, the guys who wanted to play cards sat in the middle, and those who wanted to sleep and the few blacks and Hispanics, or "Latins" as we called them, sat in the back. The downside to the rear was being next to the toilet and the noise and heat of the engine. We were off on a weeklong trip to play the St. Cloud Rox (a Twins farm club), the Huron Phillies, and the Aberdeen Pheasants (an Orioles franchise). St. Cloud was just three hours away, but Aberdeen and Huron were in South Dakota and a long haul, more than four hundred miles. But before we moved the bus driver, who looked and spoke like Ralph Kramden in *The Honeymooners*, got on the public address (PA) system and said we weren't going anywhere until the player who had his feet up on the seat removed them. We later learned the driver owned the bus.

We arrived in St. Cloud in early afternoon and checked into our hotel. Wags and I were assigned to room together. Since we didn't have to be at the ballpark until five, some of us walked around St. Cloud, on the banks of the Mississippi. Charlie discovered a sale, and a few of us bought Ban Lon shirts—short-sleeved nylon knit shirts, much like cotton polo shirts of today, but less comfortable. I already had a half dozen in different colors. They were just about the only shirts many of us wore.

Back at the ballpark during the pregame warmup, two young boys asked for my autograph; I spent a fair amount of time talking to them, perhaps because they reminded me of my two young sisters. During the game they handed our batboy a Baby Ruth candy bar and asked him to give it to me. A few weeks later I received a letter from them asking me for an autographed photograph. There was no such thing in the Minor Leagues in those days, but I wrote them back anyway. I didn't hear from them again until thirty-five years later, when after the publication of my first baseball book, *In the Ballpark*, they found my address on the Internet. They wrote that they had formed the "George Gmelch fan club" (they were its only members), noting that I'd taken the time to talk to them and to respond to their letter. They said they had followed my playing career after Duluth through the *Sporting News*. One is now a jazz musician in Minneapolis, and both are big Twins fans.

It was opening day for St. Cloud Rox fans with all the usual opening-day pageantry found in Minor League ballparks across the country: the high school marching band, slender majorettes twirling batons, uniformed soldiers from the local National Guard unit with their white gloves and rifles, and assorted sponsors and club officials standing near home plate. One of the team's sponsors, whose company was advertised on the outfield fence, threw out the first pitch, bouncing it in front of the catcher. And of course everyone in the ballpark had to sing the national anthem. I hummed along, never having learned all of the words. It wasn't that I was unpatriotic; rather, the national anthem didn't seem to have anything to do with baseball. Then the guard unit fired their rifles into the air. This was my first inkling of the cozy relationship between our national pastime, patriotism, and the military. I wondered what would keep some crazy guardsman from bringing live ammunition to the ballpark.

The crowd of 1,182 was treated to a well-played, tight game. The home team, Rox, won 4–3 in the eleventh inning behind the pitching of Bob Gebhard, who would later have a long Major League career and become the first general manager (GM) of the Colorado Rockies. I hit the ball well but had nothing to show for it. After such a good start in our preseason, I was now just one for eight (.125), and it was bugging me. After the game we boarded the bus for Huron, South Dakota, to play two games against the Phillies.

Tired from the all-night bus ride, we got blown out, 12–3. I made an error and went 0 for 4, or what we called an "o'fer," hitting three fly balls to right field. I thought they'd have been great sacrifice flies if only someone had been on third with less than two outs. In the clubhouse Doc berated us for our sloppy play and called a 10:00 a.m. practice.

JULY 1 . . . Back at the ballpark the next morning, we worked on fundamentals—relays, cutoffs, pickoffs, rundowns. By the time we returned to the hotel, everyone was beat, and many went back to bed until it was time to return to the stadium for that night's game. We faced their ace, Billy Champion, a red-haired, hard-throwing, string-bean six-foot-four right-hander who had been drafted in the third round out of a Shelby, North Carolina, high school. Billy would become the toast of Huron, finishing the season with an eye-popping and league-leading 1.20 earned run average (ERA). Within a few years he'd be called up to the big leagues, where he would pitch for eight years until an elbow injury.

That night I rode the hotel elevator with Phillies traveling hitting instructor Paul Waner, whose playing nickname was Big Poison. It was just Big Poison and me going down four floors. I had once read a story about him in *Baseball Digest*. Not only was he in the National Baseball Hall of Fame, but he was also one of the greatest ballplayers of the century—a three-time National League batting champion who had attained the hallowed mark of three thousand hits. He and his younger brother Lloyd, who played alongside Paul in the Pittsburgh Pirates outfield and was called Little Poison, had learned baseball by hitting a corncob ball with a homemade bat while growing up on a farm in Oklahoma. Never before had I been in the presence of such a famous athlete, yet he looked so small. During his playing days he was listed at five-foot-eight, but now he didn't even seem that and appeared frail as well. I wanted to speak to him, but I didn't know what to say, not even a good question, and soon we were on the ground floor and went our separate ways. A few months later I read in the newspaper that he had died and had been in failing health for several years. He was just sixty-two.

The crowd of nearly twenty-five hundred that night at Huron's Memorial Ball Park represented one quarter of the town's population. The fans weren't there just to watch Billy Champion. The Huron Phillies drew a large crowd every night; Huron was one of those small towns in the middle of nowhere where the Minor League ballpark was still the place to be on warm summer nights and where there was little else to do.

In a great pitching duel Billy Champion struck out fifteen of us, while our pitchers held the Phillies to three hits, until a walk-off home run in the thirteenth inning. I took another o'fer, deepening my despair.

JULY 2 . . . The next night Huron beat us again, this time the winning run coming on a blown call by the umpire who thought that I had pulled my foot off the bag on a wide throw. I was certain that I hadn't, and Doc and my teammates agreed, with outfielder Dave Pekich shouting that the ump was as "blind and dumb as Helen Keller." A heated argument ensued. Earlier in the game the plate umpire had called me out on a questionable third strike, so I was especially peeved. Later that night we saw the umpires, who were not much older than us, in a diner. They got up and left, perhaps feeling threatened or just overly conscientious about pro ball's rule that umpires must not fraternize with players.

The umpires were just as green and inexperienced as we were. Like most of the umpires in the Northern League, they were rookies, having just graduated from one of the country's private umpire schools, all located in Florida. There were few openings in the umpire ranks, so they must have been quite good to have gotten one of the available jobs. They made considerably less money than Minor League ballplayers (just $250 per month plus travel expenses), and they spent the entire season on the road, traveling by car and staying in cheap hotels with their lone partner. Unlike the big leagues where a team of four umpires worked together, in the low Minors there were only two. Like us, they had a long ladder to climb to reach the bigs, and, like us, most would wash out long before they got close.

But that night in Huron I didn't know any of that, and I didn't have much sympathy for them and wanted to let them know it. But I was also down on myself because I was now hitless in my last twelve at bats. It mattered less to me that our team had lost four in a row and was in last place. The late-night bus ride to Aberdeen was somber. In the unlit bus I stared out the window at the darkened countryside and wondered how things could be falling apart so badly. Perhaps as a diversion, I tried to locate myself in space, imagining exactly where on a U.S. and then on a world map I was traveling, a habit I would adopt on bus rides over the coming seasons.

JULY 4 . . . We were scheduled to play a split doubleheader against the Aberdeen Pheasants. Before the game I called my always supportive mother, Edna, to wish her happy birthday. Hearing her voice and news of the holiday family gathering made me homesick. Had I been playing better, I probably wouldn't have felt that way.

In the first game I went hitless again, smacking two balls deep to center, but both tracked down by a speedy fielder. Now hitless in my last seventeen at bats, I wasn't at all sure that Doc would start me in the nightcap, but there I was penciled into the lineup, down a few spots in the batting order. I broke out of my slump with three hits. *Hallelujah!* The first was a clothesline off the right-field wall, on a belt-high fastball in my wheelhouse. The last was a pop fly down the third base line, which, leaving my bat, looked to be going foul. When I realized it might not, I burst, half stumbling, out of the batter's box and gagged on the fresh wad of chewing tobacco that I had in my cheek. New to chewing, I had tried it only after being pestered by a teammate. That night in the clubhouse our diminutive outfielder and comic Dave Pekich imitated me chewing and gagging, proclaiming me "captain of the all-flaky nine." I didn't mind the ribbing, since being a rookie made getting any attention, even unflattering, welcome. But I did give up chewing tobacco shortly afterward.

After the game we watched the holiday fireworks display from the dugout. Wags, Charlie, and I bought firecrackers, and later that night we lit and threw them out our hotel window onto the street below. When Charlie bumped the wooden window screen, it tumbled four stories down and splintered on the street. Looking back, such shenanigans seem less amusing today, but they were an important part of baseball life in the 1960s. It was an era before iPads and iPods, video games and cell phones, so horseplay and pranks gave us a little excitement during our considerable downtime.

One player on the Pheasants roster was Pete Lewis, a speedy, switch-hitting second baseman and a former teammate from back home. Pete was the only player in the Northern League I had known before, and it was great to see him, although I still hadn't completely forgiven him for nearly killing me while we were attending the College of San Mateo. Just after baseball practice one day, I had squeezed into my locker, planning to scare a few teammates when they came out of the showers. Pete had seen me do it and picked up an open combination lock lying on a bench near him and locked me in. The problem was that nobody knew the combination or even whose lock it was. It was Friday afternoon. All the coaches appeared to be gone, and I was beginning to suffer severe claustrophobia. At first, my teammates didn't realize how serious the situation was and joked about leaving me there until Monday. On the verge of full-blown panic, I began pounding on the locker door and screaming for help. They managed to summon a coach, who got me out with a bolt cutter. I've been claustrophobic ever since.

Back in San Mateo Pete had been a highly touted prospect, signing with the Baltimore Orioles for a rumored twenty-five thousand dollars, a very large bonus at the time. So it was a big surprise to find him sitting on the Aberdeen Pheasants bench. Although I hadn't been in pro ball long, I knew that players who got big money were guaranteed to be in the starting lineup. I wondered what Pete had done wrong that was keeping him on the pine. Pete said he couldn't figure it out and grumbled a lot about Minor League life and about Aberdeen, saying that there was "nothing to do" and that the people were "hicks." The following spring training Pete was given his unconditional release.

We lost that night, but I got a big hit and two runs batted in (RBIs), which made the nine-hour, 411-mile bus ride home more tolerable. Nevertheless, when we finally arrived in Duluth the next morning, I was convinced that I hadn't slept more than an hour or two. Each player had two seats across, but it simply wasn't enough room to be comfortable for that length of time, let alone sleep well. Fortunately, we had our first day off. Wags, Charlie, and I moved into our own house and then went to a grocery store to stock up. After a long nap we grilled cheap steaks and went to the movies to see *Von Ryan's Express*, a World War II action film. It was the norm among ballplayers to spread out, sitting every other seat in the theater unless it was crowded; like on the bus, we wanted as much room as we could get. That night I couldn't sleep, got up at two thirty, and drove down to the ballpark, where I walked around and then climbed partway up one of the light towers for reasons I can't recall and probably couldn't have explained at the time either. Up high, I got a panoramic view of Lake Superior and the loading docks for the Iron Range Railroad. I had a premonition that I was going to be leaving Duluth, perhaps because a few teammates and I had been asked to come to the ballpark early the next morning. I had no idea what it might be about.

When I arrived in the clubhouse, teammates Benny Roop, Ray Keech, Dick Ahrendt, and Ray Bye were packing their gear. All four of them (who belonged to the Cubs) had gotten their unconditional releases and plane or bus tickets home. I was stunned. I tried to tell Ray Bye how unfair I thought it was and that I would miss him. He smiled and tried to make a joke about finally being able to go fishing and hunting, but I could see he was just putting up a good front, that at heart he was miserable and probably a bit scared. As I waited to be called into the manager's office, I began to fear that I was also being let go, fired, sayonara. Although I was still the starting first baseman and had broken out of my slump, my batting average was hovering around .200. Still, I wondered, how could they possibly make a judgment on my potential as a ballplayer after just nine professional games and thirty-five at bats?

The longer I waited, the more worried I became. My roommate Wags had gone in to see Doc before me. When he came out I learned that he was being reassigned to Idaho Falls (a Cubs farm club) in the rookie Pioneer League. Finally, Doc called third baseman Bob Felber and me into his office. Perhaps there was hope after all. Felber was leading our team in hitting at .320. Wasn't it logical that whatever was in store for him might be the same for me? I breathed a little easier. "Detroit is sending you two to Jamestown," said Daugherty, referring to the Jamestown, New York, Tigers of the Class A New York–Penn League (NYPL). He congratulated us on our promotion and told us that our flight was leaving in three hours and to get a move on it.

I quickly cleaned out my clubhouse locker and hurried home to pack up the rest of my belongings. There wasn't time to wait around to say good-bye to any of my teammates. Jamestown may have been a step up, but I had mixed feelings. I had become friends with Wags and Charlie, and now I thought I might never see them again, they being in the Chicago Cubs organization. I wrote my thoughts: *I like Duluth, I like my teammates, and I want to stay here, and now all of a sudden they have uprooted me.* As I departed Charlie and I shook hands and punched each other on the shoulder. He promised he would send me a check for my share of our '57 Ford and for the rent and groceries I had just paid for. I don't think he ever did.

3

WEARING KALINE'S PANTS

Jamestown Tigers

Although the distance from Duluth to Jamestown is just over seven hundred miles, it took us seven hours to fly there because of stops in Green Bay, Milwaukee, and Cleveland. Exhausted by the time we arrived, Felber and I headed straight to our Main Street hotel and crashed without unpacking, hardly undressing. After breakfast the next morning we walked around town to get a sense of our new home and learned that Jamestown was a furniture-making center, that it was located on the southern tip of Lake Chautauqua, that it had a population of thirty-two thousand, and that Lucille Ball had been raised there.

Then we walked to College Stadium to sign our new contracts and pick up our uniforms and gear, both of us still in shock over the suddenness of our departure from Duluth and me unconvinced that the move really represented a "promotion."[1] In the clubhouse we met Jerry Klein, who was sweeping the locker-room floor while chomping on a cigar. Short and rotund, with suspenders hiking his pants up so high that his white socks showed, Jerry seemed out of place in this athletic setting. But he was the team's clubbie as well as its trainer and driver. Sometimes he even helped out in the concession stand.

6. Jerry Klein,
Jamestown Tigers
clubhouse manager.
Photo courtesy of
Chautauqua Sports
Hall of Fame.

Jerry pointed to a large cardboard box filled with uniforms and growled, "Take your pick." It probably didn't matter which uniform we took since baseball uniforms in the 1960s were baggy affairs made of heavy wool flannel. Those in Jerry's box were also wrinkled, and a few had grass stains and repaired rips in the seat. We hardly noticed. They were Major League uniforms with the names of the Detroit Tigers who had worn them the previous season still stitched into their shirttails and waistbands. I got Al Kaline's pants, which seemed like a good omen. When I signed with Detroit, a sportswriter for a nearby town newspaper, the *Redwood City Tribune*, quoted my college coach, John Noce, as saying, "If Gmelch keeps hitting the way he has, he will make Detroit fans forget Al Kaline." It was an over-the-top remark that embarrassed Noce, who swiftly denied having said it. But here I was wearing Al Kaline's pants.

When Felber and I arrived, the Jamestown Tigers were playing in Auburn, about two hundred miles east. Jerry Klein had stayed behind in order to drive us there in one of the team's station wagons. Though still tired from multiple plane rides the day before, Jerry kept us awake with gossip about our new teammates and crass jokes:

"Hey, kid, what's a bad thing to do?"

"I dunno, Jerry, what's that?"

"Wipe your ass with a broken Coke bottle."

"Hey, kid, you don't see that very often."

"What's that, Jerry?"

"Horse shit in a garage."

Jerry talked the entire way. It was his fifth year working for the Tigers, and we would soon discover that he was a beloved character. Besides performing the typical clubhouse duties such as washing our uniforms and polishing our spikes, Jerry kept everyone loose through ridicule and raunchy jokes.

I found a copy of the morning paper, the *Jamestown Post-Journal*, in the car and came across an article about our joining the club. It also named the three players who had been released to make room for us: utility man Gene Smith, pitcher Hugh Hardin, and outfielder Barry Williamson. Any addition to a team roster meant somebody else had to go, but until that moment this fact had been an abstraction. Smith, Hardin, and Williamson, like friends of mine in Duluth who had been released, were real people who had now lost their jobs and their dreams. *Someday I might be on the other end, being sent home to make room for some other newcomer*, I wrote in my journal that night.

The Jamestown Tigers were one of six teams in the Class A New York–Penn League. The league's name struck me as odd because it had no teams in Pennsylvania. All were located in small to medium-size upstate New York towns: Batavia, Binghamton, Jamestown, Wellsville, and, in the Finger Lakes region, Auburn and Geneva.[2] Our road trip with

Jerry took us along the southern shore of Lake Erie, past Buffalo, and then a hundred miles on the New York State Thruway.

Our hotel was located in Auburn, even though the team was playing in Geneva. The Geneva hotel where visiting NYPL teams stayed had banned the Jamestown Tigers for the 1965 season. As Jerry explained, last year's Tigers "fuckin' tore up the place . . . water and pillow fights . . . soaked the fuckin' floors and left water stains on the fuckin' ceilings below. One player knocked a fuckin' hole through the bedroom wall with a fuckin' baseball bat." Felber and I were fast learning that *fuckin'* was one of baseball's favorite adjectives.

We rendezvoused with our new teammates in the cramped clubhouse of Geneva's McDonough Park. Jerry gruffly introduced us to our new skipper, thirty-seven-year-old Gail Henley, as the team was changing into their uniforms. At five-foot-nine, Gail was shorter than I had expected based on Jerry's large description of him. He had played center field for the 1954 Pittsburgh Pirates when he ran into the outfield wall, smashing an eye socket and his left wrist. After these injuries Gail bounced around AAA teams in the Pacific Coast League and Mexico until Detroit offered him a Minor League managing job. Gail made me feel welcome with a firm handshake and a smile. Nonetheless, I was nervous. Many of my new teammates were veteran ballplayers who had already played a full season. They had already formed friendships, and some of these might have been with the three guys who'd been released. Looking around the small clubhouse at them, I didn't think it was going to be easy to join the team midseason.

As I suited up, Gail asked where I had played college ball. The clubhouse was fairly silent as I began to answer. "College of San Mateo," I said, and then added that besides its having an excellent baseball program, the school also had its own TV station. As soon as the words were out of my mouth, I realized how stupid and defensive they sounded. Big fucking deal. I didn't hear much of Gail's pregame talk after that because I was busy trying to calculate just how badly I had embarrassed myself.

In Duluth I had been part of the group, one of the regular guys. Now, only a month later, I had to break in all over again, and I didn't like it.

Neither Felber nor I were in the starting lineup that game, but it was memorable just the same. In the sixth inning the sky turned dark as a thunderstorm rolled in. Lightning struck one of the outfield light poles, causing an electrical surge that knocked out two-thirds of the stadium's 165 lights, some of them shattering and popping and emitting wisps of black smoke—a Minor League version, without the dramatic musical score and super slow-mo, of the final scene in *The Natural*, where Robert Redford's mammoth walk-off home run explodes the stadium lights.

With twilight and some lights still working, the umpires decided to play on. Gail thought that poor visibility posed a danger to hitters and asked them to call the game. (Most ballpark lighting in A-ball in the 1960s had only one-tenth the candlepower as Major League stadiums.) They refused, and Gail told them he was playing the game under protest. In the seventh inning our first baseman, Ken Magown, fashioned a torch from a bundle of twigs and lit it when he went out to his position. The base umpire ordered Magown to hand it over, stomped it out, and threatened to eject him. But after conferring with the home plate umpire, they reversed themselves and called the game.

The next day Felber and I went out to explore Auburn and met two girls in the town park. After we chatted with them and told them we were visiting ballplayers, they offered to show us around town in their car. Auburn is on Lake Owasco, one of New York's Finger Lakes, and the old Erie Canal is nearby. I thought that was pretty cool because in high school I had written a paper on the canal and its importance to American commerce. Even better was seeing, smack in the middle of town, the massive Auburn Prison, with its turret-like guard towers. The girls told us with some pride that the first-ever execution by electrocution had been carried out inside, in 1890, of a man convicted for murdering his lover with an ax.[3] They boasted it was the toughest and most secure prison in the country. I said no, that Alcatraz, set in the middle of the cold waters and strong currents of the San Francisco Bay, had been even more secure before it had closed a few years before.

In what was becoming a game of one-upmanship, the girls next told us that the legendary Abner Doubleday, the Civil War general thought at the time to have invented the game of baseball in Cooperstown, New York, in 1839, was from Auburn. They showed us a plaque to prove it. We were impressed. Of course, we didn't know then that Abner Doubleday actually had nothing to do with inventing baseball and had probably never even played the game.[4] In any case, I loved learning from local girls tidbits of history and geography in the towns we visited.[5]

JULY 10 . . . I got my first start, playing first base and batting eighth against the Auburn Mets. We faced a wild and hard-throwing left-hander. During BP I told Gail that I didn't hit lefties very well. *Great*, I journaled that night. *I'm a professional baseball player, and I'm telling my new manager that I'm not confident about hitting left-handers. That's about as dumb as you can get.* The Mets pitcher jammed me in my first two at bats and in the next threw a wild pitch that barely missed my chin as I fell back from the plate, and then, on the next pitch, hit me on the elbow with a hanging curve ball. Jerry froze the bruise with a spray of ethyl chloride. After a right-hander came in relief, I doubled to left, but we ended up losing for the third straight night, plunging us deeper into the cellar.

After eating some of the unsold concession-stand food—hot dogs, burgers, and pizza—that was often put out for us after games, we piled into the team's three black Pontiac station wagons for the long trip back to Jamestown. There was no team bus. To save money the Jamestown GM, Marty Haines, who worked for a Pontiac car dealership in the off-season, had acquired the cars in exchange for advertising on the outfield fence, in the program, and on the air. Even though the station wagons were massive, there was barely room for eighteen athletes, a manager, a trainer, and our equipment.

I was assigned to the car driven by Gail, and, being the new guy, I was directed to the space in the back, where the gear was stowed. There was no seat, so I arranged the duffels and ball and bat bags as best I could to create some comfort. Ken Magown, a five-year veteran and the team's alpha male, always rode shotgun. Our car led the Pontiac caravan, ostensibly so Gail could keep the other drivers from speeding. But we routinely traveled above the speed limit ourselves. And over the next few months Gail collected three tickets. We also had no seat belts. They had been available for decades but were still optional on many American cars.

Arriving back in Jamestown in the wee hours, Felber and I were invited to sleep at the apartment of teammates Carl Solarek and Mike Small. Carl, our power-hitting catcher and a "can't miss" prospect, was nicknamed Polak. He came from a small town in Pennsylvania and was a big, solid man-boy, with thick, dark eyebrows and oversize thighs that gave him a waddle when he ran. Polak was fastidious about his locker and equipment; everything had to be in its precise place: hat on top, glove on the bottom, jersey on the left, shoes perfectly lined up. And he didn't like lending his catcher's mitt to anyone to warm up our pitchers.

Mike Small was a six-foot-four, loose-limbed lefty from Southern California who threw as hard as anyone in the league. You could hear the pop of his heater in the leather of the catcher's mitt from a distance. It intimidated batters. But Mike was a thrower and not yet a pitcher and never would become one. He often had no idea where the ball was going. Detroit must have thought they could help him find the plate because they had given him sixty-five thousand dollars to sign, the largest bonus the Tigers paid to anyone that year. Much like Nuke LaLoosh, the ditzy character played by Tim Robbins in *Bull Durham*, Mike was considered a "flake" by his teammates. He wore his belt buckle on the side and the face of his watch turned inward on his wrist. Before one road trip he bought a dozen candy bars for a nickel each and then tried to sell them on the bus for a dime. Outfielder George Zalocha called him "Pecker Head" for being so cheap after receiving more bonus money than the rest of us combined. Both Polak and Small had signed out of high school and were one year younger than Felber and myself. We were grateful they took us in that night, even if it meant sleeping on the sofa and floor.

In Duluth Felber and I hadn't been friends, but now circumstances threw us together. He was a muscular five-foot-ten with a thin face and narrow-set eyes and always impeccably groomed. He was easygoing and upbeat, considerate, and determined to be the best ballplayer he could be. "If you always give 100 percent," Felber liked to say, "you'll never have any regrets." Another favorite was "When you're hot, you're hot, and when you're not, you're not." Eager to find a place of our own and get settled, we began searching for an apartment first thing in the morning, but didn't find anything before we had to be at the ballpark for the team's sixty-five-mile commute to Wellsville to play the Red Sox.

In the New York–Penn League teams that were fewer than ninety miles apart commuted to play their opponents. This saved the clubs considerable money on hotels and food. But for players it meant making day trips whenever we played Wellsville or Batavia. It was Family Night at the Wellsville ballpark, not the best night for kids, as it turned out. Mike Small was on the mound when in trying to pick off base runner Billy Conigliaro he threw wildly and hit him in the head so hard that the ball careened into center field on a single hop. Billy—the younger brother of Red Sox slugger Tony Conigliaro, whose own big-league career would be derailed by being hit in the face by a pitch—left the game with a concussion. Small also soon left the game, walking seven in three innings of work. I struck out three times, despite Jerry's repeated "C'mon, kid, rap-a-sacky" encouragement.

Felber, who had gotten two base hits, brought his hot bat back to Polak and Small's apartment for luck, laying it beside him when he went to bed. Mike was still stewing and went straight to the telephone, talking to his girlfriend in California for the next two hours. Polak explained to us that Mike got homesick when he didn't pitch well, which was most of the time, and had spent seven hundred dollars on phone bills the previous season. Even with his signing bonus of sixty-five thousand, spending that kind of money on phone calls seemed incredibly extravagant. Mike got bombed again a few weeks later, but this time he walked to the main road and hitched a ride with a trucker, apparently with no destination in mind. He rode with him for an hour before getting out and calling Polak to come pick him up.

Whenever I was troubled by my performance and wasn't able to sleep, I would write in my journal. That night's sofa entry was as follows: *I'm thoroughly discouraged with baseball, discouraged about being sent here. I was enjoying playing in Duluth. . . . [H]ere half the pitchers are left-handed. I'm definitely not ready for this league.*

The next day Felber and I found an apartment for sixty dollars a month in a turn-of-the-century three-story brick building on Second Street, in a shabby section of town. The stairway going up was creaky and the floor uneven, but the apartment had large windows and high ceilings, making it bright. There was only one bed, however, a double that sagged in the middle. Neither of us had ever shared a bed with another man before . . . or with a woman. In fact, I'd always had my own bedroom, as had Felber, who was an only child. All season long we clung to our respective sides, trying to avoid sliding into the valley and touching one another, such was the homophobic world of pro ball. But oddly, we thought nothing of patting our teammates on the fanny, the equivalent of today's high fives, after they made a good play or got a hit.

We cleaned the apartment thoroughly. I had always kept my stuff pretty organized, but nothing like Felber. A neat freak, he washed his dishes as soon as the meal was done and dusted our place every other day. Felber even ironed his chinos, which he wore with penny loafers without socks, an East Coast preppie look that I was unaccustomed to.

To brighten up our place we went to FW Woolworths and bought two maps—the USA and New York—and hung them on our living room wall.

Arriving early at the Jamestown ballpark, I took a good look around. It had a handsome brick facade, seating for three thousand, and a press box perched high up in the rafters that reporters reached by a metal gangway. The seats, as in most Minor League ballparks, were close enough to the field for spectators to not only get a good view of the action but to see players' facial expressions and hear the infield chatter, including the occasional *F* bombs after a strikeout or error. The clubhouse sat underneath the stands but lacked the usual tunnel leading to the dugout. This meant players walked on the concourse, rubbing shoulders with the fans, to reach the field. Some fans would ogle or ask for an autograph (or both). Most players didn't mind; we liked the attention. Signing autographs was still a novelty and made us feel like professionals.

We beat Wellsville 9–5 that night, after a delay of play when a black cat strayed onto the field and to the delight of everyone except the umpires refused to be caught. I felt better about being in Jamestown after getting two hits, but I also booted two ground balls, both of them glancing off my glove.

JULY 13 . . . Felber and I walked the mile and a half to the ballpark for a midmorning departure to Binghamton, a 219-mile road trip. The Binghamton Triplets, or the Trips as the sportswriters called them, were a Yankees farm club. It showed. They played in the league's nicest ballpark—Johnson Field—which had Major League-quality turf. They drew more than a thousand fans per game, tops in the league. The Trips were also flush with new equipment. Whereas we reused balls that had gotten wet on rainy nights for BP, they had buckets of brand-new baseballs—"pearls," we called them. Binghamton was loaded with talent as well. They had won the first-half championship and were again in first place, the mirror opposite of us last-place Tigers. Playing against a Yankee farm club was special for me. Following my New York–raised

JAMESTOWN
Tigers

1965
SCORE CARD
MEMBER N.Y.P. LEAGUE

Meet Your Friends
at the
RITZ
RESTAURANT AND LOUNGE
221-23 West Third St.   Jamestown, N. Y.
Enjoy Your Favorite Cocktail In Our New Lounge
Enjoy a Meal or a Snack From Our Menu
DANCING NIGHTLY

DIBBLE PONTIAC, INC.
WIDE TRACK TOWN
—— WHERE YOU RECEIVE ——
Service With A Smile
Mile After Mile After Mile
•
1900 WASHINGTON ST.   PHONE 484-1144

YOU MAY HAVE ONE OF THE 3 LUCKY NUMBERS!

7. Jamestown Tigers program, 1965. Photo courtesy of Chautauqua Sports Hall of Fame.

father's example, I had grown up a Yankee fan, and some of the awe that I had for the Yankees carried over to their farm clubs.

But that night we beat the mighty Triplets behind the pitching of our bonus baby, fourth rounder Ricky Clarke, who combed his hair in a pompadour and had movie-star good looks. It was his sixth complete game of the season; back then pitchers were expected to go deep into the game. Managers didn't pay much attention to pitch counts. I got two hits, including a late-inning double off the left-field wall that scored the tying run. I was now hitting .375 and suddenly feeling confident. *I think I might have what it takes to make it to the bigs*, I wrote that night.

On the way back to Jamestown, Gail was pulled over for speeding and tried to argue that the calibration on his speedometer must be wrong.

The cop was unconvinced—and unimpressed that we were professional ballplayers—and wrote him up. During our meal stop we overheard on the news that the National League had won the All-Star Game, with Sandy Koufax the winning pitcher. Locked in our young and egocentric baseball world, we barely noticed what was happening in the rest of the world, which included the Vietcong inflicting heavy casualties on the South Vietnamese and the likelihood that American troop levels might be increased. Most of us, if we picked up a newspaper at all, went straight to the sports section and seldom got beyond the box scores.

The next day I arrived at College Stadium early and while waiting around fell into a conversation with the northeastern Spalding Sporting Goods representative. The rep, who was in town to check on some of my teammates who were Spalding clients, learned that I had just been promoted to Jamestown from the Northern League and that I was hitting .375. After making a phone call to his head office, he offered me a shoe and glove contract; it entitled me to a new pair of spikes and a new glove every year for as long as I was in pro ball. In exchange Spalding would get to use my autograph on a glove should I make it to the big leagues. On the spot the rep gave me a top-line first baseman's glove and kangaroo-hide spikes. I was thrilled but later hoped that he hadn't stayed for the game, as I made an error and went hitless.

While only a handful of my teammates had glove and shoe contracts, and no one had yet been offered a Louisville Slugger bat contract, everyone had signed a baseball-card pact with Topps. Topps, then the sole manufacturer of baseball cards, gave you five dollars and some bubble gum; they wouldn't produce a card with your likeness on it until you made it to the big leagues, which for most of us would be never. Dan Ardell held out for ten dollars. Topps refused. Dan did briefly make it to the majors but never had his own card, which he now says, only half joking, "was one of the biggest mistakes of my life."

I had now made three errors in six games, more than some first basemen made in an entire season. All were balls that bounced off my glove, which was hard to understand since I had always been a pretty reliable fielder. Lacking an explanation, I decided that my habit of holding the infield ball during the singing of the national anthem was bad luck. For the rest of the season, whenever the ball came to me at first base as the national anthem was about to begin, I'd hurriedly throw it to another infielder. It was highly unusual for any player to have a superstition tied to fielding, an area of the game where there is very little uncertainty compared to hitting and pitching. After all, most fielders catch and throw the ball without error 9.8 times out of 10, whereas most hitters are successful only 1 time out of 4. Most rituals and superstitions took place, and still do, on the mound or in the batter's box, not out in the field.

In the dugout shortstop Junior Lopez joked about my fielding, saying balls bounced off my glove as though it was a steel I-beam. The next day around the batting cage a few teammates called me "I-beam," and it stuck. Junior sometimes also called me "U.S.," short for U.S. Steel. It wasn't uncommon for a player to have more than one nickname or for nicknames to change from one season to the next, as mine would the following year. I didn't mind that my nickname was unflattering because being given any moniker meant that you were becoming one of the regular guys. Most Jamestown Tigers had nicknames—Pek, Moose, Ozark, Mooner, Polak, Humper, Newt, Ginny, Goose, and Pecker Head are the ones I remember. Like on all teams, it was the players who did not fit in or were not well liked who were not given nicknames. A good nickname could give a player distinction. It's hard to imagine that Yogi Berra, Dizzy Dean, or Babe Ruth would have gained the same notoriety had they been known only by their Christian names, Lawrence, Jay, and George, respectively.

Having grown up in the Bay Area, Jamestown's weather took some adjusting to. It was my first exposure to summer days with high humidity and nights that never cooled off. Few places in Jamestown then had air-conditioning, and it never occurred to me to invest in a fan. Our apartment was sometimes so hot and muggy that I was unable to sleep and would get up in the middle of the night and go for a walk in order to cool off. Whenever I did get up, I would surprise a small squadron of cockroaches in our kitchen. I had never seen a cockroach before that summer.

Nor had I ever seen coal before, not until one day when, taking a different route to the ballpark in hope of changing my luck, I walked along the railroad tracks and came across lumps of shiny black rock. I took one piece to the clubhouse, where Jerry identified it for me, holding it aloft for others to see while making a joke of my ignorance. The next day we were on the road to play the Batavia Pirates. They had more Latinos than any team in the league. Pittsburgh was one of the first organizations to scout heavily in the Caribbean, and consequently their farm system and big-league club were loaded with Hispanics. The Red Sox organization was the opposite, doing little scouting in the Caribbean and having scarcely any Latinos . . . and few blacks. So it was no surprise that the Wellsville Red Sox did not have a single black player and had only one Latino on its roster. Given the image I had had of Boston as a progressive, liberal city, it seemed odd that its baseball organization would have so few nonwhite players, while the blue-collar steelworker city of Pittsburgh supported a ball club that had so many.

The Batavia Pirates' catcher was a Panamanian, Manny Sanguillen, who was called up to Pittsburgh two years later and become an All-Star throughout the 1970s. Manny had played only a few years of organized ball before signing, having been a professional heavyweight boxer. At the plate Manny was a free swinger, equally liable to swipe at a pitch in the dirt as one at his shoulders, but he had unusually long arms and great reflexes. I learned that Manny didn't speak or understand much English when he came to first base after a base hit and I tried to make conversation with him, as I often did with base runners. When Manny made it to the big leagues, Pirates announcer Bob Prince liked to tell his listeners that Manny ordered only cheeseburgers when he was in Batavia because he didn't know the words for any other foods. Ever since, the inability to order food has been a cliché of the Latin rookie experience in pro ball.

Without any explanation from Gail, I was on the bench for the next three games. *Sitting is tortuous*, I wrote. One of the biggest adjustments young players have to make in pro ball is not playing. Always having excelled at the game, they had very seldom sat on the bench. Indeed, most of my teammates had been stars—MVPs, all-league, all-state, and even All-American. And all of our relief pitchers had been starters before they signed; back then it was unusual to scout relievers.

Restless watching the game from the dugout, I went down to the bullpen and got one of the relief pitchers to play pepper with me. After Gail motioned us to stop, telling us to get our heads in the game, I found a spot in the corner of the bullpen where I could not be seen from the dugout and read a pocket *Merriam-Webster's Dictionary*. It was the perfect book for small snatches of time, like the lulls between action on the field. Actually, with the ball in flight for only ten minutes in the average two-and-a-half-hour baseball game (about 6 percent of the time), there was plenty of time to read between the action.

After the game Felber and I went to the Jaguar Club, one of several bars along Main Street frequented by students, who in the sixties could legally drink at eighteen. A few tables away from us were two attractive girls. We started a conversation, and I was drawn to one—Claire Murphy—a slender, tanned, twenty-year-old with wild auburn hair. She was home from college for the summer and living on her family's 160-acre farm a dozen miles from town. She described herself as a "farm girl," in contrast to the "townies" or girls from Jamestown. Although Claire was raised in the country, her progressive mother had sent her off most summers to relatives in New York City to broaden her horizons. Besides her looks, she had a quirky sense of humor and an easy laugh that hid a certain shyness. She was, at times, unsure of herself, which much later she attributed to her emotionally abusive father who never praised her for anything: "If you got ninety-nine on a test, he would be disappointed because you didn't get a perfect score. He thought that was the way fathers motivated their children to do better." I could relate to that because my own father, like many fathers of that generation, held the same philosophy. Unlike most townies, Claire hunted and fished, but she also read books. I liked her.

After talking for several hours, we walked around town until she had to catch a ride home. We made a date to meet again a few days later. That night I wrote: *She is gorgeous and seems to enjoy my company!* Unlike the groupies who hung around College Stadium, Claire wasn't impressed that I was a ballplayer, though I wished she had been. How ironic—I thought baseball would be my ticket to attracting the affections of a pretty girl, and Claire didn't even like the game. She had been to only one Jamestown ball game, which she described as "fairly boring." Soon she became my steady and a regular at the ballpark, sitting with the other player girlfriends, all of whom were townies who, Claire later recalled, "liked to get their little digs in and pull that 'better than thou' stuff on me because I was from the country."

If there was any downside to dating Claire, it was that she didn't have a car. In the low Minors few players had their cars with them, so the only way to get around was to date someone with wheels. All season long, whether with Felber or Claire, we mostly walked or hitched. In the big leagues picking up a groupie was and still is nearly always about sex—usually a one-night stand. In the low Minors, however, the groupies— which we called "Shirleys" or "Annies"—often became companions for the season. In addition to dating and sex, many also ran errands, performed domestic chores like cooking, and provided emotional support.

Most of the girls were just looking for a good time, with no thought of a long-term relationship with their player. In Jamestown, as in other small Minor League towns, dating ballplayers gave girls something to do and a place to go—the ballpark—on muggy summer evenings. And after the game they'd be taken out to eat at a café or have drinks at a nightclub and then head back to a player's apartment to hang out.

JULY 21 . . . Playing Geneva that night, I was riding the pine again. *I can't take much more of this*, I wrote. Felber, who was struggling even more than I was, was also on the bench and equally unhappy. Without Felber or me in the lineup, the Jamestown Tigers played errorless ball for the third straight night. And for the third straight night, the game was played in precisely two hours and fifteen minutes, which the *Post-Journal* speculated "must be some kind of modern record." After the game I went out with Claire again, and we had some serious discussion about college and life. She had informed opinions and helped me forget my disappointments at the ballpark.

Arriving in the clubhouse each day, we were always eager to see if we had gotten mail. Letters were left in your locker by the clubby. None of us had telephones in our apartments, and calls made from a pay phone were expensive, and of course this being the pre-Internet era there was no e-mail or social media. So it was mostly through handwritten letters that we heard from family and friends. At a glance you knew from the handwriting on the envelope whom a letter was from. We read them as soon as we reached the ballpark. You'd save some letters to read again later on. In the mail that day was a letter from my scout, Bernie DeViveiros, with a lot of fatherly advice: "I know you will work on the things that you do not do well, that is the secret." About my hitting, Bernie advised,

> Don't try to be a home run hitter. Hit to all fields, because they are not going to pitch you inside so you can park them. Play just as you did in college . . . Have a lot of confidence and always think you're

one of the best players on the field. Don't tell them. They'll know it by the sound of your bat. Keep playing like the game is fun. Take good care of George; don't get down if you have a bad day. Just keep going and you will improve with each day's play. Keep your spirits high and go get 'em.

The letter was signed "Ever sliding, Bernie." Just then Jerry interrupted my reading. "Hey, kid, how can you tell when an elephant is in the bathtub with you?"

"I dunno, Jerry."

"By the smell of peanuts on its breath, you dumbshit."

I kept Bernie's letter in my back pocket for a while, hoping to absorb its message. Trying to hit to all fields was a lot easier to implement than the bit about confidence and convincing myself that I was one of the best players on the field.

I was back in the lineup that night but had another o'fer, as I did again the next night. My mother had always preached that you learn from failure, that failure builds character, and that you come away from failure a stronger and better person. In the abstract that sounded fine, but as my slump continued, I couldn't see how my o'fers were going to make me a stronger person or a better ballplayer. Instead, they were destroying my confidence, making me miserable, and breaking down my love of the game. I tried to change my luck by mixing up my daily routine. I took different routes walking to the ballpark. I put my uniform on in a different order—jersey first, pants second, and then socks. Finally, I began praying for hits, which was completely hypocritical. I'd been raised a Lutheran, and my parents had insisted I attend church until I turned eighteen, even though they seldom went. But then Steven Harris, the most religious and all-around best kid in my confirmation class, died of leukemia when I was in seventh grade; after that it was hard to be a believer. If God didn't save Steven, I reasoned, there wasn't much chance of his caring about me. Besides, why would God favor me over the opposing pitcher who might be a *real* Christian? But in a deep slump I turned to God in a superstitious way, thinking, "Hey, you never know." In the darkest moments I thought about other careers, what I might do after baseball if necessary. Perhaps with that in mind, I went to a bookstore and bought a world atlas, a one-volume nature encyclopedia, and a guide to writing college research papers.

When Felber and I got to the ballpark the next day, we learned that a new shipment of bats had come in from the Louisville Slugger factory. Bat arrival day is exciting for all position players, who always look forward to getting new lumber. I was thrilled because I was getting, for the first time, bats with my own name embossed on the barrel. When I opened the box, however, and pulled my bats from the carton, I saw on the barrels not "Gmelch" but "Smelch." My teammates thought it was funny. "Smelch like smells bad," quipped Junior Lopez. *How could Louisville do this to me?* Later, I realized that the way I wrote the cursive letter *G* looked a bit like an *S*. After that I changed the style of my signature so that it could never again be mistaken for anything other than a *G*. The first mention of me in the Duluth paper had called me "Bud Gmelch," and now my bats for the rest of the season would read "Smelch."

Jerry Klein joked that my box of bats should have come with *instructions* on how to hit. But swinging my new thirty-four-inch, thirty-two-ounce D2 model Smelch against Wellsville that night, I broke out of my slump with a two-run homer in the sixth inning to tie the game. Ken Magown, pinch-hitting for Jim Leyland in the ninth, blasted one far into the night air to win the game.

Like other ballplayers in the sixties, neither of us made a big deal of our home runs. You were expected to put your head down—conceal what smile or satisfaction your face was showing—and circle the bases in a steady trot, returning to the dugout to be congratulated there. Slowing down in order to take in the trajectory of your home run or, worse, making a show of it by pumping your fist or pointing to the heavens as players do today, all were taboo. One of the unwritten rules of baseball was never show up the opposing pitcher. It could incite him to "put one in your ear" the next time you came to the plate.

The next day we were playing Wellsville again when rain postponed the start of the game. During the rain delay I overheard our catcher, Jim Leyland, loudly debating with several teammates about whether Polak could lift three men off the ground. Others joined in, making wagers and putting money in a hat that was being passed around the room. Leyland selected three large players, including myself, for the test of Polak's strength. As a rookie, I was happy to be included. We were told to strip down to our shorts and then lay down on the floor; I was told to get in the middle. We then interlocked arms and legs. A crowd formed around us, cheering Polak on as he leaned over us, preparing to lift, and then . . . he jumped back. I described what happened next in my journal:

Everyone began dumping some condiment, ointment, soda pop, etc., on me. With my arms and legs locked, I couldn't escape. My chest was painted black with shoe polish, topped with catsup and mustard. My legs were painted pink with Merthiolate. My genitals and pubic hair were coated with analgesic balm, zinc oxide, tuft skin, and pine tar . . .

When they finished with me, Leyland called Felber into the clubhouse and did the same to him with the help of two new confederates. Luckily, the game was rained out because I couldn't have played very well. The hair on my groin and legs was stuck together, and my groin burned from the analgesic balm.

In this prank, called "lifting," and in others as well, Leyland was often the ringleader. Just a few days older than me, he had signed after high school in the small town of Perrysburg, Ohio, where he not only was a standout catcher but also played quarterback, sang in the choir, edited the yearbook's sports section, and was voted most popular boy. He didn't have all the baseball tools (in fact, he would never hit above

8. Jamestown Tigers catcher Jim Leyland, age twenty. Photo courtesy of Chautauqua Sports Hall of Fame.

.241 in seven Minor League seasons), and he wasn't nearly as talented a catcher as Polak, but he had the kind of toughness and charisma that coaches liked. Within a few years the front office would regard him, despite his penchant for furtively smoking Marlboros between innings, as an "organization player"—a company man. At age twenty-six he was offered his first managing job, the Bristol Tigers, in the Appalachian Rookie League. Fourteen years later Leyland would become a big-league manager with the Pittsburgh Pirates; soon after *Sports Illustrated* would call him "the best young manager in the game." None of us in Jamestown would have predicted that Leyland, whose greatest talents then seemed to be smooth-talking women and thinking up clever practical jokes, would go on to become a big-league manager—in fact a three-time Manager of the Year.

I met Claire for dinner, and afterward we played pool at a bar called Sodies, where the owner, Mr. Soderquist, was a big baseball fan. After Claire beat me three straight games, we walked around town and then returned to my apartment. We flirted and then wrestled on the floor; I pressed my body against hers, pinning her. We were sweating, her thick hair was soaked, and through her blouse I could feel her firm breasts. I began to think that this might eventually lead to sex, finally my chance to score. If so, this would be the first time for both of us.

I had come close several times in the past. The closest was on a double date with a girl—I'll call her Kathy—who was unabashedly "easy." She was the sister of our left fielder on a semipro team and had already slept with most of our infield. On our date four of us drove over the mountains to Half Moon Bay to find a secluded place on the beach. Kathy and I made out in the backseat, sliding from side to side as the car made its way over the twisting, winding road across the Coast Range. Kathy was clearly as horny as me, but by the time we got to the beach I was carsick. I couldn't do anything more than feel her breasts, and even that wasn't very satisfying as I felt like any minute I might vomit. The next day I could not believe my bad luck.

I had been fantasizing about having sex ever since I was a freshman in high school when I saw my girlfriend nearly naked while playing strip poker. I had also messed up that opportunity. We were in my bedroom and had gotten down to her panties and my jock—I don't recall why I was wearing a jock, but it probably had something to do with wanting to look athletic. Whatever the reason, it seemed to have the opposite effect. A few days later she broke up with me, saying I was too obsessed with baseball. Not only did I have pennants all over my bedroom walls, but I had encouraged her to read a book about the history of the New York Yankees. She started the book and then apparently decided that not only was it too much, so was I.

This all happened six years before my night in Jamestown with Claire, and I was still a virgin. Claire and I didn't have sex that night either, but it was clear that we were seriously infatuated with one another. We began hanging out together after every home ball game. She made me happy again and glad to be in Jamestown. *Things couldn't be better here. Jamestown is just swell, and I wouldn't mind playing here again next year. . . . Claire is my utopia . . . the type of girl I want to marry in ten or fifteen years.*

4

A LITTLE WILDNESS

Jamestown Tigers

Bob Felber's parents drove up from Baltimore to visit and watch him play pro ball for the first time. Along with their enthusiasm for baseball, they brought us several bags of groceries. That night Felber looked bad at the plate, went hitless, and booted a ground ball. After each miscue I looked into the stands above third base to see his parents' reaction. I figured it must be hard for them, having come all that way and then seeing their son play so poorly. I hoped that I would play well when my father and mother would someday visit.

After the game his parents treated us to dinner at a nice restaurant; I hadn't had a fancy meal since leaving home. Felber was an only child, and it was obvious that his father, like my own, cared deeply about his son's baseball career. After Bob's hot hitting in Duluth and quick promotion to Jamestown, Mr. Felber had thought his son was on the fast track to the big leagues, but now the reality appeared quite different. Bob was hitting .150 and, like me, had made a bunch of errors. He'd lost all the confidence and the jolly disposition that he'd brought to Jamestown. At dinner we talked baseball, but more about their beloved Baltimore Orioles than the Jamestown Tigers.

The next day in pregame, Leyland joked about Felber being slow afoot and challenged him: "Felber, I'll race you to the center-field fence for five dollars. I'll even give you a head start. You start from the mound, and I'll go from the plate."

Even without the head start, racing Leyland seemed like easy money. He was so slow that once as he ran the bases, a Jamestown fan had shouted, "Jesus Christ, Leyland, if you're going to carry that piano, learn to play it."

"Ready, on your mark, get set . . ." And they were off. Felber won easily, but as Leyland arrived at the fence he shouted, "That'll be five bucks, Felber. I only said I'd race you, not that I'd win." Felber, always eager to get along, paid three dollars of it.

For me the most enjoyable activity during pregame was always BP. We hit in groups of four, each player first laying down a sacrifice bunt and then getting six or seven swings in each round. Hitting well in BP could give you confidence in the game, while a poor BP could have the opposite effect. But it was never a sure thing, and no one has ever demonstrated a real connection between having a good BP and having success in the game.

I was on the bench that evening. Later I wrote, *I never seem to know when I am going to be in the lineup, and it doesn't seem to make any difference whether the other team is throwing a lefty or righty.* I was hitting fifty points higher against righties and thought I should always be in the lineup against them. Bernie's unhelpful advice to me about hitting lefties was to pretend they were righties.

The next night I was penciled in against Batavia. In my first at bat I hit a mammoth shot that sailed far over the right-field foul pole and landed next to a public swimming pool. The umpire called it foul, but running down the first base line I had a good look and was certain that it had cleared the fence in fair territory. It was the only ball I hit square all evening, further depressing my batting average and spirit. I was on deck when the final out was made in our 5–4 loss and was disappointed that I didn't get to bat again. When hitless I was always eager to get up one last time, to have a chance to salvage the night with a hit and feel okay about myself after the game.

The next day Felber and I went to a matinee at the Winter Garden Theater and saw *What's New, Pussycat?* Movies helped take our minds off our baseball woes for a few hours. Later, playing at home against Batavia, we faced Woody Fryman, a tall, broad-shouldered lefty from the tiny Appalachian town of Ewing, Kentucky. Woody had been a tobacco farmer; he had just signed at a tryout camp at the unheard-of age of twenty-five. He looked even older than twenty-five, he had never gone to high school, and when we heard his accent we imagined he was from one of those backwoods hollows where the sun seldom shines and people lived in sagging shacks with tarpaper roofs and sat on their front porches on car seats all day, drinking moonshine. But it didn't make any difference where Woody was from or that he had a weird accent because he had incredible stuff: a wicked curveball and a big-league heater. He struck out sixteen of us and gave up only two scratch hits. The *Post-Journal* called him "Mr. Untouchable." Pittsburgh Pirates scout Joe Maxwell had been trying to sign Woody for several years, but until a month before Woody hadn't been willing to give up the tobacco farm that his father had bought him and his brother. The following year Woody was pitching in the big leagues for the Pirates, where he won twelve games, including three consecutive shutouts. Three years later he was pitching for the National League in the All-Star Game. He would stick around the big leagues for eighteen seasons.

JULY 27 . . . We left Jamestown for a five-day road trip to Auburn and Geneva. Most of us were from suburbs and cities, and for us living in a small town without a car and little to do became a little boring. Road trips offered a change of scene, a chance to get away from home for a few days. As Sigmund Freud once observed, among humans the sensation of novelty is a precondition of enjoyment.

But travel could also throw you off your routine. It wasn't easy to sleep in strange beds or in the station wagon when traveling late at night after get-away games. In every town we had to find decent affordable places to eat on our meager three-dollar-per-day meal money. Then there was figuring out what to do in town during the day before you had to be at the ballpark. Fortunately, we always stayed in a downtown hotel, unlike today's Minor Leaguers, who stay at chain motels on a commercial strip among car dealerships and fast food joints, far from the action.

Our road games were broadcast on the Jamestown radio station WJTN; the announcer would get the box score each inning over the telephone and then re-create the action, making the game sound live. It was an old practice: Ronald Reagan had gotten his start in radio in 1934 doing the same, "broadcasting" Chicago Cubs games from Des Moines, Iowa.

At the ballpark Gail juggled the lineup, hoping to snap a four-game losing streak. Mike Small was on the mound. He lasted just three innings, giving up seven hits and walking a bunch as we lost again, 8–3. The loss didn't bother me because I had two hits.

After the game Felber and I met two girls in a downtown club. I left with one of them, Sally, to walk around town, which seemed to be my routine with the girls I met. In an old cemetery we read epitaphs on headstones by moonlight. As it was getting close to midnight and our curfew, I invited Sally up to my room, suggesting that we play cards. I was a bit surprised when she accepted. We were sitting on the bed in my darkened room when we heard a firm knock at the door. I shushed Sally.

"Open up, George. I know you're in there."

It was Gail. I motioned Sally to get in the closet before opening the door.

"The desk clerk says you brought a girl to your room. . . . I know she must be hiding in here, so come on out," said Gail. When Sally slinked from the closet, Gail repeated the team rule about not having girls in our hotel rooms. She left, embarrassed and hardly saying anything. Gail said I was fined twenty-five dollars. As that was 5 percent of my monthly salary, it hurt. I was frugal and hadn't yet spent any of my bonus.

The next morning Sally called my room and invited me water skiing on Lake Owasco. The lake and setting were beautiful, but her family boat and its 25-hp engine were underpowered for skiing. It dragged me in the water for some distance before I could get up on the skis. At the ballpark that night, my arms were so sore that for the first time I was grateful not to be in the lineup. We beat the Mets 4–2, winning in the eleventh inning when their pitcher threw Felber's sacrifice bunt into center field, allowing the winning runs to score.

Things were heating up in Vietnam. The headlines in the morning paper read "**SEVEN US JET PLANES LOST IN AIR RAIDS**" and "**JOHNSON DOUBLES DRAFT CALL.**" The president wanted to add another fifty thousand troops to the seventy-five thousand already in Vietnam. I didn't think the ever-expanding draft would have an effect on me, as I still had my student deferment. My teammates who felt threatened by the draft were trying to join the U.S. Army Reserves or the National Guard, which would allow them to continue playing ball after a short stint of active duty.

The next day, while walking around Auburn with Felber and second baseman "Ginny" Ginste, we came upon a great clearance sale in a men's store. I spent all my meal money on pants, leaving me with $1.20 for food for the next two days. Felber and Polak offered to loan me money. I refused, thinking the challenge of trying to feed myself for two days would be interesting, sort of an "urban survival trip." Teaming up with the batboy, who was also short on money, we split two dozen day-old doughnuts and a half gallon of milk for forty-five cents each. We ate half the doughnuts for breakfast and the other half for lunch. To quash my appetite, I went back to bed until it was time to go to the ballpark.

Playing Geneva, we faced the fifth southpaw in as many days and lost 3–2 in eleven innings. Not feeling well with a belly full of doughnuts, I went hitless. On the long ride home to Jamestown that night in the back of the station wagon, I was reading James Michener's *The Source*. The guys up front joked about the thickness of the nine-hundred-page book, suggesting that I must be "some kind of intellectual." The book was actually a light historical novel set in an Israeli archaeological dig, but I didn't mind the suggestion that I might be smarter than I actually was.

In my journal I kept a running total of all my stats, and I was now hitting just .200. I wondered if the Spalding shoe and glove rep ever checked batting averages and wished that he hadn't signed me to a contract. Your batting average was the ultimate measure of how well you were performing (for pitchers it was your ERA along with your won-lost record). Because baseball was everything to us, our batting averages had a huge influence on our feelings of self-worth. (This being the presabermetrics era, there wasn't any attention given to on-base percentage or slugging percentage, statistics that today are regarded as a better measure of a player's value to his team.)

Your batting average also influenced how much other players respected you and, to some degree, your place in the team pecking order. It was an important measure to the farm director and his player development staff in Detroit's front office, too, but they also took other factors into account in assessing your potential. Besides the standard five tools—running, throwing, fielding, hitting, and hitting with power—they also considered "intangibles" that had no statistical measure, notably your "attitude" and whether you were a team player and good for team chemistry. Like most rookies, though, I didn't understand the importance of these other factors, so my batting average assumed even greater importance than it should have. Seeing it decline depressed me; when it was rising, I was elated.

JULY 31 . . . We played Wellsville and faced another lefty, losing 11–4. The *Post-Journal* noted in a small headline that Wellsville had taken a two-game lead over us in the battle to stay out of NY-Penn League's basement. I guess there was little else to report. *The only thing that is keeping me from hating Jamestown and facing so many lefties is my new pretty girlfriend, Claire.*

After the game Claire and I hitched out to her family's farm. The next morning was already hot and muggy as we walked two miles to a stream with a swimming hole. We swam, picked a leech off Claire's ankle, wrestled, and flirted. We removed our clothes and lay down on the bank and made out. We were very close to having sex when a mother and two young children in swimwear and carrying a picnic basket appeared. We leaped up, awkwardly threw our clothes on, made our way through the underbrush, and left. Struck out again, I thought, wondering if I was ever going to have sex. Claire feared that she might have been recognized. It was a small community where everyone knew everyone else, so the mother likely would have known Claire's parents.

AUGUST 1 . . . We traveled to Wellsville for the first game of a six-day road trip. During the second inning the skies opened up, and the game was washed out. After showering we piled back into our wagons, heading for Binghamton. The game the next day against Binghamton was delayed by rain for two hours and then canceled, to be made up in a doubleheader the following day. Playing every day, seven days a week, we were always glad to get a rainout, but no one liked sitting around the ballpark waiting, sometimes for hours, for the game to be called.

After most road games the team would split into groups of four or five guys who would go out to eat and have a few beers before returning to the hotel. Drinking wine or liquor was unheard of. Team curfew was two hours after the game or around midnight, though it was relaxed if the team was playing well, which for us was rare. Once back at the hotel players would sometimes sit around the lobby or on the hotel porch talking—usually about baseball. Gail sometimes joined in with great stories from his time in the Pirates and Giants organizations, where he and Willie Mays were teammates and for a time competitors for center field. Such hotel-lobby gab sessions are rare in pro ball today, as most players retreat to their rooms and into their personal electronic entertainment.

AUGUST 3 . . . Our hard-throwing right-hander George "Moose" Korince shut down the Trips as we won the first game of the doubleheader, 3-0. Moose got his nickname from his large body—six-foot-three and 210 pounds—bulbous nose, enormous incisors, and Canadian heritage. Having grown up playing hockey, Moose had less mound experience than American pitchers, but as an exceptionally hard thrower he had great potential. Like Leyland, Moose loved horseplay, and late that night I awoke to sounds of a water fight in the hallway. Moose had dumped an ice bucket of water on his roommate's bed. When his roomie then locked him out, Moose broke the door in. The following year, just twenty years of age, Moose was called up to the Tigers and over the next two seasons pitched well but sparingly in relief, before being returned to the Minors. He was out of baseball altogether before his twenty-fifth birthday.

AUGUST 4 . . . We arrived home from our six-day road trip at four thirty in the morning and had to return to the ballpark at three that afternoon to leave for a road game against Batavia. Everyone was relieved when rain canceled the game before our departure. I took Claire to see *Dr. Zhivago*, and then we returned to my apartment to enjoy the coffee cake she had baked me—one of the many benefits of having a girlfriend. As powerful thunderstorms rolled through, we went out to walk in the wild weather. *The large cool drops crashing into us in the warm night air produced a wonderful sensation*, I wrote. At the bottom of a hill we stood in a swollen storm gutter where the torrent of water rushed against our bodies like an incoming wave at the beach.

We returned to my apartment soaked to the skin and elated from our adventure. Removing each other's clothes to dry off, we soon found ourselves scuffling on the bed. Claire was strong from the daily chores she did on the family farm. Her still damp body had that wonderful clean and fresh smell of a baby's head. A lightning flash outside the window lit her naked body in my dim candlelit bedroom. "Just like in the movies," I thought. Soon, after all those false starts, we were making love. It was the first time for both of us. Afterward, we collapsed on the bed and talked—analyzed it—and concluded that sex wasn't all that it was cracked up to be. But a while later we did it again—and this time, we agreed, it was fabulous. I still remember it clearly.

One of the benefits for small-town girls of dating ballplayers rather than local boys was that a girl could have an affair without risking her reputation. Ballplayers had no local friends to brag to, and at the end of the season they left town, usually never to return.

AUGUST 5 . . . Playing Batavia the next night, we were down by two runs in the seventh with a man on when Gail had me pinch-hit. On the mound for the Pirates was Larry Killingsworth, who would be called up the following year and would stick around for fifteen years with the Pirates, Angels, and Red Sox. His first pitch was a high heater that I got under just a bit and skied to deep center; a breeze carried well, and it cleared the fence. The home run surprised me as much as Killingsworth, because like many lefties I was a lowball hitter and my home runs usually came on pitches that were no more than belt high. My dinger tied the score, but we lost the game in the ninth when, with a man on second, Felber at third base couldn't handle a hard smash, the ball bouncing off his chest. In the previous twenty-four hours, I had finally gotten laid and hit my first pinch-hit home run. Life was good.

The *Post-Journal* that day reported LBJ as saying, "The U.S. would leave Vietnam promptly if the local population could be guaranteed self-determination free of any alien ideology," adding, "America wins the wars that she undertakes." I hadn't paid much attention to the war other than wanting my country to win and get it over with. I didn't have much sympathy for the demonstrators. That would change.

George Spencer, the roving Minor League pitching coach, joined the team for a few weeks and was at the ballpark. He and Gail were good friends, having been teammates in the Giants organization. In fact, George had been a Giant when they won the final playoff game to decide the National League championship in 1951, one of the most celebrated games in baseball history. Everyone liked George, with the only rap against him being that he sometimes seemed more interested in teaching hitting than pitching. That night we beat Batavia 6–5, and I had one bloop single in four trips. My mind was on having sex again, as soon as possible.

AUGUST 7 . . . It was the annual AFL-CIO night in which all union members were given free admission to the ballpark and a chance for prizes. The promotion drew 3,225, the largest crowd of the season, as we lost to Auburn.[1] I blasted one far into the night, which the *Post-Journal* described the next day as a "tremendous shot." I loved hitting home runs—it had been my favorite thing in life, until Claire and I discovered sex. Some of my homers, those that I got a good look at as they left the park, I can still see in my mind's eye today, a half century later. Nonetheless, I would have swapped a home run that night for four singles to raise my batting average.

The next evening, with so many fans having gotten in free the night before, our attendance dipped to 205. Few of them stuck around to see us win the game in the ninth after Batavia's shortstop booted a ground ball and their pitcher threw wild to first base on a sacrifice bunt. Fielding in low A-ball was erratic compared to the levels above us. We would sometimes go three or four games without making an error and then would fall apart, making a bunch in a single game, making our brand of baseball on such evenings look "bush."

Claire and I went to a matinee, and when the movie lasted longer than I expected I had to run the mile and a half to the ballpark. Left-hander Steve Dillon, who had briefly pitched for the New York Mets the previous season, now on injury rehab assignment, was going for the Auburn Mets. In my first at bat he threw me a low and in fastball, and I yanked it over the Caprino Furniture sign in center field. While Claire wasn't a real baseball fan, it felt good knowing that she was there and had seen it. Success was always sweeter if there was someone you cared about in the stands.

AUGUST 9 . . . Captain Dynamite Night, a much ballyhooed promotion, arrived. The Captain set up his coffin of death behind second base, and then, with the crowd counting down—3 . . . 2 . . . 1 . . . BOOM, he blew himself up. Or so it seemed. There was a tremendous bang and a lot of smoke and then a long silence. After the smoke cleared, the Captain slowly emerged, unscathed, from the coffin. The trick was that he placed blasting caps, the source of the explosion, around the coffin in a way that the blast was directed outward, away from his body. Captain Dynamite performed in Minor League Baseball stadiums nearly every night for another twenty-five years. In 1990 he brought his daughter into the act while scaling back his nightly explosions to once every three days.

We lost that night, 2–1, our ninth loss in eleven games. But I hit another home run. For this one an eighty-eight-year-old widow and season ticket holder, Mrs. Lewis, gave me twenty dollars. To get our bats going, she had announced that she would give ten dollars to any Jamestown Tiger hitting a home run. After I circled the bases, she beckoned me over and passed me two ten-dollar bills through the screen with no explanation as to why she had doubled the prize money. I planned to spend it on Claire.

AUGUST 10 . . . It was the NY-Penn League All-Star break, which I'm certain was celebrated by every player in the league as though it was Christmas. It was the only scheduled day off the entire season. Not since opening day in April, four months before, had there been a real day off. Only two of my teammates made the All-Star team: Carl Solarek and Bruce Buys. The rest of us scattered. Those whose hometowns were in the East went home for the day; Felber and two others took some local girls to Niagara Falls. I spent the day with Claire at her farm and for one of the few times all season got to watch TV—*Bilko*, *I Love Lucy*, *The Evening News with David Brinkley and Chet Huntley*, and the *Bugs Bunny* cartoon that always preceded the news. Felber and I didn't have a TV, nor did most of the hotel rooms we stayed in on the road. The one time we did, we could barely make out the picture through all the snow.

As we got ready to play Geneva at home, it was hard to believe that our day off was already over. Quality Markets Night at the Park drew 2,862 fans, who, as the *Post-Journal* noted, "came to gather up a truck load of loot," everything from S&H Green Stamps to cooking grills and canned hams. The kids were given free balloons and pencils as they entered the ballpark. Lefty Gomez, the onetime Yankee great, then traveling for a sporting-goods firm, was the emcee. The Corn Planters Drum and Bugle Corps performed, and the ballplayers leered at the comely and stacked French horn player. But best thing about promotions was being able to play before a large crowd. Despite leading the entire game, we managed to lose again, 6–4, when in the ninth a Geneva Senator hit a bases-clearing triple.

The next night, after losing the first game of a doubleheader with Wellsville, Gail scrambled the lineup, and we won the nightcap. The headline in the *Post-Journal* was "**JUGGLED LINEUP HELPS TIGERS GAIN A SPLIT.**" The article claimed that we had responded to the new lineup "with gusto." It was silly—a lucky bases-loaded bloop had won the game. Felber and I went hitless, and we each made an error as well. That we both had terrible games made it a little easier at home. For us, there was always truth in the cliché about misery loving company.

AUGUST 14 . . . *TODAY is a day I'll never forget*, I wrote, half in caps. We were playing a scheduled doubleheader against Binghamton. The first game started at 6:30 p.m. on a stiflingly hot and humid night. Six hours later, with the score tied at 4–4, the game was finally called. It was 12:40 a.m., and we had played twenty-one innings. There were forty-five strikeouts. Binghamton's star first baseman, Herb Farris, the Mickey Mantle lookalike, struck out seven times. The Trips' catcher Chuck Siebel caught the full twenty-one innings and lost five pounds doing it. Felber and I each went one for eight. Claire was one of just a handful of fans still in the stands in the fifteenth inning when she fainted in her seat—she figured from not drinking enough liquid in the heat—and had to be helped out of the stadium.

We should have won that game in the twenty-first inning when Polak singled with one out and Ricky Clark, our fastest runner, went in to pinch-run for him. John Faehr, a.k.a. Ozark, then hit a double off the fence in left-center that would have scored Ricky had he not stumbled rounding the bag at second and thus had to pull up at third. We couldn't believe it. But we still had Ricky on third with just one out. Junior Lopez then lofted a fly ball to center, deep enough to score the winning run. But at contact Ricky ran down the line toward home, and by the time Gail, in the third base coaching box, frantically waved him back, it was too late to tag up. "Fucking unbelievable" was the universal reaction. For the few fans left in the stands, it must've been hard to believe they were watching professional baseball. Ricky's boneheaded play seemed emblematic of our team's season-long disappointments. It was the longest game ever played in the history of the NY-Penn League, shattering the previous mark of nineteen innings, set in 1944.

No one was happy when we were told that we'd make up the entire game in another doubleheader the next day against Binghamton. Neither team scored in the first game until Binghamton pushed across a run in the ninth on a bad call by the plate umpire, who seemed more interested in getting the game over than getting the call right. I struck out in all four at bats.[2] From such a promising beginning, my batting average had fallen below the .200 mark. Only sleeping with Claire was keeping me from total despair.

The next day we traveled to Batavia. I got the first hit of the game in the fifth inning and afterward went deep in the eighth. *Baseball can be such a roller coaster. One day you're in the dumps, and the next day you're happy as a clam and on top of the world. . . . I love it when I play well,* I wrote that night.

Vietnam got pushed off the front page of the *Post-Journal* by race riots in Los Angeles. "**NEGROES SNIPERS BOMB LA WHITE SECTIONS—33 DEAD AS RIOTS ENTER SIXTH DAY.**" The article described "carloads of Negroes carrying snipers" and more than a thousand fires having been set, burning shops and stores. The race riots were, said the paper, "an aid to Commie propaganda overseas," as they showed the United States as a country in the throes of violence. It sounded pretty serious, but at the ballpark only one player mentioned the troubles and no one followed up with any curiosity, nor did it come up at the postgame party that night at Leyland's cabin on the lake. That muggy evening Claire and I took a small rowboat far out on the glassy lake and went skinny dipping but then discovered that we couldn't climb back in the boat without capsizing it. We had to swim back, towing the boat behind us. By the time we reached shore it was three, and everyone had gone to bed or gone home, including our rides. Sleeping on the grass together, we didn't really mind being left.

AUGUST 18 . . . We left on a five-day road trip to Auburn and Geneva. The first night we faced Geneva's Bill Hepler, a nineteen-year-old rookie from Covington, Virginia, who had signed with the Washington Senators after averaging nineteen strikeouts a game in American Legion ball, an incredible feat. The PA announced that Hepler, a beanpole six-footer, had just been voted by the NY-Penn League's managers and sportswriters the player expected to go the furthest in professional baseball. Hepler did make it to the big leagues the following year but lasted only one season. Arm trouble would send him back to the Minors, where he would bounce around for a half-dozen years before, like Moose, he was washed up at twenty-six.

AUGUST 21 . . . After getting three hits the previous night I was back on the bench. *How do you get three hits one night and benched the next day?* I watched the game from the bullpen, which was always a good place to escape Gail's harping that we "keep our heads in the game," that we pay attention to the action on the field and support our teammates.

That evening in the bullpen Gary Hart, Mike Small, and a few relievers debated the existence of God. It went something like this: "If there really is a God, how can you explain the death of so many innocent, devout Christians? Like those killed in car crashes on their way to church outings or killed by a tornado while saying their prayers." The believers side countered: "Because he's God, we don't know what he has in mind for us. We can never know his ways, and we should accept his existence on faith and shut the fuck up about it."

Bullpen debates like this one never resolved or convinced anyone of anything, but were often amusing. And they passed the time for those who weren't in the game. Another favorite bullpen activity was to scout for good-looking girls in the stands. Each girl would be rated on a 1 to 10 scale, sometimes with accompanying descriptions of what the player would like to do with her. When we got hungry one of the relievers might sneak down to the refreshment stand to bring back hot dogs, peanuts, or Cracker Jack. Eating in the bullpen that evening caused us to break into song: "Take me out to the ball game, / Buy me some peanuts and Cracker Jack, / I don't care if I never get back . . ."

AUGUST 22 . . . After buying cork guns in a shop on Main Street, Moose, Leyland, Buys, and Ginny Ginste dueled in the hallway and rooms of the hotel that night. Apart from the noise it was harmless until it turned into a pillow fight. One pillow tore open with feathers flying. Leyland emptied a wastebasket full of water on me, and I did the same to Felber, who then dumped water on my bed, leaving me without a dry place to sleep. Veteran Ken Magown, who was five years older than most of us, put a stop to it by strongly suggesting that it was, at three in the morning, time for everyone to go to bed. Felber and I slept on our box springs.

AUGUST 24 . . . When I arrived in the clubhouse Ozark and Bill Newton were packing their gear. They had just learned they were being moved up to Rocky Mount in the Carolina League, the Tigers' top Class

A club. Everyone congratulated them, saying we'd see them again in spring training in March. Their departure left us with only fifteen players on the active roster, including pitcher Gene Voss, who had just returned from his one month of service with the military reserves. That night Voss, a.k.a. "Needle Dick Bug Fucker" because of his long, slender penis, pitched us to a 7–6 win.

AUGUST 26 . . . On a two-day road trip to Binghamton, Gail shuffled up the room assignments and put me with veteran Ken Magown. *I am not sure why. Is he hoping I might learn something from Magown? Or does Gail think I was responsible for the water and cork-gun fights in Auburn and this is punishment?* Magown had been a pitcher and had put up good numbers at Montgomery in the AA Southern League when an arm injury ended his pitching career. Detroit sent him to Jamestown to retool as a first baseman and outfielder; Magown had a good bat and, like Leyland, was regarded as an "organization man." He would later marry his Jamestown sweetheart and serve on the town's police force for more than twenty years before retiring to Florida. In the 1940s and '50s, several Jamestown players had married local girls and stayed on in the town. They were generally well regarded, and one became a city councilman. But by the mid-1960s it was unusual for players to stick around the small towns where they played, and Magown was the last to do so.

That night we led the whole game until in the ninth Gary Hart walked the bases full and then gave up a grand slam. *We have only six games left in the season. I can't wait to finish.* We were in the dog days of late August where everywhere in the baseball universe, players, worn down by the grind of road trips and a game every day, were weary and eager to go home.

AUGUST 27 . . . Rain fell off and on all day in Binghamton, the tenth-rainiest city in America, with precipitation on an amazing 162 days of the year. When we got to the ballpark, the infield was a mess, with the forecast for more rain. The game should have been called, but there was a big promotion scheduled and the club was expecting five thousand fans. The Trips' GM tried to do everything possible to get the game in, no matter the conditions or the objections of the players. The grounds crew had been working on the field for two hours when, as a last resort, they poured gallons of gasoline on the puddles. The leaping flames and black smoke put on a show in itself. The field was declared playable by the umpires, but in the second inning another downpour forced the game to be called. As we caravanned out of Binghamton, the streets were flooded, the water at times lapping over our front bumper. We arrived home at three thirty in the morning with, as always, a game to play that night.

In an attempt to generate interest in our few remaining games, one *Post-Journal* headline ran: "**TIGERS CAN PLAY IMPORTANT ROLE IN WHO WINS NEW YORK–PENN LEAGUE FLAG.**" We were to play Auburn that night, and by beating them, the paper declared, we could spoil their chances of winning the second-half championship. In the real world, whether Binghamton or Auburn won the championship was of no importance to us. No one particularly liked or disliked either team. At our level the kind of rivalries common in the big leagues, like the Dodgers-Giants, Yankees–Red Sox, Cards-Cubs, were nonexistent.

Before the game the Auburn Mets catcher Greg "Goose" Goossen was called up to New York. Everybody was happy for the likable catcher. We were all aware that expansion clubs like the New York Mets, who had been in existence for only four years, offered more opportunities for young players to move up the Minor League ladder quickly than the older, established organizations, like the Tigers, Red Sox, and Yankees. A fellow Californian, Goose would stick with the Mets and then go on to play for the Seattle Pilots, Milwaukee Brewers, and Washington Senators. As I was writing this chapter, Goose died of cancer at age sixty-six, and a short while later Woody Fryman died of Alzheimer's.

Not having seen them since our baseball days, my image of them was still of strong, dominating young men; it was hard to fathom that they were now gone.

AUGUST 28 . . . A cold air mass from Canada had descended on the region, and by game time the temperature was in the low forties, with a stiff wind—you could hear it whipping the flag beyond center field—making it feel even colder. In cold weather vibrations from the bat can sting the hitter's hands. Junior Lopez went to the plate with a towel wrapped around his bat. Players from the Caribbean suffered the most, some wearing gloves and even long underwear and sweatshirts under their uniforms. In the second inning Ginny and Moose gathered some scrap lumber and built a fire at the end of the dugout. It must have been a strange sight to the few fans in attendance: smoke curling out from under the dugout roof. Felber was hit in the head by a hard throw from the outfield as he was sliding into third and had to be removed from the game. Finally, after four and a half innings, the minimum for the game to count, it was called on account of "cold weather."

AUGUST 30 . . . Ralph Snyder, the Detroit Tigers' general manager, arrived in town to meet with Jamestown GM Marty Haines and a few shareholders. The *Post* reported that Marty was going to inform Snyder that next season the Tigers needed to field a better team, and if the Tigers couldn't promise better ballplayers, the Jamestown owners would not re-sign with Detroit. Whenever front-office brass were in town, everyone felt the pressure to play well; given my anemic batting average and being a rookie, I really wanted to impress Mr. Snyder. I made decent contact, going one for three, and left the ballpark feeling pretty good.

After the game many of us went to Leyland's place on Lake Chautauqua for another party. Felber and Leyland tried to get me drunk. *I had three beers, the most ever in my life*, I noted in my journal. Inexpensive beer was the only alcohol anyone on our club drank, and no one yet smoked marijuana. In fact, I didn't know of any teammate who used a drug of any kind, although amphetamines or greenies were beginning to make an appearance in the big leagues, as Jim Bouton would reveal to the world five years later in *Ball Four* (1970).

AUGUST 31 . . . In our 5–1 loss to Auburn, the air was again so cold that we built a fire in the end of the dugout and kept it going the entire game. The Auburn bullpen also had its own little fire. After the next day's game was rained out, I went to Claire's and stayed over, planning to be back at the ballpark at three o'clock for the final game of the season. With more rain forecast, however, the team canceled the final game and told the players to meet at the ballpark in the morning to clear out their lockers. Being at Claire's, I didn't get the message. When I arrived at the park in the afternoon expecting to play that night, no one was there. With the clubhouse locked and not sure what to do, I started to climb one of the light towers to take a last look around. I was about halfway to the top when Jerry Klein drove up, apparently to let me in the clubhouse. I scrambled down, hoping he hadn't seen me. Everybody else had left town. Even my roommate, Felber, had cleared out. It was a lonely feeling, and I wondered what Mr. Snyder thought of my not having shown up with the rest of the team for our season-ending farewell and whether Jerry would tell him that he had found me on the light tower.

Our dismal season had come to a fitting end on an equally dismal day. I was relieved the season was over. Our record of forty-seven wins and seventy-five losses tied us for last place with the Batavia Pirates. It was Jamestown's worst showing since 1939. Our attendance was only 30,642 for the season, an average of about 450 per game. In the previous decade the team had routinely drawn three times that many. The Jamestown owners did not renew their "working agreement" with Detroit and instead signed a contract with the Dodgers (LA would last just one year before being succeeded by the Braves).

Mike Small had given up more than one hundred runs and one hundred walks in ninety-six innings of work. He would survive five seasons in pro ball without ever finding the plate. Our team batting average was .233. Felber, who had been the leading hitter in Duluth when we were promoted, hit .131. *Felber said that if only first base was one step closer he'd have hit .250* (slow afoot, he rarely had an infield hit). I finished at .207. Wearing Kaline's pants hadn't given me much luck after all. I wrote, *Just three scratch hits stand between me at .207 and the team batting average.* What wonders that would have done for my psyche and for my prospects going into the off-season. If there was a bright spot, it was that I hit more home runs per at bat than anyone else on the club.

Of the twenty-nine players who cycled through the Jamestown Tigers' roster that season, three would eventually play in the big leagues: Ricky Clarke, George Korince, and Wayne Redmond. Jim Leyland would make it as a manager. That was close to the overall average of 8 percent of players in low A-ball who reached the Majors, a figure that hasn't changed much over time. In the Major Leagues that year Roberto Clemente would lead the National League in hitting at .329 and Tony Oliva the American League at .321, while Willie Mays hit fifty-two home runs and Maury Wills stole ninety-four bases: two Latinos and two African Americans.

Looking back at my first season of pro ball, it's clear that I learned a good deal about the culture of the Minor Leagues—the jargon, the pranks, the importance of nicknames, the pastimes, and the need to always show respect for the game, whether by wearing the uniform properly, by not throwing your bat or helmet in disgust, or by running hard on every batted ball. I learned that, unlike amateur and school leagues, in pro ball your own personal performance was more important than your team winning the game. This emphasis on individual performance rather than the team, and the cutthroat competition that it could produce between teammates playing the same position, was something Felber never got used to and often railed about. It became clear that baseball management put great stock in the value of hard work. No matter how talented you were, coaches talked only about your having the "potential" to move up if you worked hard.

I discovered that playing a game every day was a grind—baseball by far has the longest and most grueling season of any professional sport. It leaves little time for anything else. And finally I learned that if I was going to survive, I had to do a better job of staying on an even keel—not getting too elated after getting a few hits one night or too depressed the next night after an o'fer. I had to get off the emotional roller coaster.

In retrospect, my pursuit of a girlfriend seems more than just the typical interests of a young male. I was driven equally by the loneliness of living away from home for the first time and the tremendous pressure to perform in a new occupation. Claire provided emotional support and someone to confide in. Of course, there was also the excitement of romance. Today's ballplayers, in contrast, are able to maintain their connection with family and friends at home through cell phones, e-mail, and Facebook, and far more of them today are visited during the season by girlfriends and family.

After staying with Claire during my final night in Jamestown, I left on a bus early the next day, wondering what would become of us. And of me. Would I ever see her again? Would Detroit want me back?

5

SPRING TRAINING

Tiger Town

Six weeks after I returned home from Jamestown, I received a letter from Claire. She had missed two periods. A week later, on a Friday afternoon, another letter arrived. Like the first, it came to me at Stanford University, where I had been accepted as a transfer student and was majoring in biology. Suspecting the contents could be upsetting, I took it to a quiet place in a grove of trees on campus to read. My eye instantly caught the words, "I am pregnant." *Oh my God.* I knew nothing about these things and apparently hadn't known enough to have prevented the pregnancy. I called Claire. Her father was furious, she said. He'd called her a whore, refused to let her eat at the family dinner table, and wanted her out of the house. She was sent to live with friends of her mother in town.

An abortion was out of the question because her mother was Catholic. She had not told her parents that I was the father, but they must have figured it out since she hadn't been seeing anyone else. I needed to talk to someone, but I didn't have any friends at Stanford yet, and besides what advice would another twentysomething male be able to offer? It was the start of a weekend, so I drove home to San Mateo. I couldn't bring myself to talk to my mother about it, even though we were close. I returned to campus on Sunday, having spoken to no one.

Claire decided she had no choice but to have the baby. In the sixties it was still common for pregnant girls to be shipped off to avoid embarrassing their families. Before Claire began to show, her father sent her to a home for unwed mothers in Buffalo where the girls were given false identities. Claire, now known as Joyce, met another girl from a NY-Penn League town who was also carrying a ballplayer's baby—a pitcher I knew from the Bay Area. I sent Claire what money I could. Neither of us mentioned the idea of marriage. We both had career "plans" and thought of ourselves as far too young. And could I have supported her and a child on a Minor League salary? And what would it have been like for her with an infant following me around the country, to spring training, to the town(s) I was to play ball in, and then to Stanford in the off-season? I had seen how tough that was for teammates who were married with young children. Besides, were we really in "love" . . . or was it that we were each just eager for the affection of another? We'd known each other for less than two months.

We corresponded throughout the fall, but less earnestly on my part as I struggled to keep up with my studies and perhaps because I was not eager to be reminded of the mess that I had helped create. I wondered how we could have been so clueless—but as virgins and without any sex education in schools in those days, neither of us had understood the risks. As Claire later said, "My parents were good Irish Catholics who didn't believe in sex education; all I knew was that having sex was like Russian roulette, and I guess I was prepared to take my chances." Claire said she wasn't expecting anything more from me, that she would handle it herself. Though I didn't realize it then, I would see Claire again.

In March, as my departure for spring training approached, I arranged to take my final exams early, as did two other Stanford students who were also professional ball players; one of them, Jim Lonborg of the Red Sox, would win the Cy Young Award the following year. As I boarded my red-eye flight from San Francisco to Tampa, I was of two minds. I was eager to see what spring training would be like and still proud to be a ballplayer going off to Florida, but I was also anxious and unsure of myself after not putting up good numbers the previous season in Jamestown. My confidence had been further shaken that winter when Detroit sent my new contract with a 5 percent cut in salary.

I boarded the plane wondering if I really had the tools to make it in pro ball. Despite my doubts, I was determined to work my tail off and do whatever I could to show the Tigers that I had what it took. I knew there would be more players in spring camp than roster spots and that many would be released before the new season even started. During the flight I wrote, *I'm going to give it my best shot, and whatever happens happens.*

For six weeks, from late February until the opening of the new season, Florida and Arizona were, and still are, the center of the baseball universe. Nine of the sixteen Major League organizations in 1966 trained in Florida. All but one have since moved to new taxpayer-subsidized complexes elsewhere in Florida or Arizona. Only the Detroit Tigers still train in the same town—Lakeland—where they have been every year since 1934.[1]

Spring baseball helped put Arizona and Florida on the map. While most fans today think spring training has always taken place in one of these two sunshine states, this isn't so. In the late nineteenth century, most clubs trained at their home park for a few weeks before the season; when it rained or snowed, they worked out indoors or under the stands. The first teams to head south to warm weather were the Chicago White Stockings and the New York Mutuals, who trained in New Orleans in 1870. In the mid-1880s several teams began training in Hot Springs, Arkansas, which remained a favorite for several decades. It wasn't until 1911, when the Pittsburgh Pirates moved their training camp to St. Petersburg, that Florida hosted its first Major League team. Over the next decade Florida became the preeminent spring site. Arizona didn't enter the picture until the late 1940s, when the Cleveland Indians and New York Giants set up training bases in the desert.

I arrived at Tiger Town, Detroit's spring-training complex in Lakeland, on Thursday, March 10, 1966, after traveling all night. The receptionist issued me a Detroit Tiger identification card, gave me a schedule of meal and workout times, and assigned me to room 34 in the barracks. I found it, dropped my gear, and then reported to the clubhouse, where the clubbie, George Popovich, issued me a uniform. Number 87. With so many players in camp, uniform numbers ran into the high 90s—more like football than baseball. As in Jamestown, all uniforms were hand-me-downs from the big club. The only thing that distinguished each of the camp's six teams or squads was the color of our socks. The rookie-league team wore pea-soup green. Double A Montgomery had maroon, but the best was Triple A Syracuse, who wore the same dark-blue socks as the big club. Popovich told me that the Detroit Tigers had gotten their name from the yellow and black stockings—like Tiger stripes—they had worn in the 1890s. Before I left the clubhouse he handed me a bottle of sun lotion, warned me about the power of the Florida sun, and advised me to slather up, including the tops of my ears. A few of the northern kids said they'd never before used sun lotion.

Each of the 140 or so Minor Leaguers was assigned to a team. At the bottom was Lakeland (Gulf Coast League), and then going up the ladder were Statesville (Western Carolina League), Daytona Beach (Florida State League [FSL]), Rocky Mount (Carolina League), Montgomery (Southern League), and finally at the Triple A level Syracuse (International League). Adjustments were made in the rosters throughout the spring; each Sunday, before the evening meal, new rosters were posted on a bulletin board near the cafeteria. The posting was momentous. If you were promoted, demoted, or, God forbid, no longer on a club, there it appeared on the bulletin board. While much of how things worked was a mystery to us first-time spring trainees, the hierarchy of the "farm system" was well understood by everyone. If you were a Class A player, like me, you wouldn't try to hang out with guys in Double or Triple A, even if they were of the same age, as they were of higher status.

Just two hours after arriving in Tiger Town, and working on little sleep, I was on the field with my Daytona Beach team in the middle of an intrasquad game. Although I had missed the first week of camp because of final exams, Gail Henley inserted me into the lineup. In my only at bat I hit a long triple in the right-field gap. Better still, it was off a tough lefty. *I'm off to a good start*, I wrote that night.

After the game and a shower, I walked around to look at my new surroundings. The seventeen-acre Tiger Town complex had been a flight-school training center for American and British pilots during World War II and home to squadrons of B-17s, B-24s, and P-51 Mustang fighters.[2] Its air-base heritage was evident in the two large hangars that now contained a batting cage (the first-ever indoor batting cage) and an infield and pitching mounds for workouts on rainy days.[3] Alongside the hangars an old runway was faintly visible beneath the crabgrass. There were also a military-style mess hall and two double-story wooden barracks, painted forest green. Four ball fields were arranged back to back, cloverleaf fashion, with a tower in the center from which the Detroit brass and coaches could watch several games and practices at once. There were no outfield fences; instead, a ditch ran around the perimeter. And not far off was Lake Parker, the largest lake in Lakeland.

The centerpiece of the complex was, and still is, Joker Marchant Stadium, where the big-league spring-training games were played. It had just been completed a few months before and is now the oldest spring-training stadium in the country. Despite some remodeling, it still has an old-school 1960s feel and charm.[4]

While the Minor Leaguers bunked four to a room in the barracks, the Major Leaguers stayed at a Holiday Inn a mile away. Our rooms were spartan, with little furniture and no decoration on the walls, and they were separated by partitions that did not extend to the ceiling. There were no doors. We slept a few feet apart on steel-frame cots that squeaked when you shifted or rolled over. We stored our clothing and

9. Outside the Tiger Town barracks.

10. Joker Marchant Stadium, spring-training home of the Detroit Tigers, 1965. Photo courtesy of the Detroit Tigers.

gear in upright olive-colored metal lockers left over from the army. Dormitory rules were posted on the bulletin board: "No soft drinks or pets in your room" (who in their right mind would bring a cat or dog to spring training?), "Don't hang anything on the walls," and "Lights out at midnight." Fortunately, none of the coaches lived with us, so there was little enforcement other than an occasional bed check.

We awoke each morning at eight to Herb Alpert's Tijuana Brass blared over the PA system. After shaving, dressing, and making your bed (another rule), you lined up in the cafeteria for breakfast. There more rules governed us: "Fill the rear tables first," "Eat everything on your plate," and "Do not loiter after your meal." Scrambled eggs, bacon and sausage, French toast and pancakes were constants, but despite being in the center of citrus country the orange juice was from concentrate and fruit from a can. It was rumored the Tigers put saltpeter in our food to reduce our sexual appetites. But overall the food tasted good, and there was plenty of it. After breakfast we went to the clubhouse to change into our uniforms for the day's workout and game. Ed Katalinas, the scouting director, a bear of a man with a gravelly voice and revered for having signed Al Kaline, began each day's workout with an announcement, first blowing loudly into the microphone: "Good morning, Tigers!!! It's another sunny day here in Lakeland. It's going to be seventy-six degrees and in Detroit just twenty-two degrees." Katalinas never failed to give us the Detroit temperature—probably to make us feel lucky to be in Tiger Town.

He'd then tell us which field each club was to report to. All four fields were named after Tiger legends—Cobb, Cochrane, Gehringer, and Heilmann. Our workout began with roll call, followed by calisthenics and running laps or foul pole to foul pole to get loose. After that we played catch and pepper—a game in which the hitter tried to stay at bat as long as he could by forcing the fielders to make errors, sometimes by hitting smashes off the fielders' shins. But there was little room for real horseplay or for skating by since the coaches saw to it that we followed the regimen. Except for the few with big bonuses, we understood that if we weren't in top shape and didn't work hard, we would not last long. There was always someone waiting on the bench or on the level below eager to take your place.

The first ten days of spring training stressed fundamentals (covering bunts, rundowns, hitting the cutoff man, and so forth) and conditioning, or, as one coach put it, "shaking winter out of your fat asses." Unlike today's players who train throughout the off-season, most of us were not in great baseball shape when we arrived at camp. Guys had winter jobs, and some, like me, had been in school right up to leaving for Florida. Bernie DeViveiros, the scout who had signed me, taught sliding; he had us wear heavy denim sliding pants over our uniforms, remove our spikes to avoid turning an ankle, and then run and slide on a damp, grassy incline. Bernie railed against the head-first slide, saying there was a greater risk of injury from the fielder's spikes or hard tag on the hand or head. And Bernie preached the bent-leg slide over the hook slide because it enabled you to pop up and proceed to the next base in case of an overthrow. It was the same sermon he had given at my home in San Mateo the night he had signed me.

Bernie had a hard time with names, either forgetting them or in a comical way butchering their pronunciations; Jon Warden, for instance, became Jon "Warbler." Everyone liked Bernie, and I was proud that he had been my scout. I also figured it was to my benefit that he had signed some big-league stars, like Mickey Lolich, and that the front office considered him the ultimate company man who would do anything for the Tigers.

Although the radar gun was still twenty years off, coaches did make use of stopwatches. Our foot speed from home plate to first base and then circling the bases was measured and duly recorded. My speed was just average. Running was the one skill or "tool" that you couldn't do much to improve (I had tried by joining the cross-country team in high school). While there was a lot of attention paid to physical skills, there wasn't much on the mental side—maintaining focus, concentration, and confidence. Surely, the coaches understood the importance of the mental dimension (as Yogi Berra put it, "90 percent of the game is half mental"). Looking back, I suspect they just didn't know how to teach it. And there were no sports psychologists on the staff back then.

On the field our behavior was governed by still more rules: "No player may leave his squad or the field without permission from his coach" and "There will be no altering of outer socks." And there were warnings as well: "Be careful of sunburn; use the lotion provided." "Control your temper! Breaking or throwing bats or helmets will result in disciplinary action." Despite all the rules and admonitions, there were no counselors, no one to help you deal with the incredible pressure to perform well or to offer advice about loneliness, groupies, alcohol, or money. Management's mind-set was that if you couldn't deal with it, there were plenty of other players waiting to take your place who could.

The worst workouts were those on rainy days when we were sent to the old, and always hot and muggy, airplane hangars, where the noise of bat on ball and smack of fastballs hitting leather catcher mitts reverberated.

After the first week of camp, everyone was eager to start playing real games. We began with intrasquad games and then games against the other Class A teams and occasionally the Double A club. We also traveled by bus to other spring-training complexes to play their Class A teams.

Twice we hosted a university team barnstorming over spring break. We beat them badly, such as our 22–3 trouncing of Harvard. It was then that I realized how much better was the caliber of college baseball on the West Coast. I had already noticed the difference in talent among some of my teammates from the East and Midwest, who were not as good as some of my college teammates at home in talent-rich California who had never been offered contracts. The difference didn't mean that the northern kids had less chance of advancing in pro ball than the Sunbelt kids. Rather, the mild climate and long season in Sunbelt states meant that we had played a lot more baseball and were more developed. We were closer to our full potential than players from states with real winters. The coaches and scouts expected the Snowbelt kids, once they had more playing time, to catch up to us. I wasn't convinced they ever could, especially position players, where our skills, more than for pitchers, were honed over years of repetition.

By the third week we were playing two games every day. There were no spectators other than scouts, coaches, and front-office personnel, but we could hear the roar of the crowd across the way at Joker Marchant Stadium where the big leaguers played.

Off to a good start, it wasn't long before I was hitting in the cleanup spot, where I stayed for the rest of the spring. It was such a different feeling having, for the first time in pro ball, real success. I was very happy, and for the first time I believed that I was just as good as the competition. I remember overhearing pitcher Shelby Morton and another player speculating that I must have signed for a big bonus. Any player who received more than ten thousand dollars to sign was considered a "bonus baby." I was pleased to hear Morton's remark, but it reminded me of the hash I had made of my signing when I had called the Yankees scout and tipped my hand.

Following the morning game we lined up on the grass outside the clubhouse for lunch: a tuna, peanut butter and jelly, or cheese sandwich; potato chips; an apple; a Hershey bar; and a Dixie cup of iced tea—always iced tea. Some players sat at picnic tables to eat, but most sat cross-legged on the turf. I think there was something special about sitting on the grass in the bright sunshine in the middle of winter for the northerners when their folks back home were shoveling snow. A Canadian teammate constantly reminded me how miserable Ontario winters were and how wonderful it was to be in Florida. I didn't fully appreciate his point until I lived in Montreal and then upstate New York years later. On most days we headed for the showers around four o'clock. The crowded clubhouse was so steamy, hot, and smelly from sweaty uniforms and dirty socks that you didn't linger. We then had an hour or so to relax before dinner. Oddly, what I remember liking best about dinner was being able to get refills on chocolate milk. At home chocolate milk was a rare treat. As we ate, Jerry Klein, the colorful Jamestown clubbie, would stroll along the dinner line yelling, "Chew your food! Chew your fuckin' food!" To Hook Warden he'd say, "Warden, with a snout like that, how do you drink from a mug?" And to every rookie, "Hey, kid, don't let that door hit you in the ass." To anyone who had a retort, he'd say, "Go jump in Lake Parker."

Wednesday evening was the eagerly anticipated "steak night." Even some of the big leaguers, like Willie Horton, Gates Brown, and Al Kaline, would come over for the steaks and sometimes stick around to play pool or Ping-Pong or just socialize in the large screened-porch recreation area off the mess hall.

After dinner, if I had the energy, I would join a few teammates and walk the mile or so into town to the Pizza Inn, where local girls who wanted to meet ballplayers hung out. Florida Southern College offered both girls and other forms of entertainment, including the college's basketball games. The campus was interesting in its own right. Many of its buildings were designed by Frank Lloyd Wright and had astonishingly low ceilings (six feet, six inches) in the covered walkways or esplanades that wound through the campus. We wondered how the college was able to recruit basketball players when they could never stand up straight.

I once asked out a freshman girl, named Jody, with freckles and a small pointed nose. I had to put my request for a date in writing for her resident assistant to get approval from Jody's parents. It was college policy for freshman girls. And she had to be returned to her dorm by a ten o'clock curfew. It was a memorable date, not just for the restrictions but because while walking along the shoreline of Lake Parker we spooked an alligator that charged straight toward us in its pursuit of the shortest distance to the water. With no time to think, Jody ran to the right and tumbled; I ran to the left. Jody didn't think that very chivalrous of me and asked me to take her back to campus. After all the trouble I'd gone to, my date was over by eight. I thought Claire, always fun loving, would have understood and regretted that we had been writing less frequently and seemed to be drifting apart.

Most evenings I stayed in Tiger Town. I was taking correspondence courses—Western Civilization and Sociology—in order to keep my student-deferment draft status. Bernie arranged for me to use a desk in the front office at night. During a study break one night, I peeked in some of the other rooms and discovered one in which the names of every ballplayer in the Detroit organization were listed on the wall followed by a colored star indicating his military draft status: a green star for 1-A, available for military service; a blue star for 1-D, a member of a reserve unit; a silver star for 1-S, student deferment; and so on. *This is serious stuff*, I wrote that night. It drove the reality of Vietnam and the military draft home to me and made sense of the discussions I'd heard among teammates about the different options, such as National Guard versus the Army Reserves, for avoiding the draft. And which option would have the least impact on our baseball careers.

Seeing the military draft lists gave me an idea. In the office I had use of a typewriter, and some Detroit Tigers letterhead was in the desk drawer—all the ingredients needed, I mused one night during a study break, to make up a phony set of team rosters. I could post them on the bulletin board on Sunday before the real rosters went up. It seemed like a great prank. I enlisted the help of teammate and fellow Californian Paul Coleman in compiling fantasy rosters with some unusual promotions and demotions. We posted them the next Sunday afternoon an hour before the real ones were to appear and then stood back and watched the commotion. No one seemed to realize that our rosters were not the real thing. One rookie who had been unexpectedly promoted to high-A Rocky Mount called home to tell his parents the good news, and veteran AA player Ike Brown, whom we had demoted one level, was outraged and went to find his manager. A coach saw the gathering, realized what had happened, and pulled down our counterfeits. That evening the coaches put two and two together and figured that I, having access to the front office, must have been responsible. Gail summoned me, saying I was in a heap of trouble. In the front office Ed Katalinas sternly warned that if I ever did anything like that again, I would be on my way home. Had I not been hitting so well, I probably would have been sent packing then. When, twenty-five years later, I saw Jim Leyland, then managing the Pittsburgh Pirates, the first thing he mentioned was my posting those fictitious rosters.

When not doing my schoolwork, there was Ping-Pong, pool, poker, and chess. *Chess is fast replacing poker games. Almost everybody in my barracks is playing chess. Even the colored boys are taking it up.* (The terms *colored* and *Negro* were used by both white and African American players at the time; I have no excuse for *boys*.) A college-educated pitcher from New Mexico, William Seifert, taught me how to play bridge, and for a while I was hooked.

Weekends, with so much free time, however, could drag. During moments of boredom, players often turned to pranks, such as short-sheeting a teammate's bed or putting foreign substances in a teammate's underwear, the fingers of his baseball glove, or his bed.[5] I learned to always pull back the sheets and check my bed before getting in. Someone put a snake under Cuban Julio Perez's pillow. Julio, it turned out, was deathly afraid of serpents. He freaked out. Brandishing a knife, he said he would use it on anyone who tried it again. We believed him.

At one point, in an attempt to inject some life into our cheerless room, I bought a fishbowl and a pair of brilliant goldfish, which I named Molly

11. Playing chess in the Tiger Town barracks with pitcher Paul Coleman (*right*).

and Mike. Not long after, I returned from dinner to find the fishbowl missing and a note: "If you don't want Molly and Mike hurt, leave five dollars at the flagpole at six." It was signed "The Phantom." I got Molly and Mike back the next day, by threatening retaliation.

We also passed the evenings with a lot of talk, on almost any topic from girls to religion. One conversation I noted in my journal concerned the athleticism of our "Negro" teammates and how the white guys involved in the discussion, including me, felt disadvantaged. We believed that blacks in general had faster reflexes and therefore "quicker hands," enabling them to get a baseball bat out front quicker on an inside pitch. It was the baseball equivalent of the basketball notion that "white men can't jump." *And once they hit the ball, their quicker foot speed gets them to first base that much faster*, I wrote. Over the course of the season, we figured just these two differences could add up to a lot of extra hits for black players. The feeling was that getting to the big leagues would be easier if we had their extra athleticism. When I related this spring-training conversation years later to former teammate Les Cain, who is black, he said that black players also thought they were more athletic. Today most athletes still believe this, although it's seldom talked about. The concern seems to be that if one admits to small physical differences, some people will want to make the leap to positing mental differences as well.

A few players had cars, and occasionally we could convince one of them to make a Sunday road trip. A group of us, for example, traveled to Cypress Gardens (now Legoland) to see the famous water-ski show and later to Daytona International Speedway for the big 500 race, which we found disappointing. *Watching cars circle a two-mile track over and over gets old pretty quick.* Also, the noise was deafening, and despite having paid a pricey admission, we left after an hour. My next trip to Daytona was the week before camp broke, when a few of us went to find apartments for the upcoming season.

Two of my barracks roommates were Canadian Bob Gear and Southern Californian Dennis Grossini. I can't recall my third roommate, and my journal never mentions him. But that is not unusual, as today most of my teammates do not remember whom they roomed with in spring training, probably because we spent so little time in our rooms other than sleeping. Gear stood five-foot-ten, a stocky, affable, hard-swinging outfielder from Merriton, Ontario, with a raspy voice and an easy laugh. He talked in torrents, was always fidgeting with something, and never tired of telling others how much he loved Canada. Or how much he loved Mickey Mantle and the New York Yankees.

It wasn't long before he acquired two nicknames: "Shifty," playing on his surname Gear, and "Shoes," after his odd-looking white desert boots with pointed toes and his equally odd baseball spikes that sported a white stripe along the side. In the sixties everyone wore solid black spikes. Gail ordered him to blacken the white stripes with shoe polish.

No one then could have dreamed that someday it would be acceptable for ballplayers to wear any color shoes they wished, even brilliant orange.

It was Shifty's first spring training, first time away from home, and first time on an airplane. He later admitted to being so nervous on the plane that his hands were shaking, and the woman seated next to him had to buckle his seat belt. Shifty had wanted to be a baseball player since the age of eight when every Saturday he watched with his grandfather the televised Game of the Week. During the action he would throw a baseball into the Chesterfield. Like most of the Canadians in camp, Shifty was more raw talent than polished product, despite being a consistent .400 hitter as an amateur. Growing up in a cold climate, he had played more hockey than baseball and still had much to learn about the game. But it was easy to see that he had all the tools and a strong work ethic . . . and powerful arms and shoulders. Nonetheless, Shifty worried about his chances, especially after a talented free-agent shortstop—with the great baseball name of Shag Luster—was let go, despite playing well that spring.

We probably had more Canadians in camp than any other organization. Nearly all were from Ontario and had been signed by a single Tigers scout, Cy Williams. The top scout, Ed Katalinas, once candidly explained in a newspaper interview, "Canadians are cheaper than Americans." Canada, like the Caribbean, was not part of the annual free-agent draft, and therefore, as Katalinas noted, "Any team can negotiate and sign players as it sees fit. And we have found that Canadian players do not demand high bonuses." Katalinas went on to say that the Canadian players were "greener than our other boys" but had natural ability and developed fast.

Dennis Grossini was an eighteen-year-old hard-throwing left-handed pitcher who had been a bonus-baby sixth-round pick. He signed out of a Lompoc, California, high school. As a Little Leaguer, he had once struck out every batter he faced but one. He was good looking and, unlike Shifty, confident that he would not only make the grade but soon be in the big leagues. Midway through camp Tigers manager Charlie Dressen invited Dennis over to pitch for the big club in a split-squad game against the Red Sox. Dennis, wanting to look good, went to Popovich, the clubhouse manager, and requested a pair of big-league stirrup socks for his outing in place of his green rookie socks. It was something that less confident Shifty Gear would never have done. Thinking this was his big chance to make an impression on Dressen, Dennis overthrew and hurt his arm. Nevertheless, he pitched well, and Charlie told him that he had plans for him. The *Sporting News* reported that Charlie liked the young lefty and mistakenly reported that he had received a bonus of forty thousand dollars, double the actual figure, which greatly enhanced his status among players. When Charlie died from a kidney infection during the season, Dennis was dismayed over having lost his most important supporter. And then, unbelievably, in the off-season, Charlie's replacement, Bob Swift, who had also been impressed with Dennis, also died—at fifty-one of lung cancer.

Rookie League and Class A players, like Shifty, Dennis, Felber, and me, fell into one of three categories. First were the true "prospects." Usually, they were high draft picks and bonus babies, but also some low-round picks and free agents who had put up good numbers the previous season. Next were solid players who were assured of making a team, but were more "suspect" than prospect. They provided the necessary bodies for the prospects to play with and against. Finally, there were the rookies and other unknowns who had not yet proved themselves and were straddling the fence between success and failure. That was me coming into camp. Many of the players in this category would be gone by the end of spring training, and for them every game or outing on the mound could have consequences and was pressure packed. Regardless of status, nearly all players worked hard to impress the scouts, coaches, and front-office brass. Everyone hoped to someday be regarded as a "prospect"—as someone who could someday play in the big leagues and contribute to the big club winning.

The names of players to be released were usually called out over the PA system: "Will the following players please report to Mr. Snyder's office . . ." When the voice began reading the names, nobody moved. Silence. Players who were struggling prayed they would not hear their names. Having gotten off to a hot start, I didn't have to worry that spring. Although every ballplayer knew that one day he would be let go, few were ever prepared for it. While players were released throughout spring training, the numbers really increased toward the end, when rosters had to be trimmed before camp broke and the teams headed north to begin their seasons. After getting the bad news, the now ex-players returned to the barracks to pack belongings and say farewell to their buddies. Some, whether out of humiliation, embarrassment, or not knowing what to say, simply slipped away. Years later farm director Don Lund told me that releasing players was the hardest thing he ever had to do in baseball. Some players, he said, begged to be given another chance, and some broke down.

Tiger Town was culturally and ethnically diverse. My Daytona teammates were from all parts of the United States, Canada, and the Caribbean. White, black, and Hispanic. Protestant, Catholic, and Jew. From farms, small towns, and big cities; from lower-class and middle-class families. There were a few college graduates and some who hadn't finished high school. Coming to spring training directly from Stanford, I was more accustomed to such diversity than many others and probably more interested in it than teammates with only a high school education. A little shy at first around blacks and Hispanics, I soon discovered that I enjoyed learning about the places and backgrounds they came from. I enjoyed being among a varied group of guys. Also bunking in the barracks were a half-dozen umpires who had been assigned to Tiger Town. Among them was Ron Luciano, who had played briefly in the

NFL for the Buffalo Bills before injury forced his retirement. Being a first baseman—the most sociable position on the field—I often spoke to base runners and the umpire stationed near me, and I got to know Luciano this way. He was then developing the flamboyant style that he became famous for and that would make him a fan favorite in the Major Leagues. After ten years umpiring in the American League, he retired to become a sports commentator with NBC and to write several witty and popular books about his umpiring days, including *The Umpire Strikes Back* and *The Fall of the Roman Umpire*. It came as a shock years later when he committed suicide via carbon monoxide poisoning in his garage. Ron left a note providing funeral instructions, but gave no indication what prompted him to end his life, nor did his family members have any idea. He had been in good health, and the autopsy found no disease. He was just fifty-seven.

Besides enjoying my success on the field, I liked being in Tiger Town for other reasons. *I like the freedom of just having to play ball and nothing else. I don't have to cook or clean or study for exams. I feel free; everything is taken care of for us.* By the end of camp, I thought Tiger Town had furnished me an education in how professional baseball worked. In one locale I could see the entire Minor League system, and nearby was the big-league club. I got a sense of my competition, what it was going to take to move up the ladder (players were always sizing up the competition), and what qualities the coaches and front office looked for in players. I learned that those who signed for large bonuses, like Mike Small, were going to be in the lineup every day regardless. They would get more chances to succeed than anyone else because the organization had invested in them their money and their scouting reputations.

One morning near the end of spring training, Ed Katalinas summoned me to the office. I was one of three players being offered a bat contract by Louisville Slugger. In the 1960s nearly every player swung Louisville Sluggers, unlike today, with numerous companies with bats in the game.

The recommendation for a bat contract had come from the coaches, as the Louisville representative hadn't seen any of our games. I was bowled over, for to be offered a bat contract was a big deal. It meant from that point on all of your bats would carry your signature on the barrel, rather than block letters. That signature announced to everyone who saw your bats that you were worthy, a true "prospect." I wrote out my signature with great care, unlike my usual sloppy scribble. I wanted the name to look good and legible when it was reproduced on my bats; I didn't want another mistake like SMELCH from the previous season.

Louisville offered its standard contract, a choice between one hundred dollars in cash or a set of Louisville golf clubs. Even though I didn't play much golf, I took the clubs because they were worth a lot more than a hundred bucks. I still have them, but they never got much use.

Of the many different Louisville Slugger bat models known to players, the D2, M110, R43, and K55 were the most popular. Each model number represents different dimensions in thickness of the handle and barrel, shape, and style of the knob. Every position player was to submit a bat order so that your shipment of bats would be ready for the start of the new season. Besides choosing a particular model, you also had to decide what weight and length you wanted. Since the baseball bat was our most important tool, this was a big decision, as we each wanted bats that felt just right and had good balance. Most players favored bats weighing thirty-one or -two ounces and thirty-four inches in length. Our bats were lighter than those of previous generations. Ty Cobb and Joe DiMaggio had played with forty-two-ounce lumber, about 25 percent heavier than our bats. And Babe Ruth broke into the big leagues swinging an unbelievable fifty-two-ounce hickory bat, although a few seasons later he had dropped down to a still hefty forty ounces. Even on steroids, Mark McGwire and Barry Bonds never used bats that weighed more than thirty-five ounces. I still have one of my D2 thirty-four-inch, thirty-two-ounce flame-treated Louisville Sluggers standing in the corner of my study. Occasionally, I take a swing, and each time I can't believe I was once strong enough to have gotten it around on a 90-plus-mph fastball. I wonder how Babe Ruth, who early in his career was exactly my size and weight—six-foot-two and 190 pounds—could ever have used a forty- much less fifty-two-ounce bat.

On April 4, with just over a week of camp left and eager to get the season under way and have the hits and wins count, we narrowly escaped a violent tornado. As the horizon turned black and the skies opened up, over the PA system Ed Katalinas told us to immediately return to the barracks and take cover. A few of us lingered outside to run and slide on the wet grass in the downpour. We were probably all from places that never experienced tornadoes. This F4 twister (F5 being the highest intensity) passed just a quarter mile from Tiger Town. It had cut a wide path across central Florida, demolishing two hundred homes, scrambling power lines, and leaving one Lakeland neighborhood in shambles. Statewide, eleven people died, and in Lakeland ninety-two were injured, many by flying glass. It still ranks as the fourth-deadliest tornado ever recorded in Florida.

After the storm passed I went out to a nearby neighborhood to look at the damage. Debris was scattered everywhere, and houses were without roofs. A citrus grove had been destroyed, turning the ground yellow with fruit. But what I remember best was a two-by-four sticking into the side of a tree like an arrow. Only then did I realize how lucky we had been. Had the tornado passed through Tiger Town, the wooden barracks where we had taken shelter would have been blown to bits.

With the new season and a fresh start only a week away, players talked about their hopes. The new season allowed a chance to reinvent ourselves and set new goals. I listened to brawny six-foot-three outfielder Tom Hamm, headed to Daytona Beach with me, calculate that he should be able to hit one home run in every 10 at bats. He had worked it all out and was convinced that he could do it. But that season in Daytona he hit only three in 354 at bats (one-tenth the production he had hoped for), and two years later he was trying to become a pitcher. My hopes, I wrote, were to *improve my fielding, finish my correspondence courses, and not waste time by sleeping late.* Curiously, there was no mention of hitting. It had been a great spring at the plate for me, one that had restored my confidence. I had arrived in Tiger Town wondering if I would survive the cuts and left camp six weeks later as a prospect.

On the twelfth of April we broke camp, with each squad heading north to begin the new season. Our team had only to drive 110 miles across the state to Daytona Beach. We had heard stories about playing in Daytona from teammates who had been there the previous season. One that stood out above the others was of pitcher John Sculley driving the team's van into the ocean. He had been hit hard one night, his third consecutive bad outing, and after some drinking he took the team van for a spin on Daytona's famous beach—where compacted sand makes it possible to drive. Agitated over his pitching failures, John snapped and drove the van into the sea. The van was a total loss, but he was able to walk back to shore.

6

PUTTING UP NUMBERS

Daytona Beach Islanders

We arrived in Daytona Beach with twenty-one players, including three African Americans, three Hispanics, and three Canadians. All of the catchers and infielders were white; most of the outfielders were Hispanic or black. And we were all between the ages of nineteen and twenty-two—that is, if you believed the understated ages some players gave to the Tigers when they signed their first contracts. We felt fortunate to be in the Florida State League since most of its ten teams played in Major League spring-training ballparks with top-notch fields, clubhouses, and grandstands—far better than any Class A and most Double A stadiums in the country. The stadium in Daytona was not as good as the others, but still not too bad.

Daytona Beach was the oldest franchise in the league, having joined in 1936. Since then it had been aligned with five different Major League organizations. The Tigers had arrived in 1965 and would leave after the 1966 season. We were called the Islanders because our ballpark—City Island Park—sat on a small island in the middle of the Intracoastal Waterway. A bridge connected it to the mainland.

As a town Daytona had more going for it than Jamestown or Duluth; its smooth, wide strand had been dubbed in the 1920s the "World's Most Famous Beach." By the 1960s Daytona was the principal city on Florida's

12. Main Street, Daytona Beach, circa 1966. Photo courtesy of Halifax Historical Museum.

"Fun Coast" and drew crowds of college students on spring break. The area also became known for auto racing. Its hard-packed sands made it a destination for high-speed automobile testing in the early 1900s, but by 1959 the beach gave way to the city's celebrated racetrack, the Daytona International Speedway, home of the 500.

APRIL 17 . . . We opened the season, with me batting cleanup, on the road against the Tampa Tarpons, a Cincinnati Reds farm club. José Cepeda, brother of future Hall of Famer Orlando Cepeda, was in right field, hitting sixth. Batting behind him, playing third, was my Jamestown roommate, Bob Felber. The opening-day fanfare featured prancing majorettes, a marching band, and a military color guard. The team's attention focused on the majorettes.

Our first six batters struck out. The pitching wasn't overpowering, but our eyes hadn't adjusted to our first night game of the year. By the second time through the batting order, most of us had accommodated. I drove in our first run with a gapper to right center, but also let in Tampa's first run with a wild throw. Our starter, Jim "Dizzy" Dietz, gave up back-to-back home run blasts to dead center. Skipper Gail Henley came to the mound. He smiled and said, "Son, that's a record for the longest consecutive homers ever given up." Dietz settled down, and we came from behind with four runs in the seventh to beat the Tarpons 5-4.

All was not cheerful, however. A foul tip broke the index finger of our catcher Tim Garner. Just one game into the season, he was put on the disabled list and would never again see much action and would be out of baseball before the season ended.

Except for a two-day All-Star break in the middle, we would play every night for the next four and a half months—144 games in all, and that was on top of the 30 games we had already played in spring training. We would not finish the season until Labor Day. It was to be my first full season of Minor League ball.

Coming off a great spring, I had high hopes. Part of my delight over being in Daytona was our classy accommodations. We lived in the Pendleton apartment complex, which advertised itself as "Daytona's most exclusive address with the cordial atmosphere of an exclusive country club." It was on the Intracoastal Waterway and just a short walk over the bridge to the ballpark. The Pendleton had its own private dock, putting green, shuffleboard court, doorman, tasteful landscaping, and large swimming pool where we would pass many hours doing cannonballs off the diving board, standing on our hands underwater, and playing Marco Polo. We could afford the three hundred dollars of monthly rent by sharing—five players to an apartment. Altogether fifteen of us lived at the Pendleton. For my teammates from blue-collar backgrounds, this was the nicest place they had ever lived. I doubt any one of us had ever lived in a building with its own doorman.

We were only a short distance from the ocean. Some days I got up early to swim and then walk on the beach or the boardwalk. The manager's unusual ideas limited my morning activity. Gail thought that swimming for more than a short time would "waterlog" us and affect our play on the field. He also set a curfew for being off the beach—a twenty-five-dollar fine if you were seen anywhere near it after eleven in the morning. The rule was not closely followed since Gail rarely went to the beach himself.

The Pendleton didn't rent to blacks or Hispanics. Even had they been able to live with us, they probably wouldn't have chosen to do so. In 1960s pro ball, players lived and roomed with their own kind—whites with whites, Hispanics with Hispanics, blacks with blacks. This was especially so for the Hispanics because of language. After ball games the players of color vanished, and we wouldn't see them again until next day in the clubhouse. I don't recall anyone ever asking them where they lived or what they did at night.

Beyond race, pitchers preferred rooming with other pitchers and position players with other nonpitchers. There were always exceptions, of course: two of my four roommates happened to be pitchers—Phil Bartelone and Jon Warden, a.k.a. "Hook" on account of his bent penis. Most of the other residents of the Pendleton were wealthy retirees who at first seemed to like having ballplayers around. One woman baked us cookies; another introduced her granddaughter to Bob Felber, and they began to date. After a while the retirees' enthusiasm waned as some players caterwauled at night and were boisterous around the pool. It wasn't long before the apartment manager issued a warning that if we didn't tone it down, we'd be told to move out.

APRIL 19 . . . The day of our home opener the *Daytona Beach Morning Journal* ran a front-page picture of Gail handing the ball to our starting pitcher, Hook Warden. Next to it an article reported the number of U.S. troops in Vietnam was approaching 250,000. I paid more attention to the news now, especially from Vietnam, than I had the year before in Jamestown. My childhood buddy Chris Nelson had been drafted and deployed.

Being a witness to the demonstrations at Stanford raised my interest in the war. There had been many protests, some of which I attended, more out of curiosity than commitment, until I heard a stirring speech by student body president David Harris. Harris said that if a country is going to war, then everyone should have to fight, not just poor people who couldn't avoid the draft by going to college. He told the student crowd that he had mailed his student-deferment draft card back to the Selective Service folks with a letter that he "opposed killing people . . . to prop up tinhorn dictators." His defiance of the draft laws and his organized civil disobedience would send him to prison, but not before he married fellow activist Joan Baez. Harris's conviction and personal sacrifice caused me to think more deeply about the war and my own passivity. In the off-season I began watching the evening news, eventually noticing the suspiciously high and obviously inflated counts of Vietcong killed and the daily images of body bags of American soldiers arriving home.

In the clubhouse Gail reviewed his expectations of us and the fines that would result for such things as throwing a helmet, missing a sign, being late for the bus, or using profanity within earshot of the fans. The latter was not always easy for players accustomed to venting their frustration with *F* bombs and using them as their favorite adjective: "Did you see the fuckin' break on that curveball? Fucking amazing."

We sat through another opening-day ceremony, much like the one in Tampa except that Daytona's mayor, throwing out the first pitch, bounced it ten feet before the plate. Shifty remarked, a bit too loudly, "He throws like a girl." There were 593 spectators on hand to see us blow a seven-run lead with four errors late in the game and lose 8–7. "Tampa players started crossing the plate as if someone had unlocked a prison gate," reported the *Morning Journal*'s sportswriter Neil LaBar. At the concession fans could buy a hot dog for a quarter or a snow cone for a dime or a cigar for fifteen cents. Back then fans could smoke in the grandstand.

We left the next morning for a three-day road trip to St. Petersburg and Orlando. No one wanted to be late getting on the bus because it could mean you wouldn't be able to get a two-seat row to yourself. The strategy was to put your bag down and spread out your stuff on the empty seat next to you. If there was a threat of someone taking the extra seat, you'd sprawl out your body and pretend to be napping. Having a seatmate made it difficult to stretch out and sleep. And you might be forced to listen to him ramble on about some inanity, like Doc Olms did to his seatmate in the row behind me on the way to St. Petersburg. Doc had just read a Dear Abby column in the *Morning Journal* about the sex of angels. Abby had concluded that they were neither male nor female since the sole purpose of sex was to fulfill God's commandment to propagate the earth, and, supposedly, angels weren't into procreation. Doc didn't agree that angels could be sexless. "There wouldn't be no fuckin' happiness in heaven without sex."

Pitchers were told not to sit with their pitching arms next to the air-conditioning vents. It hardly mattered since the air-conditioning was so weak. Even on really hot days—which after mid-May was virtually every day—some guys opened the windows, figuring the breeze had to be cooler than the feeble AC.

At the start of each road trip we were given meal money in an envelope, usually in two-dollar bills. Our general manager, Warren Keyes, was a denizen of the dog track where two-dollar bills were the common betting currency. With fresh money in our pockets, a poker game usually broke out at the back of the bus. Often some guy would lose his grub money before we reached the first stop. When the bus stopped for our late-night meal, twenty-one players would descend all at once, a real challenge for the small dives we frequented. The few waitresses didn't look happy, probably because ball players were lousy tippers.

As the bus pulled into a diner for our first road meal, Shifty Gear, upon retrieving his brown wing-tip shoes from under the seat, discovered that someone had firmly tied the shoelaces into a hundred small knots.

APRIL 20–21 . . . We beat future Hall of Famer Sparky Anderson's St. Petersburg Cardinals by one run both nights. The first night we had only two hits, but those combined with a few walks and a bases-loaded single by José Cepeda were enough. We were off to a good start, winning three of our first four games, and I was hitting well, driving the ball up the middle and poking outside pitches to the opposite field.

Once back in Daytona my roommates and I bought an old Packard for a hundred dollars. It was the same color—pea-soup green—as the rookies' spring-training socks. The rusted floorboard allowed us to see the pavement below. The Packard stood out like a sore thumb among the Cadillacs and Lincolns in the Pendleton apartment parking lot.

One of the Pendleton old-timers told me that Jackie Robinson had played at City Island Park in 1946 in the first racially integrated exhibition game. I later looked it up. Sure enough, the Dodgers had played in Daytona after attempts to play in Jacksonville and Sanford had been thwarted by intimidation, locked stadium gates, and excuses like faulty lighting. In 1989 the name of Daytona's stadium was proudly changed to Jackie Robinson Ballpark and soon was nicknamed "the Jack." The 2013 film 42 re-creates scenes of Robinson playing in Daytona.

Baseball greats Stan Musial and Rocky Colavito each spent a full season playing for the Daytona club. Stan was a pitcher for the 1940 Daytona Beach Cardinals and, like Babe Ruth two decades earlier, had hit so well that his manager began playing him in the outfield between starts. Following an arm injury, he switched permanently to the outfield to become the Man, probably the greatest National League hitter of his time. Rocky hit a league-leading twenty-three home runs for Daytona in 1951, which seemed unbelievable unless the fences were a lot closer back then. Our entire Daytona Beach team would hit only thirty home runs in 1966, and that was a dozen more than the year before.

APRIL 24 . . . We lost a tough one to the Cocoa Beach Astros, 3-2, on a walk-off double by their pitcher. Shifty Gear, who was now our starting left fielder and hitting in the three hole, was called out on a key play at first base when he was clearly safe. It killed a rally, and Gear tossed his helmet in the air in disgust. "Pick it up or you're outta here," the umpire threatened. Gear ignored him and was tossed. Gail warned him that if he got tossed again, it would cost him twenty-five bucks.

Larry Calton slammed the team's first home run of the season as we beat the Miami Marlins 10-5. Even balls hit square did not carry well in our ballpark or elsewhere in the Florida State League, as the air was humid and heavy. Baseballs are also less lively in humid climates because the moisture in the air is absorbed by the wool in the core of a ball. That, say the scientists, reduces the carry of a baseball by 10 percent, a boon for pitchers, a downer for power hitters. Making things even tougher for lefties like me were the prevailing winds in most of the FSL's ballparks, which blew in from right field.

APRIL 27 . . . We beat Miami 3-2 on a wild pitch in the bottom of the twelfth. I had a base knock to center that set up the winning run. It was my fourth hit of the night. *I'm now hitting .327. I am on a tear . . . Can I keep this up?* I wrote that night. I was in that mystical zone where you play beyond your usual abilities and hope and pray—and try to do everything the same so that you can keep it up. Other Islanders weren't so fortunate.

Hard-luck pitcher Hook Warden got another no decision despite pitching brilliantly for eight and two-thirds innings and striking out twelve. And our bonus-baby infielder, eighteen-year-old Mickey White from South Carolina, again struggled mightily at the dish, taking another o'fer. Mickey, who liked to say, "I ain't takin' nothin' from nobody," hadn't had a base hit all week. Mentally, I connected my good fortune that night with having changed my baseball undershirt midway through the game, something I rarely did. For the next week, as I continued to hit well, I continued to change my shirt around the fifth inning.

The *Morning Journal* reported that Lyndon Johnson said discrimination and racial practices still existed in many American communities despite the sweeping reforms of the 1964 Civil Rights and 1965 Voting Rights Acts. Johnson urged Congress to enact new legislation, calling for new tactics "to strike at night riding terrorism and the intimidation of Negroes." I didn't know anything about "night riding terrorism," but it sounded so ominous and un-American that I was astonished that LBJ's proposed legislation might not survive a southern filibuster in the Senate. *What do these southerners dislike so much about colored people?* It was hard to imagine anyone feeling threatened by, much less hating, the people I knew, the likes of my black teammates, two of whom were fast becoming my friends. Daytona Beach, by the standards of northern Florida, was a fairly progressive place. In fact, the Kansas City Athletics had moved their Minor League spring-training site to Daytona that spring because they felt their black and Hispanic players would be treated better there than elsewhere in Florida. Nevertheless, Daytona's blacks had to use a separate beach from whites and until the 1950s weren't allowed on the peninsula after dark without a written letter from the home owners who employed them as maids and gardeners.

MAY 1 . . . We played the Deerfield Beach White Sox at their home park in Pompano Beach. Because their new stadium lights had not yet been installed, games usually started at 2:00 p.m., when it could be brutally hot. When summer arrived it got worse. Our uniforms were a heavy wool blend, making it even more uncomfortable. In Daytona, two hundred miles to the north, the average daily high in June, July, and August was right around ninety degrees, and the evenings, unlike what I was used to in California, didn't cool off all that much. I decided that I never wanted to live in Florida again.

My Daytona teammates did not call me "I-beam," my Jamestown moniker; now I was "Moonbeam." *I'd like to think they switched because my fielding has improved, but I don't think that's it.* No doubt being left-handed was a factor—there is a universal stereotype in sports that left-handers have a different mentality. But the other left-handers on our club weren't called Moonbeam. Years later second baseman Larry Calton explained, "We called you Moonbeam because you were from California, and like most California guys you were kind of flaky. I mean, you read books on the bus and you were a little unorthodox . . . more free-spirited than us, like getting up early on the road and wandering around town and hanging out in a library. But Mike Small was a lot flakier than you." Incidentally, the books I read that summer, which some teammates mistook as scholarly, were *The Bridge over the River Kwai*, *U-Boat*, and Tom Wolfe's *The Kandy-Kolored Tangerine-Flake Streamline Baby*.

Before going to the ballpark we usually cooked our big meal of the day in our apartment—typically Swanson TV dinners from the Winn-Dixie. We drank a lot of cheap soda, too. For one dollar we could buy seventeen cans of Chek Cola. Diet soda was not yet widely available. I hate now to think of the huge amount of sugar we consumed each day. Overall food wasn't that expensive. One dollar could also buy us three cans of tuna or two frozen enchilada dinners. Sometimes I went to the Eckerd drugstore before the game to get their lunch-counter special: ham and cabbage, boiled potato, hot vegetable, roll and butter, coffee, and Jell-O, all for ninety-seven cents. Once we celebrated a rainout by going to a real restaurant, the Skyline, where Hook and I shared the charbroiled sirloin-steak special for six dollars. Unlike today's players, we had little understanding of the effect of diet on our performance, apart from the need to avoid eating too many doughnuts and Twinkies.

I received another letter from my scout, Bernie. This time, perhaps because I was hitting well, he advised me only on my fielding, "It takes more than a good bat to make it. Work on that glove. . . . Give the ball [grounders] a chance to get to the glove. . . . [A]lways take at least one step towards the ball but don't play the bouncing ball on a run as you will find yourself in between the hops and that is tough." Bernie closed with, "Keep your spirits high. Every time you have a good day it is just like me having one too. Go get 'em. Ever Sliding, Bernie." I appreciated his letters not just for the guidance but because none of my teammates got letters from their scouts. And of the two dozen scouts in the Tiger organization, mine was an instructor as well.

On our first road trip Shifty bought a red portable record player. From then on he sat in the back of the bus, amid the engine noise and vibration, playing his 45 rpm records, and if you were near the back you heard hour after hour of Simon and Garfunkel, the Beatles, Roy Orbison, the Mamas and the Papas, Jefferson Airplane, the Box Tops, and the Byrds. It was quite unlike today's earbud-wearing iPod ballplayers, in which all music is private and silent.

There were always a few players who would look out the bus windows into the passing cars below, hoping to see a pretty girl. Whenever one was spotted, there would be a shout, "Beaver on the left!" or "Beaver on the right!" whereupon everyone would rush to the windows to get a good look. Once we hit the jackpot, seeing a partially naked girl giving the driver a blow job. When our new catcher Dave Bike arrived, he worried that the sudden shift of weight would tip over the bus, as though we were on an overloaded ferry boat.

Some guys passed the road time playing trivia games. When they were stumped, they sometimes shouted to me for the answer, assuming that because I read books and went to Stanford I would know. Most of the time I didn't, but that didn't keep them from asking. And, frankly, I enjoyed playing that role. After a while I sensed that our left fielder Tom Hamm, who had signed out of Georgetown, felt slighted. He must have had other grievances as well, because one day in the clubhouse, as we were getting dressed and had a small disagreement over whether the swamp lights in nearby Tomoka State Park were real, he charged across the locker room and threw a punch and pushed me into my locker. Larry Calton jumped in and broke it up. *There has been tension between us, and the argument over the swamp lights I guess was the final straw. He sure was agitated, red-faced and all. I don't know what set him off.* I didn't like Hamm, but mostly because he didn't like me. Nonetheless, I was saddened when I learned years later that he had been killed, run over by a cement truck while jogging in Florida on vacation.

I usually got along well with all of my teammates, so I was puzzled why Hamm seemed to dislike me so much. I never did find out exactly, but in asking around I discovered that I had also annoyed his roommate, a pitcher, because I used to walk over to the mound from first base when he was struggling to find the plate and say, "Just throw strikes." I was simply trying to provide encouragement, but it was a ridiculous thing to say. Obviously, there was nothing in the world that he wanted to do more than to throw strikes. His problem was figuring out what adjustment in his mechanics was necessary to regain his command. Years later, when I coached Little League, hearing other coaches tell their struggling hurlers to "just throw strikes" drove me nuts.

Coming back from a road trip to our ballpark and its cinderblock bunker of a clubhouse was a letdown. The space was cramped, always seemed to have sand on the floor that got into our socks and shoes, and lacked ventilation. "It was so steamy," remembers Polak, "that after you showered, you were sweatier than before you went in." Our stadium lights were also weaker than any other ballpark in the FSL. Playing in nice ballparks made you feel more professional, gave you more pride in being a ballplayer. Because of this I think we all enjoyed playing on the road more than at home.

I was always nice to umpires for the same reason I have always been nice to secretaries. They both control things and can make your life miserable, if they wish. With umpires I made small talk, and rather than show them up by making a stink over a bad call, I'd usually ask where the pitch was. I figured the next time they might give me a break, maybe shrink the strike zone a little. I can't say for sure that it worked, but I did sometimes see the strike zone expand for the whiners.

MAY 4 . . . It was *Sporting News* night at the ballpark: the first fifty fans through the gate received a free copy of the baseball weekly. In a thrilling come-from-behind 5–4 win over Leesburg, I was robbed of a hit when my perfect drag bunt was ruled an error. The first baseman briefly bobbled my bunt, but I would have beaten his throw to first base even had he fielded the ball cleanly. While taking my lead off first base, I glanced at the scoreboard to see how it had been ruled. You never wanted to be seen blatantly looking at the scoreboard, as it made you look selfish— preoccupied with your own numbers, which of course every player was. The red error light flashed. I couldn't believe it. When playing on the road you might expect the hometown scorer to favor his pitcher's ERA by calling it an error, but we were playing at home. I wanted to plead my case the next day, but scorers were off-limits.

The loss of that hit probably means five points off my batting average. It isn't fair. As I said earlier, like all position players, my batting average meant everything to me—it was the yardstick by which I measured my baseball worth.

Playing at home against Tampa the next night, we had another drag-bunt issue, this time involving Canadian Shifty Gear. We led by

13. Bob Gear's rookie postcard, 1966. Photo courtesy of Bob Gear.

seven runs late in the game when Shifty laid down a perfect bunt for a base hit. Gail took him aside and, to Shifty's surprise, told him that he wasn't sure how the game was played in Canada, but in America you didn't show up your opponent by piling on runs when you already had a big lead late in the game. Shifty kept his head down and did not argue.

Since the Pendleton was such a nice place to hang out, we often went back there after games rather than go out. We'd have beer and pizza and sit around the pool or on the dock. When I had a bad night at the ballpark, it preyed on my mind, and I would be pretty quiet. Other guys drank to try to forget their o'fers or, in the case of pitchers, having gotten shelled. But I was never much of a drinker, so I moped. Sitting on the dock, we'd occasionally see a manatee making its way along the channel, and once we saw a calf and its mother who had an ugly open wound on her back, most likely from having been hit by a powerboat prop. One time a few players went swimming in the waterway, spotted some large fins breaking the surface, and practically flew out the water. They pointed out the "sharks" to others on the dock, only to be corrected by a bemused Pendleton retiree, who said were merely curious porpoises.

Every club had a few pranksters, and chief among the Islanders was my roommate Hook Warden, a burly, funny, and endlessly energetic left-hander. Hook had grown up on a large corn and livestock farm outside Columbus, Ohio. His father had deserted the family when he was three, and despite not having an adult male at home to teach and encourage him in sports, Hook became a high school star in football, basketball, and baseball. Having a golden arm, he knew that pitching would be his ticket off the farm. Warden was a fourth-round draft pick and just nineteen when he arrived in Daytona Beach. He sometimes unwittingly telegraphed his pitches to the opposing hitter, but he threw so hard that it usually didn't matter. For luck, when on the mound at the start of each inning, Hook would throw exactly five warm pitches, then toss a pebble over the third baseline, and finally touch the rosin bag. On days he wasn't pitching, Hook sometimes brought his binoculars to the ballpark to scan the stands for good-looking girls. He was always on the lookout for a good time, which he often found in pranks.

Typically, pranksters were well liked, which enabled them to get away with tricks such as the three-man lift and hotfoot without pissing off their victims. Once Warden put a match to my shoelace while I was sitting in the dugout during a game in Miami. I walked to the on-deck circle unaware it was burning. I heard laughter in the dugout, but it wasn't until I got into the batter's box that I felt the heat. I jumped and grabbed at my hot foot and managed to smother the burning lace with the heel of my other shoe. The fans could have had no idea what my gyrations were all about. Such pranks are less common in pro ball

14. Jon Warden, who one year later would pitch for the 1968 world champion Detroit Tigers. Photo courtesy of Jon Warden.

today, and I wonder if it's partially a result of today's players having learned baseball in adult-organized and adult-supervised leagues, like Little League. In that setting coaches have little tolerance for horseplay, unlike the youth-centered, freewheeling sandlot ball of my childhood.

Two years later Hook had a brilliant spring and made the final cut with the big club and stuck with them through their World Series championship season. He went 4-1 with a respectable 3.42 ERA. Then, his world caved in, his career scuttled by a "dead arm," the generic term used back then for a torn rotator cuff as well as other shoulder injuries.

MAY 7–8 . . . It rained for three consecutive days, canceling our games against the visiting St. Petersburg Cardinals. Normally, we wished for and celebrated rainouts, despite having to make them up later as doubleheaders. When the forecast was iffy, we sometimes chanted "Rain, rain, wash us out today, we can play some other day." But for me, these two rainouts really hurt because my father had come all the way from California to watch me play. This would be the first time he would see me play pro ball, and he was really looking forward to it. But the rain was unrelenting. With nothing else to do, I suggested that we drive his rental car along Daytona's famous fifteen-mile beach. Daytona was then one of the few places in the world where ordinary cars could be driven on an ocean beach. Our ride was very pleasant until I got careless and tried to go a little too far. We got stuck in loose sand, and in spinning the tires I dug us in even deeper. The tide was coming in, and there were no other vehicles in sight. Probably sensing my embarrassment, my dad kept his cool throughout, even when it looked as if we might lose the car. Thankfully, someone reported our predicament, because eventually a pickup truck with a winch came to the rescue.

The next day Dad had to return to California, and he never did get to see me play. It was a pity because he had always been my biggest fan. He was the one who introduced me to baseball, had often played catch with me in our backyard, attended most of my high school and college games, and always gave me encouragement. My becoming a professional ballplayer meant almost as much to him as it did to me. After he died in 2003 I was able to place some of his ashes behind home plate at PacBell Stadium (now AT&T Stadium), home of his beloved San Francisco Giants. I was on the field with a media credential and standing behind the batting cage during BP; I removed small handfuls of ashes from my pockets and, pretending to tie my shoelaces, furtively spread them on the ground. I did it while standing next to Felipe Alou, the Giants manager and one of my father's favorite players, who apparently did not wonder why my shoelaces kept coming undone, nor did he notice the whitish gray ashes on the red-brown earth.

Felber's girlfriend, Margie Emmons, told me that she knew the perfect girl for me. By this point Claire and I had drifted apart; we hadn't written much after she went to the maternity home, so I was eager to meet Margie's friend. Her name was Audrey, and she was away at Tulane University in New Orleans but was due home any day. We met and I was smitten. Flaxen hair, pretty, fit, free-spirited, and majoring in anthropology. Like Claire, she was well read and had informed opinions. When it came to Vietnam, politics, and the place and treatment of women in society, she held strong positions. She was a feminist, although that term wasn't yet popular. She rejected the idea that the only proper role for women was to be a wife and mother. With a smirk and a laugh, she once pointed out an ad for a secretary in the *Morning Journal* that stated that the applicant should be "pretty."

Audrey lived in Daytona but had been raised in Pennsylvania. Unlike many southern girls, she had no interest in going to college or joining a sorority to find a husband. She didn't believe that women needed to be dependent on men. She was thinking of a career and hoping to go to grad school in anthropology. Audrey was not the kind of woman whom Felber and most of my teammates were attracted to, although they were quick to acknowledge that she was very pretty. In Felber's mind Audrey's good looks didn't outweigh her outspokenness, which sometimes came across as cynicism. I think Felber also detected that she, unlike the groupies we knew, didn't think ballplayers were so special. She had been athletic as a child, winning her middle school's sprint contest, but at age twelve she was cut from the boys' baseball team after the boys conspired against her. After that, she recalled, "I hated all organized sports. Besides the only 'sport' open to girls in Florida then was cheerleading. Cheerleading for boys! Argh."

On our first evening together Audrey and I got into a discussion about religion. This was on a different plane than the usual bullpen and bus dialogues on the subject. Audrey believed in karma as a basic principle of the universe and explained that karma did not require a supernatural being. In short, she felt there was no God controlling or intervening in human actions. To her it was simply illogical that any God could orchestrate or even oversee the actions of all the world's 3.4 billion people at once. In one evening she convinced me that the idea of karma had a lot to offer, although I think my simplistic interpretation of what she said was more like, "What goes around comes around." In any case, before long I became an adherent to her belief.

MAY 9 . . . We were playing Orlando at home. Just before each game Warren Keyes, our general manager, announced over the PA system, "Ladies and gentlemen, please rise for our national anthem." Arriving at the ballpark early, Larry Calton sneaked into the press box, took "The Star-Spangled Banner" out of its sleeve, and replaced it with a record by the surf-rock band the Ventures. That evening, as everyone stood for the national anthem, rock-and-roll music boomed from the PA system, followed by a loud screech as Warren Keyes in his rush to remove the alien record knocked the needle across the turntable. He must have known that one of us had done it, since we could see his pudgy red face in the rooftop press box glaring our way.

15. Larry Calton, Daytona Beach Islanders second baseman who later became a broadcaster. Photo courtesy of the author.

Keyes was cheap, which was perhaps justified given that the ball club struggled to break even. Hoping to save money on groundskeepers, he purchased a small tractor to drag the infield. The first night he used it, during the usual fifth-inning infield grooming, it chugged along so slowly that the umpires impatiently waved it off the field for good.

The club released José Cepeda, despite his hitting .291. Before coming to us he had been let go by Cincinnati and St. Louis. Detroit had picked him up, hoping that he might have some of his older brother Orlando's potential. José could hit a lot better than he could avoid getting into trouble off the field. He was the first ballplayer that I met who smoked marijuana; coming from California, it didn't seem that big a deal, but the Tigers coaching staff thought otherwise. Some of the older coaches subscribed to the *Reefer Madness* view of the evils of cannabis, regarding it as a stepping-stone to "dope addiction," with the next step being insanity. Just a few years later Red Sox lefty Bill "Spaceman" Lee would get away with saying, "There are a lot worse things in baseball than marijuana and peyote if used in moderation. Such things as walks, designated hitters, and Astroturf."

MAY 12 . . . More news about the worsening situation in Vietnam, but it still wasn't a subject of conversation among the Islanders; hardly anyone read the front pages or listened to the world news. Of more interest was the opening of the St. Louis Cardinals' much-heralded new multipurpose (football and baseball) ballpark—Busch Memorial Stadium. Polak and Calton talked about how much they would love to play there someday. Later referred to as the cookie-cutter style, similar multipurpose stadiums soon followed in New York, Houston, Atlanta, Pittsburgh, San Diego, Cincinnati, Philadelphia, and Minneapolis. Like Busch, they were all eventually criticized for being overly uniform and soulless. A wrecking ball finished Busch Stadium in 2005, and a new "retro" ballpark took its place.

MAY 13–14 . . . We arrived in Miami for a two-game series with the Marlins and were staying at the Miami Colonial Hotel on Biscayne Boulevard in downtown. A few guys brought water balloons to the room I shared with Hook on the fifth floor, overlooking the street. We dropped a few from the window, aiming for pedestrians. The first few missed, exploding harmlessly on the pavement, but then one landed on the shoulder of a nicely dressed man, also splashing his female companion. He looked up as we quickly closed the window. The sodden couple went to the front desk and reported what had happened. Gail was summoned and, accompanied by the hotel manager, checked all our rooms, looking for the perpetrators. When we heard them in the hallway, we quickly splashed water on the outside of our window, so that when they came into our room we could claim that the water balloons must've been dropped from some floor above us. "Just look at the water on our window." They believed us and no one snitched, so we got off. But at the ballpark Gail delivered a stern lecture about the seriousness of pranks involving innocent bystanders. On our next road trip to Miami, we were assigned rooms away from the street. As Shifty remembered, "When we opened the drapes we were looking into a brick wall."

With the arrival of catcher Dave Bike, our receiver Tim Garner, who had been injured on opening day, was let go. Bike had stayed in school for the entire academic year to protect his student military deferment (that is, a draft exemption for full-time collegiate study that lasted until graduation or age twenty-four). Detroit had flown him to spring training during his two-week college spring break, and I had gotten to know him then. Every time he'd introduce himself to someone in camp, he'd say, "Hi, I'm Dave Bike from Bridgeport, Connecticut," as if Bridgeport was some place special like Paris or London. If you asked Dave about Bridgeport, he'd proudly tell you that it was not just a manufacturing center, but had great athletic teams and was the birthplace of P. T. Barnum. Dave, who soon acquired the nickname Alex, which no one could recall a reason for, was easygoing and confident, which may have come from his enormous size—six-foot-four, 220 pounds, with extra-broad shoulders. We likened him to Joe Palooka, the American comic-strip character who was not only a heavyweight boxing champion but an upright if naive sports hero.

Despite his massive size, Bike choked up several inches on the bat and had just warning-track power. Only later would he hit long balls commensurate with his size and strength. Bike was also bowlegged and sluggish down the bases; as Gail said more than once, "Bike, you're as slow as a bus going uphill with a load of people on it." Despite that, he had been an excellent basketball player and had turned down college basketball scholarships to sign with the Tigers. After his baseball career stalled eight years later at AAA, he became a college basketball coach.

MAY 15 . . . In a 4–2 road loss to Fort Lauderdale, I was hitless and on deck when the final out was made. When hitless late in the game, I was always eager to get up one last time to have a chance to salvage the night and feel okay about myself after the game. I'd had quite a few o'fers in the last ten days as I wrote, *I'm in a miserable slump. It's brought my average down to .260. . . . The games are a nightmare.* Like most players, when I was going bad I changed my routine, mixed things up, whether it was the foods I ate, the order in which I put on my uniform, the number of warmup swings I took in the on-deck circle, or even the route I walked to the ballpark—all in hopes of breaking the jinx and of finding luck.

Dave Yoakum, our third baseman, pointed out that it was difficult to pick up pitches against the backdrop of a white sign on the center-field fence. I thought, yeah, maybe that's affecting my hitting. I bought a gallon of dark-green paint and a large paintbrush and at dawn went with Felber to the ballpark and painted over the offending sign. The GM, Warren Keyes, grumbled that the sign's sponsor might want a refund. But everyone else agreed that the backdrop was better, but it didn't immediately pull me out of my slump.

Sometimes slumping players developed taboos that were usually born out of some personal misfortune; for me during this slump, it was pancakes. I had eaten pancakes a few weeks before when I had a terrible game and struck out three times. After another bad game, post pancakes, I swore off them for good. Taboos like this almost always grew out of particularly poor performances. Instead of trying to repeat a good performance by repeating a particular behavior, like changing my sweatshirt every night in the fifth inning, I tried to prevent a bad performance by avoiding the somewhat unusual behavior I thought might have caused it. Oddly, for Orioles pitcher Jim Palmer, a short stack of pancakes was a requisite part of his pregame ritual, hence his nickname, "Cakes."

Like most slumping players I got a lot of advice, not always solicited or solid, from teammates. Jim Mabry suggested that I drive a few tenpenny nails into the end of the barrel of my bat to give it more weight. This, he claimed, much like Ozark had in Jamestown, would slow down my swing and give me more bat control, and the extra weight would make the batted ball travel farther. Looking back on it, despite the illegality of putting nails in one's bat, Mabry's suggestion reveals how ignorant we were back then about the relationship between the weight of the bat, bat speed, and the distance the ball traveled. Mabry was correct that a heavy bat made the ball travel farther. The problem was swinging the extra weight—getting the bat around on a fastball.

1

MOVING UP

Daytona to Rocky Mount

When I got to the ballpark, waiting in my locker was a letter from my San Mateo, California, draft board, stating that my student deferment had been revoked because I was no longer enrolled in school full-time. Therefore, I was to report to the Armed Forces Examining and Entrance Station in Jacksonville, Florida, for a preinduction physical. I immediately wrote back, reminding the draft board that I was taking correspondence courses, which they had said would enable me to keep my student deferment. No reply. The monthly military draft call had risen to ten times what it had been in 1965: the government was in need of more bodies to wage the war in Vietnam.

Two of my teammates, Norm McRae, who had a gap between his front teeth and called himself "Cool Mac," and Rudy Burson, who had a perpetual red nose, also received notices to report to Jacksonville for physicals. Together we made the two-hour journey on a Greyhound bus. After listening to the antiwar speeches at Stanford, and afterward beginning to follow the war in the news media, I no longer believed we had any business in Vietnam. Nor did I still believe in the "domino theory"—that if Vietnam went communist, it would set off a chain reaction in which other countries would likewise become communist. I wasn't sure how, but I was determined that I would not go to Vietnam. Even if it meant going to Canada. On the bus trip to Jacksonville, Norm, Rudy, and I talked about the various strategies that others were using to fail their physical. Everything from eating soap to raise your blood pressure to drinking huge quantities of soda pop to raise your blood sugar or wearing pink underwear and claiming to be homosexual. It was too late for any of the dietary tactics, and claiming to be gay was out of the question. Rudy, who always struck me as cautious, patriotic, and conservative, was as eager as Norm and I were to avoid the military. I did my best to fail the hearing test by counting for two seconds before pressing the button for each sound I heard, even though it was supposed to be foolproof. After the initial hearing test I was examined by a specialist, pretending that when my name was called out in the waiting room that I didn't hear it. All three of us failed our physicals, and we were each designated "4-F," unacceptable for military service due to our inability to meet physical, mental, or moral standards. *Flunked my physical. Failed the hearing test. I'm disqualified unless there is a mass mobilization*, I wrote in a jubilant letter to my brother, Walt.

I had no qualms about cheating, though I imagined my father, who proudly served in World War II, and my grandfathers who served on the front lines in World War I, would have disapproved. But they never said anything. Audrey, who was staunchly antiwar, was thrilled for me but wondered how three healthy professional athletes could manage to fail their physical exams and be excused from military service. Her cynicism about professional sports and its pampered athletes increased. Thinking back to the large bulletin board that I had seen in spring training, with the names of all the players matched to color-coded stars indicating their draft status, I wondered if we'd gotten help from the Tigers' front office. For years I believed we had, but then in 2012 the Tigers' former farm director Don Lund, then in his nineties and in a retirement home, insisted that we had not gotten any help. Detroit had done all it could to get us into the reserves, but,

Lund claimed, "We had no influence on your preinduction physicals. You guys were just lucky."

Rudy's career ended the following winter when he was injured in a car accident, hit at a stoplight by a drunk driver. He worked in sales for steel and concrete pipe companies for thirty years before retiring in Fort Wayne, Indiana. Norm made it to the big leagues, pitching in relief for the Tigers for two seasons, and then bounced around for the next fifteen years, finishing up coaching for Los Dorados de Chihuahua in the Mexican League, where he married the daughter of the team owner. He died of cancer in Garland, Texas, at age fifty-five.

MAY 19 . . . The *Morning Journal* reported the Islanders "barely averted another Little Big Horn" when we scored four runs in the last frame to take the second game of a twin bill. No ballplayer understood the allusion to the famous Indian massacre. I collected three hits on the night, breaking a mini slump, and drove in the go-ahead run. *It feels great to be back on track . . . Not sure what I am doing differently at the plate, but whatever, it's working.*

Hitting requires making adjustments. Once your opponents detect a weakness—or as we liked to say, once they "know your number"—they feed you a steady diet of whatever pitch or location that you aren't hitting well. For me, it was sliders and fastballs up and in, on the fists, not allowing me to extend my arms. Gail had me move off the plate, so that I could get the bat head out front on tight pitches. It worked, and I began hitting again. I wrote out a reminder to myself on an index card: *Stay loose. Take a deep breath as the pitcher winds up. Get the barrel head out quick.* I added the new card to the small pile that I flipped through each morning. Most of my cards contained sayings culled from books I read, particularly Norman Vincent Peale's popular book *The Power of Positive Thinking*. In starting the research for this memoir I found my old cards—yellowed and tied with string. Most of them seem corny today. Some encouraged me to be industrious and focused:

"Impossibility is only in the dictionary of fools."

"Ambition has no rest."

"Purpose is what gives life meaning."

"Fortune favors the best prepared."

Some reminded me of character traits I wanted to develop:

"Speak briefly and to the point."

"We weaken when we exaggerate."

"A modest man never talks of himself."

Finally, a few reinforced the then popular notion that we are in control of our own destiny:

"Life is what you make it."

"Mind moves matter."

MAY 21 . . . The Leesburg A's George Lauserique struck out thirteen of us in seven innings, while our normally reliable starter Richie Williams struggled again. Richie was a shy African American from the South who kept his eyes down and his thoughts to himself. His supersize wife, Rosebud, was the opposite. She had a booming voice, always louder and more frequently heard than any girlfriend or fan in the Daytona stands. Rosebud thought Richie wasn't pitching well because he was wearing himself out in the bedroom. She went to Gail and asked that he have a word with Richie to cut back on the sex. "For the next month of the season," Gail later told me, "I had complete control of Richie's sex life."

The club released outfielder Jim Mabry after he had arrived at the ballpark slightly intoxicated and misplayed a fly ball. Gail pulled him from the game, sent him to the showers, and later that night sent him packing. Mabry, hitting just .178, had been in a funk over being in a long slump and might have been drinking for that reason. He was from Florida and told us that in the off-season he made money "rassling 'gators" for their hides.

After a good start to the season we had lost twelve in a row; I wasn't too troubled because I was hitting again and my batting average had climbed back up to .316, leading the team. During the skid Gail juggled the batting order almost every night in hopes of breaking the jinx. After any loss but especially after a string of defeats, Gail, like most managers, didn't want to hear noise or horseplay on the bus. I suppose being subdued and quiet was to show our unhappiness with losing and that we were reflecting on our mistakes. My Hispanic teammates—Julio, José, and Hector—came from a different tradition and sometimes had difficulty or simply forgot to repress themselves. Their approach was to leave the game on the field, that is, to play their hardest between the chalk lines and when the game was over to forget it. They figured there was nothing you could do about the outcome, and there was always another game the next day, so why get down? Occasionally, Gail chewed them out for being loud or laughing on the bus after a defeat.

In the stands several young men, who'd had too much to drink, were obnoxiously razzing us throughout the game. Gail sent Dennis Grossini, Ralph Foytack, and Doc Olms to an early shower and told them to wait for the offenders outside the ballpark and "convince those bastards not to come back." They did and the offenders never returned.

Nor was Gail opposed to ordering one of our pitchers to knock down or plunk an opposing batter who had been hitting us hard. But nice guy Jim Dietz, from suburban Long Island, wouldn't always go along. Some thought he feared retaliation—with no DH back then, pitchers had to hit and therefore were vulnerable. But no one really knew why he ignored the skipper. Dietz was often quirky. Whenever someone asked how he was doing, he'd say, "Day Tripper," after the Beatles song, and nothing more.

I frequently went out with Audrey after the games. Occasionally, she talked about Vietnam or deteriorating race relations that had led to riots in Cleveland and Los Angeles. She was well versed and contributed to my growing disillusionment over the war and encouraged me to question authority. In a fashion she became my teacher, getting me to think more critically, to ask questions that I never imagined asking, and to formulate a position and to defend it. Audrey was five months younger than I was, but sometimes it felt as if she were five years older.

JUNE 2 . . . We beat Fort Lauderdale 5–1 behind a revived (no sex the night before) Richie Williams, who pitched a complete-game five-hitter. Felber had a good night, getting two hits and driving in three runs. He was thrilled after the game and hopeful that his new batting stance would continue to produce hits. It didn't. Felber, Margie, Audrey, and I went back to the Pendleton after the game and, as we often did, sat around the pool and talked. While Felber went for a dip, Margie confided to me, "Bob is awfully self-absorbed with his baseball. . . . He doesn't seem to have any other interests." Had Margie known the other Islanders better, she would've realized Bob wasn't different from the rest of us. Surviving in pro ball didn't allow for other interests, at least during the season.

JUNE 3 . . . When we got to the ballpark a new shipment of bats from Louisville Slugger was waiting. We were always eager to get new bats, and upon opening our boxes we immediately inspected them, felt their heft, took swings, and looked at the width of grain. Some players wanted wide grain, while others preferred narrow grain. I preferred narrow grain, thinking it meant the wood was denser. Today experts say the width of the grain is less important than its being straight, from the knob to the top of barrel. Swinging my new lumber, I had a big night—three hits, including a double in the ninth that drove in the winning runs, in a 3–1 win over the White Sox. *It's hard to believe I've been gone since March. When you're playing well time flies. This is the life!*

A few days later we were playing a doubleheader at West Palm Beach when at the start of the first game Julio Perez bolted in from his right-field position after he spotted a large snake. Julio refused to return to the outfield until the grounds crew removed the snake—an eastern diamondback rattler—and declared the area safe. I recalled Julio's hysteria after discovering a snake under his pillow in a spring-training prank. We lost both games to the Braves that night, 7-1 and 1-0, single-handedly beaten by their red-headed, fresh-faced eighteen-year-old third baseman, Wayne Garrett, who drove in four runs in the first game and then scored the Braves' sole run in the nightcap. Wayne, the youngest of three Garrett brothers to sign with the Milwaukee Braves, would have a ten-year big-league career with the "Ya Gotta Believe" Mets and Expos and then play his last two seasons in Japan. He returned to baseball in 1989, at age forty-two, playing in the Senior League until it folded. (The Senior Professional Baseball Association, based in Florida, was a winter baseball league for players age thirty-five and older. Its players were former Major and Minor Leaguers. The league folded halfway through its second season in 1990, due to poor attendance.)

JUNE 7 . . . On the way home from playing Leesburg, we heard on the radio that a civil rights activist, James Meredith, the first black student to have been admitted to the segregated University of Mississippi (1962), had been shot on a march across Mississippi. But that news was overshadowed by the results of the annual baseball draft. This was only the second draft ever. In the first draft (1965), the number-one pick, Rick Monday, had signed with Kansas City for a $104,000 bonus. Monday was currently hitting .249 in AA ball. That night we learned the Mets had taken Steve Chilcott, a hard-hitting high school catcher from California, as the first overall pick. Casey Stengel would go to his California home to sign Chilcott, whom the Mets had taken ahead of Reggie Jackson (taken second by Kansas City). Jackson, of course, became a Hall of Famer, while Chilcott never made it to the Majors.

We beat Leesburg that night by scoring two runs with two outs in the ninth without the aid of a base hit. Hector Soto led off with a walk, Tim Martíng was hit by a pitch, a ground ball moved up both runners, and then Dave Bike bounced a grounder to the shortstop, who threw it over the first baseman's head, allowing the tying and winning runs to score.

Audrey has been coming to my games, and last week even brought her mother and father. Sometimes I can see her reading a book instead of watching the action. After some games I could tell that she hadn't paid very close attention, sometimes not knowing how well I had done. First Claire and then Audrey: I had fallen for girls who didn't like watching baseball.

JUNE 8 . . . We began an eight-game home stand by losing to league-leading Leesburg, 3–2. Hook, who had lost another tough one, pitching eight innings and giving up only one earned run, became so distraught that in a corner of the clubhouse he wept. Gail tried to console him. My luck was only a little better, as I hit three balls on the nose and had but one single to show for it.

JUNE 9–10 . . . Hurricane Alma rained out both home games against Tampa. While moving across Honduras, Alma killed seventy-three people and then swept ashore near Tallahassee, Florida, with winds of 125 mph. I recorded Gail's advice in my journal: *"Stock up on groceries, fill your bathtub and stay in your apartments."* After getting groceries, several of us changed into swimsuits and went to the beach for the best body surfing of the season, like with the tornado in Lakeland not taking seriously our coach's warning. While the main path of the hurricane passed over the Florida Panhandle, Daytona experienced gale-force winds, heavy rainfall, and a power outage that left us in darkness for a day. Though the Bay Area home I'd grown up in is only a few miles from the San Andreas Fault, the tornado in Lakeland and then Hurricane Alma were more extreme natural disasters than anything I had ever experienced. *And people ask if I'm afraid of earthquakes in California. That's nothing compared to this.*

JUNE 12 . . . Before coming to the ballpark, I listened to Defense Secretary Robert McNamara say on the news that although military successes in Vietnam have "exceeded our expectations," more U.S. troops were needed "to counter the continuing infiltration from the communist North." Another 18,000 GIs were ticketed for South Vietnam duty, boosting the total to 285,000. *Incredible! They must think we're stupid. If the war is going so well, why would they need more troops?*

That night we lost a doubleheader to the St. Petersburg Cardinals, 6–3 and 7–0, in front of 2,300 spectators, attracted by a giveaway promotion. I went one for three in each game. *Lately I seem to be getting one hit each night. Does that mean I'm not bearing down as much after I get that first hit? I need to keep up the intensity.*

JUNE 13 . . . Before our scheduled doubleheader against St. Petersburg, Mickey White was released. He was hitting just .105 and hadn't fielded all that well, either. A phenom at his South Carolina high school, he had signed for eight thousand dollars and come to spring training looking like a prospect, but a prolonged slump and too many errors shattered his confidence. All Mickey cared about was baseball; it was all he talked about. At times it seemed to be all he knew. While we all had passion for the game, his was exceptional. Now headed home, he would have to figure out what he wanted do with the rest of his life. As we said our farewells and wished him luck, he said to me in his Carolina drawl, "I'd better not be readin' anything by you tearin' down baseball, or I'll come lookin' for you." I was stunned. What gave him the impression that I was tearing down baseball? He had read a few of the newspaper features I had written about Minor League life, but I didn't think there was anything in there that was unfairly critical of pro ball. And what did he mean, "I'll come lookin' for you"?

JUNE 14 . . . The Orlando Twins dealt us our third straight doubleheader loss in three days. Dennis Grossini, his elbow ailing, lasted only two and two-thirds innings and got the loss in the first game. So upbeat after his spring-training outing with the Tigers, Dennis now moaned about his aching arm and declining fortunes. Being a bonus baby, he was sent to a hospital in Detroit to have his elbow evaluated and then home to California, shut down for the season. The arm problem began on his first pitching assignment in Daytona, after being sent down from

Rocky Mount, Detroit's advanced Class A team. "I was pulled off the bus in Rocky Mount just as a road trip was beginning and told that I was being sent to Daytona," recalled Dennis.

> I cleaned out my locker, gathered my belongings from the house I shared, caught the train, traveled all night, and once in Daytona went straight to the ballpark. I hadn't even found a place to stay, and with my bags sitting in the clubhouse Gail told me I was starting that night. I should have put my foot down and said, "Hey, I just traveled all night on a noisy damn train, haven't slept, I am tired and in need of some rest, and you want me to pitch tonight?" But I didn't. I pitched that night, and I remember feeling something was wrong with my elbow. As I look back, it was the beginning of the end. My arm problems escalated from there. I should have said "NO! GODDAMN IT, NO!" But that wasn't how things were done back then. And I paid dearly for it.

JUNE 15 . . . On the way to a road game in Cocoa Beach, we spotted the white vapor trail of a rocket being launched from nearby Cape Canaveral. Just the month before another launch at Canaveral had put an unmanned spacecraft, Surveyor 1, on the surface of the moon. None of us had ever seen anything like it. The Cocoa Beach Astros beat us 4–2 after a seventh-inning two-run blast by Bob Watson, their young black catcher from Los Angeles. Nicknamed "Bull," he would be called up to Houston that September and would stick in the big leagues for eighteen seasons. On May 4, 1975, while playing for the Astros, he scored the one millionth run in Major League history. There had been a nationwide Tootsie Roll sweepstakes with fans predicting who would score the millionth run. As the goal came closer, there were scoreboard updates in every ballpark. Watson edged out Cincinnati's Dave Concepcion by four seconds and was awarded one million pennies and one million Tootsie Rolls, both of which he donated to charity. In the 1990s Watson became only the second African American to be a Major League general manager (Astros and later the Yankees).

JUNE 16 . . . We lost to Cocoa Beach again by the same score, 4-2. The highlight of the game Julio Perez's overrunning a fly ball down the left-field line and at the last instant reaching back and catching it barehanded. It was one of the most singular feats of athleticism I ever witnessed, as good as Kevin Mitchell's famous 1989 barehanded catch of Ozzie Smith's fly ball. A few weeks earlier Julio had picked up the wrong glove on his way to his outfield position at the start of an inning. It was not only someone else's glove but the wrong hand—right rather than left. Rather than go back to the dugout, he used it on the opposite hand and caught a fly ball. The team was amused, but it didn't surprise anyone. And Julio always seemed to get a great jump on fly balls, more adept than other outfielders at telling how hard, and therefore how far, a ball would travel from the sound of the crack of the bat. Julio, who in Cuba had been a poor kid from the streets, didn't understand much English. We spoke to him in a simplified pidgin, such as "Julio hit ball hard, *si!* . . . Julio strong boy, *si!* . . . Julio no like hamburger, *si?*" It sounds demeaning now, but no one thought of it that way at the time. Julio, who had a deep voice and a powerfully built body, and sometimes played with his dick in the back of the bus, was probably five years older than the twenty-one listed on the program, and for reasons we never understood he didn't get along with our Dominican teammates. I guess we expected all Hispanics to be friends with one another.

JUNE 17 . . . After losing to the Miami Marlins 3-1, Hook, Calton, and I were out walking near our hotel when a black guy approached us. "Hey, would you like some girls? I can get some girls for you." After a little hesitation, as we were all inexperienced at these things, Hook said, "Sure, I guess so." We followed the guy into an apartment building, where he took fifteen dollars from each of us and then said he would get the girls and be right back. We sat there for ages, and just about the time we had concluded that we'd been taken to the cleaners he returned. He said the girls were ready, but that they weren't trustworthy and that we should give him our wallets for safekeeping. Calton and Hook did, and the pimp then left to get the hookers. We waited and waited and waited. It was probably an hour before we realized it was a scam.

JUNE 20 . . . We lost to Fort Lauderdale 5–1, and after the game our slick-fielding Canadian infielder, Steve Oleschuk, who was hitting an anemic .134, was released. I had enjoyed his company and his stories about growing up in Quebec. *Quite a few of my teammates from opening day are no longer with us—Cepeda, Mabry, Garner, White, and now Oleschuk—all released, and some of them are pretty darn good ballplayers. It's scary.* Losing teammates whom you hung out with was tough, but that was pro ball and you became hardened to it, and you soon forgot them.

JUNE 22 . . . The first game of a twin bill against Deerfield Beach went eighteen innings before we pushed across the only run of the game, the longest scoreless game in the FSL since 1947. Deerfield took the second game, 11–3, after midnight. Much like the twenty-one-inning marathon in Jamestown, we had played twenty-seven innings over a span of nearly seven hours. While worn out by the end, I was happy, having gotten three hits in the first game and two in the nightcap. We dragged ourselves home to the Pendleton and went to bed, grumbling that we faced another doubleheader the next night.

Shifty clipped the article about the previous day's game from the *Morning Journal*, as he did every day. Each week he'd mail the batch of cuttings home to his parents in Meritton, Ontario, for them to enjoy and then paste in his scrapbook.

After splitting the next night's twin bill with West Palm Beach, 2–1 and 2–1, a few of us got beer and pizza and went to Tomoka State Park to look for some weird lights that supposedly appeared in the swamp at night. With Margie as our guide and our car lights out and one player sitting on each fender, feet up on the bumper, we drove slowly, looking for the mystery light. Margie told us of some young people who had turned off their car lights while chasing the swamp light and had been killed when they drove off the road and into the water or quicksand. We didn't see anything that night but saw what we thought was "the light" a few weeks later, flickering in the distance. Swamp gas, Margie told us, was nothing supernatural but rather methane produced by decaying vegetation in the stagnant water of the swamp. In some places the light went by the name of will-o'-the-wisp or jack-o'-lantern. The mystery was not that it existed, but what caused the spontaneous ignition. And that remains a puzzle to scientists. Nearly thirty years later Margie, who had become a reporter for the *Daytona Beach Morning Journal*, would write a feature about the swamp luminescence.

JUNE 25 . . . Playing Leesburg on the road, our new pitcher, Les Cain, got his first start. A fourth-round pick, Les had signed a few weeks after graduating from El Cerrito High School in Northern California. Unlike others, Les would never reveal to us the amount of his signing bonus. He said it was none of our business, which was probably right. Gail had Les pitch in relief a few games before starting him. We had a lead in the bottom of the fifth when rain began to fall. Les, thinking the game was already official, slowed down to secure the victory. But it wasn't quite official yet, since he had not retired the side in the bottom of the fifth. Gail yelled from the dugout, "Pitch the goddamn ball. . . . Get a move on it." Les either didn't hear or didn't understand. The rain fell harder, and the umpire called play and then canceled the game, one out shy of completion. Gail came down to the end of the bench where Les was toweling off. "Good game, kid. Unfortunately, it doesn't count for anything. You only had one fuckin' out to get, but you just dallied around and now you won't get the win. From now on, El Cerrito hot dog, you just throw the ball and let me do the thinking." Neither Les nor Gail ever forgot it.

Two years later Les was with the Tigers in their World Series–winning season. But arm trouble cut short his promising big-league career at age twenty-four, just as it had for my other Islander teammates Dennis Grossini, Jon Warden, and Norm McRae. After being forced to pitch with a sore arm by Detroit manager Billy Martin, Les sued the Tigers over permanent damage to his arm. The Tigers fought him. But in a landmark decision the Michigan Bureau of Worker's Compensation awarded Cain $111 per month ($475 in today's money) for the rest of his life.

JUNE 26 . . . We beat Leesburg 6–0. The game was delayed by a mosquito fogger truck passing next to the ballpark and enveloping the field and stands (and us) in a white cloud of DDT. The fogger trucks were a common sight in towns with a lot of mosquitoes. Kids would ride bikes, skate, or run behind the trucks enjoying the "fog"; no one seemed concerned about possible health consequences from inhaling DDT. While the foggers helped eliminate malaria in the United States, DDT was later banned by the newly created Environmental Protection Agency (1970) as a probable human carcinogen. Today most Americans still carry traces of DDT in their bodies.

JUNE 27 . . . We were twenty-seven games out of first place when the midseason All-Star break arrived, and for the first time in more than two months we had a scheduled day off, actually two. Audrey, Margie, and I visited a well-known spiritualist camp in Cassadaga, an hour from Daytona. *It's a spooky place on the shores of a lake, with moss hanging from big trees and kind of misty. The medium's house we went to was dimly lit with kerosene lamps, and a bit creepy.* Audrey and Margie had been there before and told me they had seen a spiritualist medium, Ann Gehman, levitate a chair off her front porch. (But when I asked them again, in 2012, they were both unsure what they had seen.) Gehman later gained national media attention for supposedly helping police solve a crime and for locating oil and missing persons. I really wanted to see levitation. But the night we arrived Gehman was away, so we had to settle on another medium. We each got a personal reading. The spiritualist claimed to be putting her body in direct communication with my "higher soul" and that through "channeling," she would help me understand the why and purpose of my life's mission. It all sounded far-fetched, but I was happy to give it a try; besides, I didn't want Audrey to think that I wasn't open to new experiences. *The medium said some things that are pretty accurate and makes me wonder how she could know these things, like my being far from home and that I am involved in some sort of athletics.* But later I realized that most of what she had said was fairly general, much like the stuff of astrology, or could have been deduced from my clothing and appearance. None of her predictions panned out, with the exception of my experiencing "a big change in my profession." She wasn't any more specific than that, but I was indeed in store for a change.

Two weeks later I heard the Tigers were sending first baseman Bob Welz, one of their top draft picks, to Daytona. Welz had signed out of Harvard for a bonus of twenty thousand dollars, meaning he was guaranteed to be in the lineup. He arrived in town driving a new sports car bought with his bonus money and with hair, brilliant white teeth, and a Boston accent all reminiscent of John F. Kennedy. He exuded a Northeast patrician air, though later I learned that his father was an electrician. Welz didn't understand the power of the Florida sun, and a few days later he was red as a lobster after having sat out too long without protection. Undeterred, Welz was set on having a good tan and before long turned as dark as the Hispanics. Actually, many of us had good tans, which prompted the sportswriter of the *Tampa Tribune* to call us the "Daytona Beach Boys. . . . [T]he Islanders may not be in first, but they have the best tans in the league." Beneath the gloss Welz was an easygoing, happy-go-lucky guy who never seemed to get too down when he wasn't playing well, unlike the rest of us. Some said that with his Harvard education, he just wasn't as hungry. Also unlike most of us, he believed deeply in himself.

The first few nights after Welz arrived he got penciled in at first base, and I was on the bench. Welz had a quick bat with some pop, but I still led the club in hitting. I was upset and began to wonder about my future, especially after hearing that my former Jamestown teammate Wayne Ginste, who played well at Jamestown the year before, had been released. I wrote, *Everybody has an identity and mine is baseball. "Oh, George Gmelch, he's the ballplayer, isn't he?" That would be the hardest thing about getting released, to lose my identity. . . . Besides, think of all the people back home I'd be letting down. I can't bear the thought.*

On the third day after Welz's arrival, Gail asked if I could play the outfield. I had played only one year of outfield in high school and a few games in college. I said, "Sure, I can play the outfield," though I wasn't sure I wouldn't embarrass myself. Either way, it was better than riding the pine. That night I became the Islanders' new right fielder. Ensconced in the relative quiet of the outfield, I became aware of the hum made by the electric light towers, something I had never noticed playing the infield near the noisy grandstand.

JUNE 28 . . . We opened the second half of the season with a 3–0 win over Tampa; I drove in two runs, and Hook shut down Tampa for eight innings. It was the fifth consecutive game in which Tampa had not scored a run—their scoreless streak of forty-six innings broke the league record. "**I'S HANG ANOTHER BLANK ON TAMPA**" was the sports headline in the *Morning Journal*. It was hard to believe that any team could go five consecutive games without scoring a run, but then Tampa had a team batting average of .215 and not one of their players would ever make it to the big leagues.

The Tampa hotel where we were staying had housing for nursing students on the top floor. There wasn't any way to gain access to their floor without a key, so Warden and Doc Olms climbed the fire escape. The girls teased them, and when some of them returned to our floor a water fight started. It began with glasses of water, then a wastebasket full, and ended with Hook pulling out the fire hose. Gail, staying on the floor below, was awakened by the hotel manager and stormed upstairs. As he walked down the hallway the water-saturated carpet squished beneath his feet. He fined us all and threatened bigger fines if there was another complaint.

JUNE 30 . . . We beat the St. Petersburg Cardinals in both games of a doubleheader in front of a small crowd, many of whom were senior citizens from nearby retirement communities. I watched the first game from the bullpen bench and yakked with the relief pitchers. We were talking about girls when I said offhandedly, "Boobs are overrated. I am a leg man." The relievers looked at me like I had two heads. I tried to defend my remark with a comment about the new miniskirt craze sweeping the country, at least on college campuses, and how nice it was seeing a girl's legs. No go. I went for a graceful exit by adding something like, "I mean, fondling breasts is okay, but it's nothing compared to getting laid." They still thought I was a bit off as I went back to the dugout.

We pulled a good one on our reliever Nick Ross the next night against St. Petersburg. All season long Nick had been going on and on about his fiancée—how beautiful Pam was, how smart Pam was, how much he missed Pam, how he was looking forward to their fall wedding. It got to be a bit much, and several of us hatched the idea of sending Nick a telegram, supposedly from Pam, saying that the wedding was off, that she had met someone else. We figured the best way to do it was to have the telegram sent to the Cardinals' manager, Sparky Anderson. Sparky agreed to go along and delivered our phony telegram to Nick during BP. Nick was beside himself in shock. Actually, we were surprised that he wasn't a little suspicious, that he didn't see through the ruse. Gail didn't know Nick's state of mind when he summoned him from the bullpen in the eighth inning with the game tied and runners on base. Nick threw a wild pitch over the catcher's head, letting in the winning run. After the game, when we told Nick it was just a prank, he was enormously relieved, but blamed me for the wild pitch. "Moonbeam, that is your fuckin' wild pitch, you bastard." As was customary, he warned us that he'd be getting his revenge, which he did a few weeks later, lighting up my shoelaces.

Gail was fairly tolerant of pranks as long as they didn't spill over onto the field or cause him to be awakened at night with complaints from the hotel staff. Although he tried not to let on, he seemed to enjoy the ingenuity of the telegram to Nick. But not all managers were so tolerant, especially if the team was losing. Winning, which we were now doing, made all things a little looser.

St. Petersburg infielder Lenny Boyer got himself into a pickle that same night when his girlfriend and a groupie he had picked up both showed up at the ballpark using Lenny's complimentary tickets and unwittingly sat one seat apart. After the game he saw both girls standing outside the clubhouse waiting for him. Not knowing what to do, he sneaked out the center-field exit and drove home. Lenny was one of seven brothers from tiny Carl Junction, Alabama, to play professional baseball. Three of them—Ken, Clete, and Cloyd—made the big leagues, all as third basemen. "Back in those days, there were only two things to do in Alabama," explained one of their schoolmates when Clete died from cancer at fifty-one. "You either played baseball or went and watched somebody else play baseball."

JULY 5 . . . We were playing the Cocoa Beach Astros when just after we took the field for batting practice, Gail called me aside. He walked me down the left-field foul line and held out his hand. "Congratulations," he said. "You're going to Rocky Mount." Rocky Mount was the Detroit Tigers' high-A team in the Carolina League, the next rung up in the Tigers' farm system.

My reaction caught him off guard. "That's great," I said, "but I'd be happy staying here in Daytona for the season." I wasn't saying no to the promotion. No Minor Leaguer in his right mind would turn down a chance to move one step closer to the big leagues. Rather, I was expressing my ambivalence about being moved again, as I had been the previous season when yanked out of Duluth and sent to Jamestown. Besides, I was enjoying success in Daytona, had made friends, and was crazy about Audrey. Staring at me with a "Now I've heard it all" look, Gail shook his head, muttered something like "Get ready," and walked off. Before I left I ordered a subscription to the *Daytona Beach Morning Journal* so that I could keep tabs on my former teammates. I left Daytona the next day with a batting average of .293, tops on the team and ninth in the league. On the fourteen-hour bus ride to the coastal plain of North Carolina, I jotted in my journal, *The big leagues might be within reach.* Little did I know that Rocky Mount and the Jim Crow South I encountered there would dash my dreams.

8

DOUBLE PASSAGE

The Carolinas

Rocky Mount was and still is a regional center on the coastal plain of North Carolina, then with a population of about thirty-four thousand. In the 1960s the town was known for its large tobacco market, thus the name of my new team: the Leafs. Although I was excited to be stepping up, after being a Duke, a Tiger, and an Islander, becoming a Leaf—a tobacco leaf—hardly sounded like a promotion. But tobacco had been a mainstay of the town's economy since the late 1800s when the cigarette industry took hold. *This is big-time tobacco growing country,* I scribbled on a postcard home. *Even the towns we play in—Winston-Salem, Raleigh and Newport—all have brands named after them.*

Rocky Mount's ballpark was a step down from the Major League spring-training ballparks and facilities I was used to in Daytona and elsewhere in the Florida State League. The outfield was hard. Its grass was patchy, with white football yard marks still faintly visible from the previous fall's games. On top of that, its lights were dim. A dirt tunnel leading to the dugout always smelled musty. And after games its cramped clubhouse looked like a laundry, with uniforms and undershirts draped from hangers everywhere to dry. Only the crowds and the fans' enthusiasm were better.

Before my first game the skipper, Al Federoff, told me that I would be starting in right field, replacing Ronnie Woods, who was in a prolonged slump. The Leafs were tied for first place. I knew a few of my teammates, like Jim Leyland, from Jamestown, plus a few I'd become acquainted with in spring training. The players were welcoming and seemed to be aware that I'd put up good numbers in Daytona. Two of them had arranged for me to rent a spare bedroom in the house where they boarded, a short walk from the ballpark. When the lineup card was posted on the dugout wall, I saw that I was batting fifth, which was flattering, as many of my teammates were seasoned veterans. Eight would eventually play in the big leagues, with a few, like pitchers Jim Rooker, Bill Butler, and Dick Drago, sticking around for a good while.

In my first at bat I hit the ball on the nose, a one-hopper at the shortstop. A few innings later I hit another ball well, but it too didn't find a hole. From that point on, it was all downhill. After thirteen games I had only four hits and was hitting .129. In Daytona I'd had confidence and thought the pitchers were more afraid of me than I was of them. Now it was the other way around. *I think I am opening up my hips and shoulders too quickly and pulling off pitches,* I noted in my journal. Pulling an outside pitch usually produces a weak ground ball to short or second. I had a lot of them. The root of my problem was what coaches call "trying to play beyond one's ability." It is a common affliction. Whether it's a player's first spring training or a promotion to the next level, he often tries to do more than he is accustomed to. On arrival in Rocky Mount, I wanted to hit with more power because I thought that's what the front office wanted—more home runs. That meant pulling the ball, as I had in Jamestown, instead of spraying hits to all fields, as I had in Daytona.

What I needed was a coach to remind me to just continue what I had been doing that brought me success in Daytona. Federoff probably told me that, but I don't remember. And if he did, it didn't sink in. As soon as you start tinkering with your swing or stance, you're liable to upset your mechanics. Voilà, you're in a slump. And slumps are especially tough if you haven't already had success at that level of play; it's easy to think that you're overmatched by the competition. A veteran player can look back and remember having been successful and know that he can do it again. I couldn't.

I became homesick for Daytona—for the place, for the ocean, for the triumph I enjoyed as an Islander, and for my girlfriend. My longing for Audrey was made worse when the *Daytona Beach Morning Journal* showed up one day with a large picture of her in an ad for the London Symphony Orchestra, which was coming to town. She looked so pretty; I worried I might never see her again.

When I told Claire that I had been reassigned to Rocky Mount, she suggested taking the train down from New York City to visit. I didn't have the heart to tell her that I had fallen for someone else, and I really wasn't sure what my feelings were. Arriving in Rocky Mount the night the team returned very late from a road trip, Claire was waiting for me in the hotel I had arranged. We ended up having sex and then talked for hours. I learned about the birth—it was a boy. Claire said she didn't look at him for fear of developing an attachment and then longing for him after the adoption. She didn't say a lot about it, and though curious I didn't press her. It was hard to comprehend that I was a father. Claire's own father had accepted her back in the house, but she chose instead to move to New York City to pursue art. She was living in Greenwich Village and working in an art gallery.

The next morning when we dressed for breakfast, Claire looked like a hippie—tie-dyed shirt, large loop earrings, flowing dress, and sandals. Her clothes expressed her individualism and her new life. I half-admired the disregard for political and social orthodoxy they represented, but the attire was not a look I was accustomed to or felt comfortable with. I never did wear bellbottoms, tie-dyed shirts, or the other fashions of the sixties, although I did, after leaving baseball, grow a beard. I suppose that was the best I could do; beards were also the fashion among anthropologists.

After breakfast as we strolled around town, I noticed some heads turn. No other female in Rocky Mount dressed like this. Thank God she didn't have a flower in her hair or a necklace with a peace symbol. When we chanced upon my teammate Wally Sherer walking with his girlfriend, he gave her a raised-eyebrow stare. She might as well have been a Gypsy or from Haight-Ashbury. I cut the conversation with Wally short. Although I didn't understand it at the time, Claire was simply more freethinking than others. It was part of who she was and partly the influence of living in Greenwich Village—the bohemian capital of the East Coast. She told me how she had met Bob Dylan and Timothy O'Leary. I had become antiwar and my politics were turning left, but I wasn't part of the counterculture and my appearance was still decidedly straight or square, that of a clean-cut jock. My social awareness, like my dress, was constrained by my immersion in the world of pro ball, a world that was clean shaven, didn't wear jewelry, didn't question authority, and was patriotic.

It didn't take long for Claire and me to realize that we had drifted apart, lacking the passion we shared for one another the previous summer. I didn't mention Audrey, but perhaps she sensed my conflict; I was never good at hiding my feelings. Claire was hurt that our relationship wasn't what it had been. I felt guilty. She had planned to stay four days but left after three. I can still see her departure, clearer than any other memory of that summer: It is late at night. She has just boarded the train for New York and is visible through the Pullman-car window, her head in her hands, crying. She doesn't look up to return my wave as the train pulls out of the station. I feel awful. Had I been insensitive? Had I betrayed her? I never saw Claire again.

In 2012 I located Claire in western New York and called her. It was only the third time we had spoken in forty-eight years. After her visiting me in Rocky Mount in 1966, she had returned to Greenwich Village but a few years later abandoned her ambition of becoming an artist and returned to western New York. She married, settled on a large farm, and had three children before losing her husband to cancer. Now remarried, she and her new husband own a four-hundred-acre farm and are active in local conservation efforts. She sounded happy and modestly alluded to a summer cabin, a house in Florida, and trips on their forty-two-foot boat on Lake Erie. Working on this memoir, I was interested in hearing what she remembered of our relationship that summer of 1965. She didn't say much, until I began relating details from my journal. As we each added new pieces, a more complete picture of our time together emerged. Reconstructing our romance was unexpectedly exciting for me. I dreamed about it for several nights. I finally asked Claire what it was that had attracted her to me. She said it was the thrill of being with someone different, my being from California and being curious about things and always eager for adventure. As an afterthought, she added that I was tall and not bad looking. I liked what she said, but not in that order.

Claire seemed amused that I had reconnected with her and was curious about our courtship in Jamestown. She tried to be helpful, but made it clear that it was "ancient history" and that she wasn't interested in exploring it too deeply. She had never heard from the child and had not been interested in locating him; he would now be in his late forties. Sometimes I wonder what became of him: Where does he live? Is he smart? Is he athletic? Does he have his mother's good looks? Has he had a good life? Will he someday contact me? Sadly, after that call my voice-mail messages were never returned, and I never heard from Claire again. I suspect that her husband did not approve.

Al Federoff finally decided that I wasn't going to solve my hitting problems and therefore wasn't going to help the club win. He benched me and put Ronnie Woods back in right field. It was a good call. Woods, whom we called Mr. Clean after his shaved head, found his groove and hit well the rest of the season, finishing at a respectable

.265. He went on to a six-year career in the big leagues with the Yankees and Expos.

After I spent a few games on the bench, Al called me into his office and told me Detroit was sending me to Statesville, their low Class A club in the Western Carolinas League. I could hardly believe my ears. "Statesville?" That was a full step below the Florida State League, where, as Gail had said, I had already proved myself. In fact, statistically, I was still Daytona's leading hitter. Al didn't offer much explanation; rather, he directed me to the general manager's office to make my travel arrangements.

Other than Claire's departure, what I remember most vividly about my short stay in Rocky Mount that season was not my failure—I must have repressed that—but one of the longest home runs I had ever seen, a high-towering drive that disappeared into the blackness, beyond the reach of the left-field lights. It was hit by the visiting Peninsula Grays catcher Johnny Bench. Bench went on to hit a league-leading twenty-two home runs. "Trying to get a fastball by him," said Federoff, "was like trying to sneak a sunrise past a rooster." Bench was also a brilliant defensive catcher. He had huge hands that could each hold a half-dozen baseballs! It was no surprise to anyone when he was called up to Cincinnati the following season.

The next day I was on a Greyhound bus, making the 204-mile trip to Statesville. The journey took me from the flat Carolina coastal plain to the Piedmont, a region of hills and ridges, and Statesville, the gateway to the Appalachian Mountains, which stretched for twenty-one hundred miles from Alabama to Canada and millions of years ago were as tall as the Himalayas before being ground down to the smallish and rounded mountains they are today.

Soon after I arrived and checked into a downtown hotel, I went out to see the town. I noticed a lot of black people; they made up one-third of the population. Statesville was called a "city"—a Chamber of Commerce tag—but it sure didn't look very big. In fact, the town was just one-third the size of Rocky Mount, and I wondered what there was to do other than play baseball. But I did like that it was hilly and hoped that, being eight hundred feet higher in elevation than Rocky Mount, it might be cooler.

The ballpark stood next to the high school and was unimaginatively named Senior High Stadium. Built into the hillside, the stands were very close to the field, with home plate so near the backstop and screen that you had to think twice before going home on a passed ball. It was a stark reminder that baseball fields do not come in a single standard size, as do basketball courts and football gridirons. The Statesville Tigers were a terrible team, with weak pitching and anemic hitting. They would finish the season firmly in last place, winning only thirty-nine games. Forty-eight players passed through Statesville that season; only one ever reached the Major Leagues, and that was Gene Lamont, who, while in Statesville, hit .197. Not only had I been demoted, but I had gone from a first-place to a cellar-dwelling team.

And there wasn't any indication that the struggling Statesville Tigers were happy to have me in their lineup. My new manager, Al Lakeman, said almost nothing to me. He never mentioned how he planned to use me and except for one start found no use for me other than pinch hitting. *Am I going to sit on the bench the rest of the season? This is crazy! What are they thinking?* Riding the pine was not just frustrating but, oddly, more tiring than playing. Nor did I make any progress in finding a place to live.

On my fifth day in town, I called the Detroit front office collect and asked to speak to Don Lund, the farm director. After a long wait he came on the phone, surprised that I had called. Trying to control my nerves, I told him how unfair it was for me to have been sent down to Statesville after putting up good numbers in Daytona and that it only seemed right that I be returned to the Florida State League. Sounding sympathetic, though also irritated, he told me to sit tight and that he would get back to me. Several days later I was on a Greyhound again, heading back to Florida.

When I reached Daytona that evening, Gail seemed cool. Perhaps he was disappointed that I had not performed up to the favorable assessments he had given the front office. Or perhaps he thought I had been uppity in calling Lund and asking for a return to Daytona. Gail said he didn't have a roster spot for me and that I would be on the inactive list for a week or two. I was to report to the ballpark every day for practice and then watch the game from the stands. *Why doesn't he want me sitting on the bench in uniform with everybody else?* (Years later, Gail told me that nonuniformed players were not allowed in the dugout during games.) Nevertheless, it felt good to be back; I was able to move in with my old roommates at the Pendleton. I hadn't had time to tell Audrey that I was coming back, so as soon as I unpacked I went to the women's clothing store where she worked, Furchgotts, and surprised her with a bear hug.

Sitting in the stands, having to watch my teammates play when I wanted to be out there on the field as well, was tough. Even in the best of circumstances, I had never been a good spectator. After a few nights I figured Gail wouldn't miss me if I left the game early; I went with Audrey to see the London Symphony Orchestra—the event that she had modeled for in the newspaper ad that I had seen in Rocky Mount. My absence from the ballpark hadn't been noticed, so a few days later I slipped away again to take Audrey to see Hollywood star Jayne Mansfield perform live. Mansfield was a leading blonde sex symbol of the time. Gail noticed I was gone and fined me twenty-five dollars, along with giving me a reprimand. Apart from disappointing Gail, I thought it was worth it because Audrey and I had found two empty seats a few rows from the stage where Ms. Mansfield sported her platinum-blonde hair, hourglass figure, and a lot of cleavage. I had never seen a movie star before, and there she was right before my eyes; Audrey wasn't impressed. A year later, at age thirty-three, Jayne Mansfield died in a car accident. Late at night her car crashed into the rear of a tractor trailer that had slowed for a fogger truck spraying for mosquitoes. Her Cadillac went under the rear of the trailer, killing her and two companions instantly. Following the accident, legislation was passed requiring a protective steel bar or underride guard on all tractor trailers; it is still called a "Mansfield bar."

AUGUST 16 . . . With just three weeks left in the season, I finally got off the inactive list and back in the lineup in right field. I took an o'fer while Les Cain pitched a four-hitter, and we beat West Palm 1–0. The next night I banged out two singles, as we beat West Palm again, 8–3, and were just one game behind Sparky Anderson's league-leading St. Petersburg Cardinals. We were all excited to be in a real pennant race. Even though it was late in the season and everyone was tired, it was easy to get up for the game when the outcome really counted for something.

AUGUST 19 . . . We swept a doubleheader against Leesburg, pounding out twenty-seven hits, scoring twenty-one runs, and extending our winning streak to nine. I had three hits. Life was good. The *Morning Journal* ran a nice piece about the success of the team, along with Gail's assessment that we had a good shot at winning the second-half championship. The sportswriter noted that, as they spoke, "Gail drew a bead on a wandering bug in front of the dugout and buried it in a splash of brown tobacco juice and dust." I wondered what Gail's wife thought of kissing someone who must always smell and taste of tobacco. I knew Audrey wouldn't stand for it.

AUGUST 20 . . . The Tampa Tarpons beat us 6–1, snapping our win streak. We fell back two games out of first place with two weeks left. It was Max Patkin Night at the ballpark. "The Clown Prince of Baseball" was a former Minor League pitcher who became a ball-field clown after hurting his arm. Wearing a baggy uniform that hung loosely on his lanky frame, his cap tilted sideways, and with a question mark instead of a number sewn on the back, he performed slapstick antics that delighted fans. Some were performed between innings, and others were done from the first or third base coaching boxes during the game. This was the second time I had seen him. The first time I had been playing first base and had a close-up view; he stood directly behind me, mimicking my warmup throws to the other infielders. Hook had come out of our dugout, stood behind Patkin, and mimicked him mimicking me. (Today, Hook, on the Major League banquet circuit, is often introduced as "the New Clown Prince of Baseball.")

Most players enjoyed Patkin's act, though a few purists thought it an unnecessary distraction. As a barnstormer Patkin appeared in Minor League parks across the country for fifty-one years, making more consecutive appearances on a diamond than Cal Ripken. He later played himself in the movie *Bull Durham*. He was a goofy baseball comedian long before the Phillie Phanatic and the San Diego Chicken.

AUGUST 21 . . . Farm director Don Lund came to town for the next two games; everybody, except maybe Bob Welz, felt the pressure. Lund, more than any other person in the Tiger organization, could determine your fate. In front of him you really, really didn't want to play badly. I felt extra pressure, being unsure whether he was still sore about my calling him from Statesville. In my first at bat I had a triple down the right-field line, driving in two runs. I looked in the stands to make sure he'd seen it. He had. But I didn't do much after that, as we beat Tampa 4–1.

The next evening we played a critical game at home against first-place St. Petersburg. In a squeaker their star center fielder, Sweet Pea Davis, scored the winning run in the eleventh inning on a high chopper to third and a questionable call by the plate umpire. With that loss our pennant hopes faded.

One of the Cardinal players asked me why our second baseman Larry Calton always had a toothpick in the side of his mouth. I didn't know, but I agreed that it seemed hot doggish. Only years later did Larry reveal that he chewed on a toothpick to keep dentures in place.

AUGUST 26 . . . We split a doubleheader with the Cocoa Beach Astros. I smacked three hits in the first game, including, on a pitch right in my wheelhouse, a towering home run that sailed far beyond the right-field fence. Audrey was in the stands, and I hoped she saw it. She had but didn't make much of a fuss about it after the game.

We won the second game behind the pitching of Doc Olms. His real name was Jim, but we called him Doc because his father was a pediatrician. Olms sometimes talked about his father's work delivering "colored" babies whose grateful parents either named them after him or invited him to name them—which he often quite inventively did. For luck, Olms placed a penny inside his athletic supporter cup after each game he won. As the season wore on, you could hear the coins clanging against the plastic cup as he ran.

AUGUST 29 . . . With a week to go in the season, my batting average stood at .289, tops on the team. *I am really hoping I can finish the season near the .300 mark.* We were playing in Miami, where Hook, Shifty, Calton, and I got up very early to go out on a charter fishing boat. We caught a load of snappers, but the boat was late getting back to the dock and we had to sprint to the hotel in order to catch the team bus to the ballpark. In hurriedly putting on my contact lenses, I dropped one in the sink and then in a panic turned on the faucet, washing the lens down the drain. Without an extra set of lenses, I played that night with only one good eye. I went hitless in our ten-inning 6–3 win over the Marlins in front of 8,853 fans. It was always nice playing in Miami and St. Petersburg, where the crowds were larger than at home. Like playing in good ballparks, a good crowd made us feel more *professional.*

Exhausted from being out on the sea all day, I went to bed early. A few hours later, however, I woke up with a strange man in my room wanting to get into my bed. I chased him out and called the front desk. The next morning I learned that the gay intruder had been sent up to my room by Calton and Warden, who had met the guy in the hotel bar. To them, it was just another baseball prank.

Hook, Doc Olms, Jim Dietz, and Ralph Foytack—all pitchers—purchased two .22-caliber starter pistols and staged a gunfight on the street outside the hotel. Shooting at one another from behind the palm trees that lined Key Biscayne Boulevard, the pretend victims would fall on the grass in view of the road. For a moment their gunslinging slowed traffic; one motorist got out of his car to check on a fallen ballplayer. When they repeated their fake shoot-out on a hotel roof terrace, someone called the police. I wrote about the gunfight in my next newspaper article, which the sports editor titled "**MONTH OF HITS AND GUNFIGHTS**." My parents were so annoyed over the outrageous prank, which I made light of in the article, that when I arrived home at the end of the season, they didn't come to the airport to pick me up.

On our return trip to Daytona, another conversation about religion took place in the back of the bus. Most road-trip talk was pretty superficial, usually about food, girls, hitting, or pitching, so for me topics like movies, politics, and religion were a welcome break. Recalling some points that Audrey had made, I argued that if the Bible was really the Word of God, why had it been altered, edited, and changed over the years, yet still contradicted itself? "Harvard Bob" Welz chimed in, supporting me, "And if God really performed all those miracles ages ago, like parting the Red Sea and Jonah and the Whale, why isn't he doing anything like that today? All he'd have to do to make people believe in him would be to come down and do another big miracle. He'd save his faithful a lot of effort, too, because they wouldn't have to work so hard trying to convince the world's nonbelievers."

As usual the response of the believers was, "Because he is God, we can never know his ways. So watch what you say, or you might burn in hell."

AUGUST 30 . . . We beat Fort Lauderdale 5–4 after scoring all of our runs on a two-out rally when a windblown pop fly fell safely. In the eighth inning I ran into the left-field fence, chasing down a fly ball. I wasn't hurt badly, but by limping back to my position I indicated to Gail that it might be better to come out of the game. It was getting late, and I wanted to call Audrey on her birthday.

The next morning Gail sat down next to me at breakfast in the hotel café—he and I were the only ones up. In the course of reviewing the season, I told him that next year I would love to be able to play in Japan, to experience another culture and a different brand of baseball. As I returned to my room, I realized how foolish I had been, telling my manager, who at the end of the season would write a full report on each of us for the front office, that I wasn't committed to the Detroit Tigers. Besides, Japanese Major League teams didn't sign Class A Minor Leaguers, not even .300 hitters.

SEPTEMBER 1 . . . We split a doubleheader with the Deerfield White Sox, 2-1 and 1-0, in which the winning team in both games got only one hit. In the second game I managed the lone hit—a sharp comebacker that deflected off the pitcher's glove—driving in the winning run.

SEPTEMBER 3 . . . Chamber of Commerce Night at City Island Park attracted, according to the next morning's paper, "a large and excited crowd of 2,100." Larry Calton, who played with flair all season, even though he hit only.239, was voted MVP by the fans and given a large trophy. I wondered if I'd been in contention. With the end of the season in sight, there was a lot of chatter about going home and what we planned to do in the off-season.

A curious thing happened during BP when I left the batting cage and tossed my bat to the side and it came to rest on top of Julio Perez's bat. The brawny Cuban outfielder came over and with his foot flicked my bat aside. He asked that I not do it again, explaining that my bat might steal hits from his bat. I'd seen some strange superstitions but none quite like this.

After striking out, Julio would sometimes angrily stare at his bat as he returned to the dugout, as if his failure to make contact was the bat's fault. Julio also thought bats contained a finite number of hits and that when those hits were used up, no amount of good swings would produce any more. I had once heard or read that Hall of Famer

Honus Wagner, who played in the early 1900s, believed that each bat was good for only one hundred hits, at which point he would discard it in favor of new lumber. That belief had little relevance in the 1960s, though, and even less today in the era of light bats with thin handles—so thin that the typical modern bat is lucky to survive a half-dozen hits without breaking.

SEPTEMBER 5–6 . . . We played Leesburg, winning 6–5 on a ninth-inning homer by Harvard Bob. The next evening, Labor Day and our last game of the season, the visiting Athletics were nowhere to be seen as game time approached. They were already in the postseason, having won the first-half championship, so some of their players, who wanted a day off and were disgruntled over their shabby bus that no longer had AC, had sabotaged it by putting sugar in the gas tank. Without a vehicle they hoped to avoid the trip to Daytona. But the Leesburg GM had hurriedly chartered a bus, and the team made the journey, arriving in Daytona two hours late.

It was a record-setting game. Their speedy outfielder Al Lewis stole two bases, tying the modern professional baseball season record at 116. (The Major League record was then 104 steals, set by Maury Wills in 1962.)[1] Each time Lewis got on base, we knew he was going to steal. Each time he stole second successfully, but each time he tried to swipe third Dave Bike gunned him down. Following Lewis's second steal, the umps stopped the game so they could remove the base and send it to the National Baseball Hall of Fame. Although not a strong hitter, Lewis's explosive speed and base-stealing proficiency earned him a call up the following year. Nicknamed "the Panamanian Express," after his birthplace and speed, he stuck around for six years with Kansas City and then Oakland as a pinch runner and reserve outfielder.

In our 5–2 victory in the season finale, I took an o'fer, despite the Leesburg catcher tipping me pitches—that is, telling me what was coming. "Okay, I'm going to give you a fastball up and away." "Okay, here comes a hook." He even asked me what pitch I wanted. I'd never seen anything like it and didn't know why he was doing it. Was he still unhappy about having to travel to Daytona for a meaningless game? Was he mad at the pitcher? Unfortunately, it didn't do me any good. Thinking I could hit the ball to the moon, I became overanxious, uppercut, and skied three fly balls to the outfield. We finished in second place with a 45-26 record, almost exactly the reverse of the first half of the season, and we drew 12,195 fans, almost twice the attendance in the first half. Winning did bring out more fans, although teams always draw more in the summer months when school is out. Finishing my second season of pro ball, and after more than two hundred recitals of the national anthem, I still didn't know all of the words.

1966 FLORIDA STATE LEAGUE STANDINGS
(both halves combined)

TEAM	AFFILIATION	RECORD	WINNING PERCENTAGE	GAMES BACK
St. Petersburg Cardinals	St. Louis	91-45	.669	—
Leesburg A's	Kansas City	87-44	.664	1.5
Cocoa Astros	Houston	81-55	.596	10
Miami Marlins	Baltimore	75-63	.543	17
Orlando Twins	Minnesota	71-68	.511	21.5
Daytona Beach Islanders	Detroit	71-70	.504	22.5
Fort Lauderdale Yankees	New York Yankees	63-75	.457	29
Deerfield Beach Sun Sox	Chicago White Sox	55-83	.399	37
Palm Beach Braves	Atlanta	45-89-1	.336	45
Tampa Tarpons	Cincinnati	47-94	.333	46

Source: baseball-reference.com.

Of the twenty-one players on the opening-day Islanders roster in April, only six were left on Labor Day. I was the only player from our opener still in the lineup. I started the season batting cleanup and finished hitting third. I batted .280, second to Dave Bike. Bob Felber hit .215. Shifty Gear hit .271 and was invited to the Fall Instructional League for favored prospects.

We had worn out our welcome at the Pendleton—too much noise, too much horseplay around the pool, and too many girls. The manager of the Pendleton promised his regular tenants that he would not rent to ballplayers again. The Tigers, unhappy with the poor conditions at City Island Ballpark, did not renew their contract and moved the franchise to Lakeland the following season.

On our last day in Daytona, with no time to sell our Packard, we drove it to the ballpark, parked it outside the clubhouse, and destroyed it with baseball bats. Charging our teammates fifty cents for three swings, they smashed all the windows and then worked on the body. Audrey, when she heard about it, considered it unconscionable, saying, "How could you waste something that could have been given to someone less fortunate?" or something like that. That night Calton, Warden, Bike, and I went back to the ballpark, climbed through the clubhouse window, and took our uniforms and bats as mementos of the season. We thought we were entitled to them.

The next day Audrey and I flew to New York to spend a few days together before she departed on the ocean liner RMS *Queen Elizabeth* for a year abroad in Manchester, England. We made plans for me to join her over my long Christmas school break to travel in Europe. Breaking open my journal on the plane home to San Francisco, I wrote, *How ironic it is that I've spent so many years in quest of becoming a big leaguer, and now that I'm getting close—maybe, if I keep hitting, just three years away—I'm thinking of quitting. Why? Well, I now realize there are more important things in life than being a ballplayer.* And under the heading *Plans for the Future,*

I added, *I want to spend more time outdoors, be close to nature, spend time with Audrey, meditate, and maybe someday write articles for "National Geographic."* . . . *Writing, teaching, and research are occupations I would enjoy. But I never want to work in an office at a desk all day.* When I came across this passage, the first time I'd seen it in decades, I was appalled and deeply disappointed that after all the years of sacrifice and hard work, I could have talked so nonchalantly about giving up baseball. I am still puzzled over what really shook my dream of being a big leaguer. I suspect that the changes in society with the Vietnam War and the rise of the counterculture began to diminish the importance of baseball for me. Many young people at the time had become critical of, or rejected outright, the traditions and institutions of mainstream America. And to many nothing was more "establishment" than America's national pastime. Claire and Audrey, the two women who had the most influence on my thinking, were both of this persuasion. Audrey argued that there were more important things for me to be doing than playing ball. Perhaps I had begun to believe her.

Back at Stanford life couldn't have differed more from baseball. Following a dramatic escalation in casualties in Vietnam and the end of automatic student draft deferments, antiwar protests picked up on campus. Students who had stayed on the sidelines the year before were now turning out for antiwar rallies. I was angry over the war. No longer having to worry about being drafted because of my new 4-F status didn't lessen that.

Despite coming off my best baseball season yet, I felt discontent. *I wish I'd never taken philosophy. I seem to question everything now . . . . The world is such an ugly mess, with Vietnam, race riots, out-of-control population growth, and young Americans dying in a far-off land for politics. It's ludicrous and I don't want any part of it. I wish I could return to my old thinking, not questioning anything, just doing as everybody else does, working toward my own selfish little goals, just worrying about my batting average.*

As my commitment to baseball weakened, a new interest in anthropology was emerging. *I find people fascinating. Speaking to strangers can be a hobby . . . one that costs nothing and can be done anywhere and never becomes dull.* I wrote that passage one weekend while working with black longshoremen on the Oakland waterfront, shoring cargo headed to Vietnam. It was a weekend job during the school semester arranged by my shipping-executive father. During the downtime on the ships, I often talked to my coworkers, who came from an entirely different world than mine. I enjoyed these men and their stories, just as I had enjoyed my black and Latino teammates, and found the differences in our backgrounds and experiences fascinating. Looking back, though, I wonder how I reconciled my opposition to the war with my well-paying job shoring (securing with carpentry) military cargo on ships headed to Vietnam.

9

SOUTHERN EXPOSURE

The Rocky Mount Leafs

During the break between Stanford's fall and winter quarters, I flew to London to meet Audrey for four weeks of travel. It was my first time outside North America, and we ended up going to England, France, Austria, Germany, Italy, and the Netherlands. Like most students in the sixties, we traveled by train, stayed in pensiones, ate on the cheap (bread, cheese, and jug wine were mainstays), tramped through museums, gawked at cathedrals, and hung out in Europe's great public spaces by day while attending concerts, movies, and the theater at night. In a rare letter home, I noted, *Audrey is so much fun. . . . We cover each town on foot, setting out in the morning, not returning until evening.* It was adventure but also an education. Conversations with strangers often compared our culture with theirs, which made me realize that others saw the world differently from Americans. We met Europeans of all ages who viewed the Vietnam War more as a nationalist struggle and America's involvement as an anticommunist crusade. *No one here really seems to believe in the domino theory*, I noted. Their views steeled my own opposition to the war and caused me to liken my country's foreign policy to the behavior of privileged campus jocks—loud, brash, and arrogant.

When I returned to campus I attended more antiwar rallies than

I had the year before, though still as a sympathetic observer rather than an activist. At a demonstration on February 20, 1967, students shouted down Vice President Hubert Humphrey as he tried to make a speech. When Humphrey leaned out the window of a building to shake the hand of a student, others grabbed his arm and tried to pull him to the ground. Egregious as this was, a wire-service story made it sound even worse, and as other media picked up the story Stanford soon sounded like a hotbed of antiwar radicalism. It was a reputation the university did not fully deserve, until the following year when demonstrations led to the burning of the campus Reserve Officers' Training Corps (ROTC) building. Nevertheless, the campus environment I left as I departed for my second spring training on March 9, 1967, was more politically charged than that of other college players and certainly the hometown experiences of the rest of my teammates.

Upon my arrival in Tiger Town, I was assigned to the Rocky Mount team, the Leafs, where I would join former Daytona teammates Carl Solarek, Dave Bike, Larry Calton, Shifty Gear, Bob Felber, Doc Olms, Hector Soto, and Hook Warden. The rest of my Daytona teammates either had not been promoted or had been released. Mike Small, my former Jamestown teammate, was also on our squad. He arrived in camp wearing new glasses. The front office, worried about their sixty-five-thousand-dollar investment in him, hoped Mike's inability to locate the plate had been due to poor vision. But the new specs would not help.

When my teammates learned that I had traveled in Europe over the winter, with Audrey no less, they were quite surprised. Even though it was common for college students to travel abroad during their undergraduate years, it wasn't something ballplayers did. Only Dave Bike asked me much about it; the others just wanted to know if I'd had a good time. Hook remarked, "Betcha got shagged every night."

Our skipper, Al Federoff, had been a slick-fielding second baseman for the Detroit Tigers in the early 1950s and then spent six years playing in AAA before becoming a Minor League manager. He was a hard-nosed, old-school baseball man. Al's language was so salty and laced with F bombs that few would have guessed that he, unlike most coaches, had been to college—two years at Duquesne University. Everyone described Al as a "red ass." He had a particularly short fuse when it came to umpires and had been tossed out of more games than any manager in the Tigers' system. But Federoff also had a reputation for developing young players, whom he pushed hard to get their best. Al didn't waste time on anyone who didn't have the right attitude, and he had definite ideas about what was good for us. He instructed starting pitchers, for example, to lay off sex the night before and not to eat steak the day of a game. When Dick Drago got married in midyear, Al predicted he wouldn't pitch well the rest of the season. But Drago proved him wrong, going 15-9 with a 1.79 ERA, and was soon promoted to the big leagues.

Just as I had the previous spring, I got off to a good start. Before long I was again batting in the cleanup spot. I kept track of my numbers, and at the end of spring I was hitting .330. On the eve of breaking camp on April 12, I wrote: *Still swinging a hot bat . . . three homers in the last five games. I am optimistic about the upcoming season. Sure hope I can keep this up. The ranks of the Islanders* [former Daytona teammates] *have been decimated. Only a handful of us remain. Some were let go to make room for the boys being moved down from* [AA] *Montgomery.*

The next day we boarded the Silver Star in Lakeland for the eighteen-hour train trip north to Rocky Mount. Federoff, who was driving his car there, made Hook and me cocaptains of the team and asked us to take charge during the journey. We were flattered and a bit surprised, given that there were older, more seasoned players on the roster. Two other Carolina League teams were with us on the Silver

16. Rocky Mount manager Al Federoff and pitcher Dick Drago. Photo courtesy of Dick Drago.

Star—the Peninsula Grays and the Tidewater Tides. For hours I stood on the observation car's platform at the end of the train, taking in the scenery. The tracks sometimes ran right down the center of the Florida, Georgia, and Carolina towns we passed through, offering a backyard view that you don't get from the highway. I was surprised by the poverty I saw and noted in my journal: *I can't believe all the Negroes sitting on benches and car seats on porches or in front of shacks near the rail line.*

They look incredibly poor. I wonder what Europeans would think of this; it's something you wouldn't expect to see in one of the richest countries in the world. I thought I might write one of my newspaper stories about the team's trip north at the beginning of a new season—so much hope for us ballplayers contrasted with the utter lack of it for the blacks the train passed by. Or so it seemed.

APRIL 12 . . . Arriving in Rocky Mount around three in the morning, we were bused to a downtown hotel and told to be ready to go to the ballpark at two for a workout and to meet the press. The "press" turned out to be the local sportswriter for the *Rocky Mount Telegram News*, Tom Ham, and a photographer who took individual and team pictures. The *Telegram News* would give our games extensive coverage, even more than the papers in Jamestown, Daytona, or Duluth. Like many small-town newspapers, the *Telegram News* devoted as much space to local events and high school sports as to coverage of national and international news. We received more column inches than the war in Vietnam or the war on poverty. Like some of my teammates, I bought a subscription to the paper for my parents, to be mailed directly to them in California. Shifty still clipped articles and mailed them home each week.

With the team paying the tab only for our first few nights at the hotel, we all scrambled to find places to rent. Shifty, Polak, and I found rooms in a brick bungalow owned by a widow, Betty Lou Searls, not far from the ballpark. The rent was just eight dollars each per week, but we didn't have use of the kitchen, there was no TV, and, much worse when summer arrived, there was no air-conditioning or fans. On hot, humid nights, I would lie awake, longing for Daytona's air-conditioned Pendleton Apartments.

Hook and Gene Lamont, whom we called "Granny" after he was seen mailing a letter to his grandmother in which the envelope was addressed to "Grandma Lamont," found rooms with a Southern

Baptist family. When they moved in the head of the household, Willie Denson, laid down the rules: "There'll be no loud music and no women in your room. You're not going to eat with us, and we are not going to do your laundry." It made my setup look a little better. But after a few weeks Mrs. Denson was doing their laundry and often inviting them down for meals. They became close to the family, and after the season ended Gene began a lifelong correspondence with them. The Densons named their next child Jonathan, after Jon Warden.

APRIL 14 . . . We opened the season with twenty-three players on the roster. Average age: twenty-three. Apart from being older, there was also a fourfold increase in the number of married players. Only two in Daytona had had wives; now there were eight. A few other players were engaged, and most of the remaining ones had girlfriends back home. Mine—Audrey—was still in England and beyond contact except by mail. Her letters were often exasperating, full of arcane pronouncements and lofty observations, such as "It is difficult to live in times such as ours when the breakdown between good and evil has been so complete. I would like so much to identify with a strong moral order." What I wanted to hear was how much she missed me and perhaps plans for our future. She seemed to sense my frustration. At the end of one letter she noted, "We now have three pages between us yet I have said so little." Yes, exactly how I felt.

No matter how well a player performed the previous season or during spring training, he started with a clean slate on opening day. Batting averages recalibrated to zero. If you had been doing well, you had to prove yourself all over again. For those who hadn't had much success the previous season, it was a fresh start. For fans, too, opening day was a symbol of rebirth. Even if the team was a perennial cellar dweller, fans might still believe they were in contention for a pennant.

We played our opener on the road in Wilson and lost 3-2 to the Tobs, short for Tobacconists. Maybe being a Leaf wasn't so bad after all. Batting cleanup, I had a double and almost tied the game in the eighth when, according to the next day's account in the *Telegram News*, "With a runner on board, Wilson center fielder Jim Pitt made a dazzling grab of first baseman George Gmelch's tremendous wallop to deep center field." I had a strange feeling about that ball being caught; it would have been a home run in any other ballpark. I thought it was a bad omen.

The next night we played our home opener in frigid temperatures before a shivering crowd of 1,285. Hook got hit hard, while we only had two scratch singles and lost again. Before the game Federoff told us— perhaps to lighten the mood—how the previous season pitcher Mike Small had been slated to start opening day but hadn't shown up at the ballpark. He'd been driving to Rocky Mount from spring training with his new wife, and they'd stopped at a café for dinner where, as Al explained, she had a "hissy fit" over something Mike had done and grabbed the car keys and drove off. Mike had to find his own way to Rocky Mount, and by the time he got there he'd missed the opener. Apart from a good anecdote, the subtext of Al's story seemed to be: don't mess with this new generation of assertive, college-educated women.

There were twelve teams in the Carolina League spread across North Carolina and southern Virginia.[1] The league schedule called for a game every night and a day game on Sunday. As usual, no days off. The Sunday day game became our way of reckoning time. In the other leagues I had played in, where all games were played at night and you followed the same routine every day, it was easy to lose track of what day of the week it was. But that would be less true in the Carolina League.

At the start of the 1967 season what struck me most about Municipal Stadium was seeing blacks and whites sitting in different sections, ordering food from different concessions, drinking from separate fountains, and using separate restrooms. Today I wonder why it hadn't made a bigger impression on me during my first time in Rocky Mount the season before.

Before Rocky Mount I had only once in my life seen racial segregation, and that was at the Laundromat my teammates and I used in Lakeland, Florida, during spring training. It had a room for whites and another for blacks. When my teammate and fellow Californian Les Cain had gone to the black side for the first time and seen water on the floor and broken machines, he decided to wash his clothes on the white side. His black companions who were from the South tried to talk him out of it. Les dismissed them, explaining to me later, "If my brothers want to live by those rules, that's okay, but it ain't for me because I truly know that I am free." Les washed his clothes on the white side, where the only other patron that day turned out to be a middle-aged white woman who engaged him in a pleasant conversation while their clothes sloshed and spun. Les had crossed the Laundromat's color line without incident and felt good about it. When he left baseball years later, after pitching four seasons for the big-league Tigers, he bought a Laundromat in Richmond, across the bay from San Francisco.

Lying just beyond third base in Rocky Mount and screened off by chicken wire was the "Negroes only" section of the stands—an area some whites called the "coal bin." A regular there was Buck Leonard, one of the most famous Negro League players of all time, although, like my white teammates, I didn't know much about him. Born and raised in Rocky Mount, Leonard had left school at fourteen because there was no high school for blacks in the 1920s. He went to work in a textile mill and also earned money as a shoeshine boy at the railroad station until he received an offer to play pro ball. Within a few years he was batting cleanup behind Josh Gibson for the Homestead Grays during the 1930s and '40s, one of the greatest teams ever assembled. Buck became known as the "black Lou Gehrig" and in 1972 was belatedly inducted into baseball's Hall of Fame. Although Buck was a board member and vice president of the Rocky Mount Leafs club, he still sat in the black section of the stands. I never learned whether he sat there because he had to or wanted to. He was said to be friendly, but regretfully I never had a conversation with him. Buck died in Rocky Mount in 1997.

Audrey wrote, asking how Rocky Mount was able to skirt the 1964 Civil Rights Act that was supposed to make this kind of segregation illegal. I wrote back that I didn't know but that I would ask. The segregation at the ballpark turned out to be no different from Rocky Mount's neighborhoods, where an ordinance banned blacks from living, or even sleeping over, in white areas. Under antimiscegenation laws, interracial marriage or even interracial sex was a felony.

On the edge of downtown stood a large monument to the "Confederate States of America." During the Civil War North Carolina lost forty thousand citizens, and the Confederate flag still flapped above some of its buildings. To whites they were proud emblems of their southern heritage. To me they were shameful reminders of slavery, and I wondered how local blacks felt about them.

It was hard to find things to do in Rocky Mount. In desperation, my teammates and I sometimes strolled downtown to window-shop and kill time before going to the ballpark. But there wasn't much to get excited among the Watch Shop, the Jewel Box, Chandler's Five Cents to One Dollar Store, Fields Leaf Tobacco Company, Planters Cotton Oil Company, or the Dixie Letter Service. I found myself hanging out at Oakwood Park Sundries, where I treated myself to a chocolate milk shake made by a teenage soda jerk who handed me my glass along with the sweating steel container the shake had been made in. I also tasted my first Moon Pie and my first Dr. Pepper there—two products then barely known outside the South.

Nothing ever happens here, I wrote in my journal. *This place is so boring that I don't know what to write about.* Of course, locals didn't find Rocky Mount boring. They were attached to its small-town virtues—friendliness, community, safety, relaxed pace—and its citizens' love of God and country. They were also obsessed with its sports. *People here live and die*

17. Train tracks and downtown Rocky Mount, circa 1967. Photo courtesy of Braswell Library, Rocky Mount, North Carolina, and the Charles S. Killebrew Collection, University of North Carolina–Chapel Hill.

for their sports, I wrote. *They just named a street after a star high school athlete. What a crazy world we live in!* As a ballplayer I should have been grateful for their interest. Instead, I was critical. My view of sports as opiate of the masses was a product of being a student at Stanford, where 1960s social justice and political activism were in the air. Had I been playing a decade earlier, I probably wouldn't have been so troubled.

The main attractions for most ballplayers in Rocky Mount were two single-screen cinemas—Cameo and the Center—and the bowling alley. About the only place open to go after games was the bowling-alley restaurant. It became the white players' hangout; our black and Latino teammates were not allowed. Occasionally, I and other position players bowled a few games, but pitchers never did. They wouldn't risk hurting their arms and had to make do with the pinball machines. Local girls in kneesocks and penny loafers, false eyelashes, or plenty of mascara also came to the bowling alley to flirt. I became friends with Nell Odom and Barbara Jean Davis. Unlike most groupies, neither was to be easily seduced by a ballplayer. *Our friendship*, I noted in my journal, *never came to anything.* Some of the girls who came to the bowling alley owned cars, which ballplayers lacked, and many of us relied on them to get a ride home at the end of the night. Having a car was a big deal. When Barbara Jean sent me a letter when I was back at Stanford that fall, she wrote, "Now for Rocky Mount news: Marcia has a new '68 Le Mans, white with black vinyl top, Nancy has a '68 baby blue Mustang with black vinyl top and is working in Raleigh with the Highway Patrol. . . . Barbara still has no car, just school." The last comment was followed by a sad face.

Unlike many of my teammates, especially those from the South, cars never interested me. Even if I had gotten a large signing bonus, I wouldn't have spent the money on a new car like my bonus-baby teammates. My first vehicle was an open-air World War II Willys Jeep, great for exploring but not for taking out girls. When I reconnected in 2013 with pitcher Shelby Morton, who'd grown up in Paragould, Arkansas, I was amazed that he remembered both the hometown and the make, model, and color of every car owned by our teammates as well as a few of the girls in Rocky Mount.

"Shelby, what do you remember of Gene Lamont?"

"Yeah, Granny, solid guy, number-one draft pick, from Kirkland, Illinois, drove a two-door blue Dodge Charger."

"How about Larry Calton?"

"Feisty. Always had a toothpick in his mouth. Good glove, fair power for a little guy . . . from Springfield, Missouri. Drove a yellow Oldsmobile Cutlass Supreme with mud flaps."

"Okay, Shelby, how about Jon Warden?"

"Gawd dang, what a character. Big-time prankster. From Columbus, Ohio. Bought a red Chevy Chevelle, four in the floor, with his bonus."

Like all players, I had a daily routine. Most of my teammates slept late, skipped breakfast, and then went out for a large late lunch. An early riser, I was off to get breakfast by nine. I usually plunked myself down on a vinyl-covered swivel stool at the drugstore whites-only counter and ordered two poached eggs and grits. The grits came with a puddle of melted butter in the center. I'd never heard of grits growing up.

After breakfast I'd walk to the Braswell Memorial Library, often for its air-conditioning as much as its literature. I skimmed back issues of *Life*, looking at the pictures and reading the captions. But I also read books that had been urged on me by Audrey, such as *Pygmalion* and other George Bernard Shaw plays. I read them mostly to please Audrey, but I would not admit that to anyone. More to my liking was *Catch-22*. After finishing it I immediately recommended it to my mother, wanting her to see the parallels between the insane system that the protagonist in the book, a U.S. Air Force bombardier named Yossarian, found himself in during World War II and the world we now lived in—the world of 1967—which to my mind was equally crazy. In the library I sometimes practiced the "speed-reading" technique I was trying to learn. Like many college students, I had taken an Evelyn Wood reading course that promised to triple your reading rate while increasing retention. Though always interested in efficiency, it took the joy out of reading for me. The only other Leaf to grace the Braswell Library was pitcher Paul Coleman, who went to check on the prices of his penny stocks. He became a broker after his baseball career ended. None of my black teammates were allowed in the library. The "colored library" was a small shared room at the black high school, Booker T. Washington.

I usually left the library around one to eat my big meal of the day. Rocky Mount's sultry heat and midday glare smacked me as I left the supercooled library to make my way to the Carolina Café, where I usually joined my white teammates Hook, Polak, Shifty, and Bike. Like the bowling alley, the café did not serve blacks or Hispanics, a fact we white ballplayers never mentioned. The food was cheap and the servings large. Salisbury steak and fried chicken were our favorites, washed down with free refills of heavily sugared iced tea. Everyone in the South seemed hooked on the stuff.

The Carolina Café, whose ads boasted of "home cooking" and "air-conditioning," also had great desserts, so we'd finish with lemon meringue or Boston cream pie. We thought it strange when Shifty, a Canadian, ordered Jell-O. But then for breakfast he sometimes had a bowl of ice cream with his eggs and bacon. Dave Bike noted that Shifty never flushed the toilet after he peed and figured it might be another Canadian custom, perhaps for water conservation, and maybe a good idea.

Around three we began making our way to the ballpark in order to be dressed and on the field by four. On the way I'd sometimes pass a cast-iron plaque on the street that read "World-Famous Athlete Jim Thorpe." During the 1912 Olympics in Stockholm, Sweden, Thorpe had won gold medals by wide margins in the pentathlon and decathlon. Later, officials took them away after discovering that he'd played semipro baseball in Rocky Mount. Even though Thorpe was paid as little as two dollars a game, this violated the Olympics' rules of amateurism. Unlike some other Olympians and college athletes who had also played professionally, Thorpe had not used an alias. I became interested in his story and read up on it in the Braswell Library. Thorpe, predominately American Indian (Sauk and Fox), not only had won Olympic gold medals in the world's two most challenging track events, but later became a star in professional football, played six seasons of professional baseball with the New York Giants, and barnstormed with a professional basketball team. He was probably the most versatile athlete in modern sports. The U.S. Olympic Committee restored Thorpe's medals to his family in 1983, thirty years after Jim died, broke and an alcoholic. Sometimes, as I passed the Thorpe plaque, I rubbed my fingers across the lettering for luck. But this was not to be a season in which I'd have much good fortune.

We were usually dressed and on the field with time to spare. No one wanted to risk a fine or incur Federoff's wrath. I learned pretty quickly not to get on Al's bad side. The pregame routine, no matter what league you were in, never varied—running, stretching, and throwing to loosen up, followed by forty-five minutes of batting practice and, finally, "infield," in which the skipper first hit fly balls to the outfielders and then sharp ground balls to the infielders, each making the throw to first base or turning the double play. This was a time-honored ritual, although lately some teams have decided it's unnecessary—that it doesn't really add anything to the players' pregame preparation—and have dropped it. After infield we had about twenty minutes to change out of our sweat-soaked undershirts and put on our "game face."

No one knew about "visualizing" in those days, so our mental preparation was minimal. Often I'd sit in the dugout soaking in the sights and sounds, sometimes reminding myself that this was professional baseball and that I needed to play my hardest. Occasionally, I would try to quiet my mind in order to focus on what I needed to do in the batter's box. Like most position players, the focus was on hitting, rarely fielding. We never got "psyched" or pumped up, as in football, where athletes play only one game a week. Playing every day, we would have exhausted ourselves with the kind of rah-rah, high-intensity emotional energy expected on the gridiron.

The first pitch was thrown at seven thirty, with the average game lasting two and a half hours, a full half hour less than today. We were usually back in the clubhouse showering and changing between ten and eleven o'clock. Our curfew came two hours after the ball game ended, which didn't give us a lot of time to go out, eat, have a few beers, and unwind before heading home. For me, going home often meant another restless night in my hot, unventilated room.

Because Sunday was always a day game, it became our big night out, the one night we could plan for. Most of the unmarried guys, except for my black and Latino teammates, went to the bowling alley for dinner—the only place open on Sunday—and then to a movie. North Carolina, like most of the South, had restrictive blue laws designed to enforce observance of Sunday as a day of worship and rest. The sale of alcohol was prohibited, so while we could get a meal at the bowling alley, we couldn't buy beer to wash it down or to celebrate a good game. *I think it's fine if they* [conservative Christians] *don't want to drink on Sunday, but why are they allowed to impose their will on others who don't share their beliefs? And these are the same people who rail about this being a free country. Fucking Hypocrites.*

Sunday was a serious day of religious observance for folks in Rocky Mount, mostly observant Southern Baptists and Methodists. But on our ball club only Dave Bike, a Roman Catholic, went to church. Playing day games on Sunday made it difficult to worship, but even in Duluth, Jamestown, and Daytona where we were free all day, hardly any ballplayers went to church. It would be another decade before Baseball Chapel would arrive in the Minor Leagues, with a minister or "chapel leader" directing a short Sunday service for interested ballplayers and umpires in every ballpark in the country. But even had Baseball Chapel existed in the sixties, I doubt many of us would have attended.

APRIL 18 . . . A rainout gave us a chance to go to our first movie of the new season. It was called *Moonlighting Wives*, in which an ambitious suburban housewife converts her stenography business into a profitable prostitution ring with neighborhood wives turning tricks. This seemed to be typical fare for Rocky Mount, despite its conservatism and family values. But I also caught *The Sound of Music* one Sunday, which, reminding me of my travel to Austria with Audrey, made me long for her company. The Cameo had separate seating for black patrons—upstairs in the balcony. After I had been to the Cameo a few times, I began to wonder what the conditions were like up there, but never dared to find out.

Not once during my entire baseball career did we see a baseball movie. With good reason—not a single baseball film was made between 1962 and 1973, probably due to the declining popularity and box-office appeal of the national pastime. And the first baseball movie to be made in the seventies, *Bang the Drum Slowly* (1973), was hardly upbeat or comedic. Rather, it was based on Mark Harris's novel about a friendship between two ballplayers, one of whom, hayseed and not well-liked Bruce Pearson (played by Robert De Niro), becomes terminally ill. Once his teammates learn the news, they treat Pearson differently, and the team's mood and play improve, with the team going on to win the World Series.

APRIL 20 . . . We beat the Raleigh Pirates 14–3, getting twenty hits. Everybody got a hit but me. Shifty hit for the cycle, banging out a single, double, triple, and home run in succession. Hitting for the cycle is one of the rarest feats in baseball, as statistically uncommon as pitching a no-hitter. Getting the hits in order from least to most total bases has been accomplished only thirteen times in MLB's 137 years.[2] Shifty, just thrilled to have gotten four hits, didn't realize the rarity of what he had done.

APRIL 23 . . . We won our sixth straight, 5–3, over the Kinston Braves, beating their fireballer Carl Morton before 1,734 fans. The previous season Morton had been a weak-hitting outfielder with a cannon for an arm. The Braves moved him to the mound, where, with a mid-90s heater, he found success. Morton resembled my 1966 Rocky Mount teammate Jim Rooker, also a converted outfielder who went on to a successful big-league career on the mound, though not to the same degree as Morton. Carl was the National League Rookie of the Year in 1970 and later strung together three consecutive fifteen-win seasons for mediocre Braves teams. Tragically, he died at age thirty-nine of a massive heart attack in the driveway of his parents' home in Tulsa, Oklahoma, after jogging with his son.

APRIL 26 . . . On an unseasonably cool evening, only 421 fans turned out for the much-ballyhooed pregame beard-judging contest, part of the town's centennial festivities. The small crowd saw our win streak end at eight games, as we lost to Portsmouth 4–2. Jim "Brownie" Brown, our starter, was cruising toward a shutout with two outs in the ninth and nobody on when the roof caved in—four consecutive singles and an error.

APRIL 30 . . . The Peninsula Grays shelled our starter, Doc Olms, who failed to retire a single batter. Olms's struggle had begun a few games before when the plate umpire caught him loading up a ball. Doc, whose tongue was always sticking ever so slightly out of the corner of his mouth, liked to throw a Vaseline ball when he was in a jam. Doc kept a blob of the petroleum jelly under his cap, and when he needed a big out he would adjust his cap so as to get some of the Vaseline on his fingers and then apply it to the ball. Any added substance, whether spit (hence the spitball), pine tar, or Vaseline, affects a pitch's flight, due to the slightly altered wind resistance and weight on one side of the ball. Once word about Doc got around among the league's umpires, they were on the lookout, making it difficult for him to use his out pitch. The Grays beat us 11–3.

MAY 2 . . . I read in the *News Telegram* that Al Kaline was leading the American League in hitting at .383. In spring training he'd come over to our mess hall on "steak night," and I'd had a chance to talk to him. I told him that I'd worn his hand-me-down baseball pants in Jamestown. He struck me as a down-to-earth superstar—someone the organization and sportswriters reverently referred to as "Mr. Tiger." He didn't look any bigger or stronger than me, nor did he have a sweeter swing, and I wondered what it was about him—inside—that made him such a great hitter in the big leagues, while I was struggling in A-ball. Usually, great athletes can't tell you how they do it because they don't know themselves. Perhaps that's why many are always thanking God for their success. Nonetheless, forty-seven years later at a Detroit Tigers reunion at our old spring-training site, I decided to ask him. Kaline hesitated and then said, "I think, maybe, I saw the ball a little sooner. I could read the pitch a little quicker than others, and that can make a difference." Yes, indeed, and didn't Ted Williams say the same?

When Kaline was my age, twenty-two, he'd already been in the big leagues for three years and had won a batting title. It was obvious that I was never going to fill his pants.

10

WHEN THE CHEERING STOPS

The Rocky Mount Leafs

"**STOPPED AGAIN! ANOTHER LONG NIGHT FOR THE PUNCHLESS ROCKY MOUNT LEAFS**" ran the lead in the May 7, 1967, *News Telegram*. After winning eight in a row, we lost eight of the next ten. Mired in a slump, my batting average dropped to .210. Like most players, I tried to change my luck by altering my daily routine, even going as far as having French toast instead of poached eggs for breakfast, wearing a new shirt, taking a new route to the ballpark, and putting my uniform on in a different order.

Letters from Audrey didn't help my mood; she seemed to relish telling me about all the exciting things she was doing in the nonbaseball world. At that time she was working on an archaeological dig in the Roman ruins of Verulaneum in St. Albans, England. She also liked to remind me there were more important things in life than playing "some game." Her views, while I was struggling, made me question my commitment. I spent even more time in the Braswell Library, reading to distract myself, which itself may have been counterproductive. Years later, after learning that periods of intense reading can cause eye strain, I wondered if the many hours I logged each day in the library had affected my hitting. In 2012 when I obtained news clippings from all our games, I computed my Rocky Mount batting averages at home and on the road. Voilà, I hit

18. Pregame at Rocky Mount Municipal Stadium, 1967.

22 points higher on the road. Interesting, but probably not enough of a difference to blame my slump on reading alone.

Things weren't much better at home, where Shifty, Polak, and I always seemed to be at odds with our landlady. Betty Lou finally asked us to move out after she spied Nell Odum in my bedroom. Nell had come over only to play chess, but it didn't look right to Bible-toting Betty Lou. She was already displeased with Shifty and me for having launched "UFOs" from her yard. We had stretched plastic dry-cleaning bags over a framework of straws to which we had attached candles. The hot air produced by the burning candles lifted the illuminated plastic bags into the sky, and from a distance they could be mistaken for some sort of flying object. After lofting several we phoned the radio station to report "something in the sky" above Rocky Mount. To our delight and amazement, the radio station reported the UFOs on the air. Betty Lou learned about it the next day from a neighbor.

MAY 8 . . . Our starter Gene "Needle Dick Bug Fucker" Voss was down. He'd had a couple of bad outings previously, and that night he gave up three runs in the first two innings, all on cheap hits—jam shots, flares, and a swinging bunt. The White Sox had not hit a single ball hard. Federoff was ejected for stridently disputing a call at first base. And earlier he had snapped at Shifty, "What the fuck would you do if you couldn't play baseball? You couldn't do shit." Shifty felt humiliated and never forgot the remark.

MAY 9 . . . "**SLUGGERS NIGHT**" declared the *News Telegram* after our dormant bats (including my own) came to life with twenty-three hits and seventeen runs in a doubleheader win over the Lynchburg White Sox. Back in the lineup and with three hits, I felt renewed. Brownie, who was in his fifth Minor League season and sometimes clashed with Al, proposed as we entered the clubhouse, "Federoff won't talk to us when we lose, so let's not talk to him when we win."

Federoff gave his college players a harder time than others. He accused us of thinking we knew everything or that we were smarter, sometimes calling us "paper-ass players." I once listened as he chewed out a teammate for "jaking it" (not working hard), telling him he was "fucking pampered" and "not hungry enough because you've got a fucking college degree." Al reasoned that any noncollege player who washed out of baseball would likely end up pumping gas or working in a mill or on the family farm and that prospect made them play hard, whereas we college boys knew we'd land on our feet because we had a degree to fall back on, which made us less hungry to play ball. I doubted that it was true, as we all wanted to succeed. In any case, I learned not to remind Al I was working toward my degree in the off-season.

At the ballpark it was not uncommon to hear fans, usually older white males, shout "Nigger" or "Brillo head" at black and dark-skinned

Hispanic players. One fan—whom locals called "Country"—liked to yell, "Niggaaa, you couldn't hit a hog in a ditch." He uttered the *N* word with derision, drawing out the second syllable as if to say, "You dumb, worthless piece of shit." I'm sure some fans, perhaps a majority, frowned upon such racial slurs, but in 1967 no one spoke out against Country. Two seasons later, however, when a blond-haired California infielder named Steve Smith walked up to the screen and told Country, "Go fuck yourself," the Rocky Mount crowd cheered.

The racism so evident at the ballpark was mirrored in Rocky Mount's neighborhoods. During a walk one Saturday, I stopped to watch a Little League game and started a conversation with one of the fathers. He fixed me with the instant friendliness that southerners often adopt with strangers. But when I asked him why there were no black kids on the field considering that nearly half the population of Rocky Mount was black, he replied matter-of-factly, "We don't let niggers play in our Little League. They have their own league across town." Like other towns in the Carolina League, Rocky Mount was skirting the 1964 Civil Rights Act, which outlawed discrimination in public facilities.

A few days later I crossed the tracks to check out "Happy Hill," a black neighborhood he'd mentioned. Its ramshackle houses, with peeling paint, litter-strewn yards encircled by bent chain-link fences, beat-up cars parked or abandoned in front yards, and tall weeds sprouting from sidewalk cracks, were unlike anything I'd ever seen. After that walk my antennae were fully up, and I recalled the conversation I'd accidentally overheard outside Leaf general manager Joe Summrel's office a few days into the season. Members of the Chamber of Commerce had been reminding Joe—who happened to be a dead ringer for Kentucky Fried Chicken's Colonel Sanders—that the town wouldn't support the team if there were too many "colored boys" in the starting lineup.

While looking for a drinking fountain one day, I wandered into the black waiting room at the Greyhound bus station. Everyone looked up as if to say, "Whitey, what the hell you doin' here?" Later, black teammate Norm McRae, pointing to a drinking fountain with a "colored" sign above it, told me he spit into the white fountain when no one was around. I understood his motive; it made me wonder what the black patrons at the movie theater, sitting in the balcony above me, might be doing.

When the team stopped for meals on road trips, my black teammates were sometimes refused service, forcing one of the white players to take their orders and bring their food out to the bus. Once, when we stopped at a combination restaurant and gas station and all started to walk in, the attendant who was pumping gas, motioning with his head toward Harvey Yancey, a black infielder, said, "You fixin' to take him inside?" It wasn't really a question, just a roundabout way of saying that Harvey wasn't welcome.

Larry Calton shot back, "You goin' to stop us?"

"Might do," said the attendant, as he held up a cigarette lighter to the container of gas he was filling. "Y'all just try me."

Harvey returned to the bus, and Calton brought him his food.

The extent to which our black and Latino ballplayers—Cool Mac, Brownie, Rufus, Harvey, Richie, Hector, and José—lacked the privileges, even the common decency, I took for granted was startling. I could sit wherever I wanted, and no restaurant or Laundromat would deny me entrance. I could walk anywhere in town at night without worrying about my safety, and of course I never had to deal with racial epithets. Rocky Mount made me understand the importance of the civil rights movement in a personal way, something Audrey already knew from living in the South.

For my next newspaper article I decided to write about segregation in Rocky Mount. I first spoke to one of our pitchers, Jim "Brownie" Brown, who was in his fifth year of pro ball, including several seasons in Rocky Mount and Montgomery, Alabama. He told me that until the 1964 season, black players stayed in separate hotels and boardinghouses on road trips and that they sometimes ended up in incredibly hot attic rooms without air-conditioning. I recalled seeing it happen once in Tampa the season before, when all the white players got off the bus, while the blacks and Hispanics remained in their seats to be taken to a hotel across town. By 1967 all the hotels where the Carolina League teams stayed had been integrated, but that did not include white and black players sharing a room. Whenever there was an odd number of black players on the team, it was Detroit's policy that one would room by himself rather than share with a white player. In 1969 Dave Bike became the first white player in the Tiger organization to have a black roommate when he paired up with John "Duke" Young. They became lifelong friends and visit one another today.

I also interviewed our shortstop James Cornelius Speight, who was born and raised in Rocky Mount. Jim, ever with a bulging chaw of Red Man tobacco in his cheek and a brown dribble in the corner of his mouth, told me that the town's police chief was a member of the Ku Klux Klan and that the chief's brother was a grand dragon (the leader of a Klan organization). Taking Speight at his word, I included the information in my story. I wasn't writing as an informed civil rights activist—far from it. I was writing as a young California newcomer encountering Jim Crow for the first time and taken aback by what he saw and who assumed his readers at home—what few there were—would be too. The sports editor would assign them titles: "**TRAINING CAMP CAN BE AN UNEASY HOME**," "**BASEBALL HAS A NAME FOR IT**," "**THIS IS WHEN LIFE GETS MEAN**." He would call my new piece "**LIFE IN ROCKY MOUNT WITH THE KLAN**." Teammate Shifty Gear, who read drafts of all my articles, warned me that claiming that the police chief was a member of the Klan was dicey and could land me in trouble. I dismissed his concern, as Shifty was overly cautious about everything. I mailed off my article, telling him my newspaper was published in California while we were clear across the country in North Carolina.

On the road I sometimes got up early to explore new towns on foot. If there was a college or university, I'd check it out and sometimes take my midday meal in the cafeteria. Even today on family vacation road trips, I like to visit local universities and Minor League ballparks. One morning while strolling around Lynchburg, a good-size town of fifty thousand in the foothills of the Blue Ridge Mountains that had been a Confederate supply base during the Civil War, I learned that it had gotten its name from its founder—John Lynch—and not from mob lynchings of blacks, as Jim Speight had said. *Maybe Speight was also wrong about the police chief being in the Klan,* I wrote in my journal that night. But then Brownie reassuringly told me of other police chiefs around the South, like Bull Connor in Birmingham, Alabama, who were avowed Klan members. The same Bull Connor who had directed fire hoses and even unleashed police attack dogs on civil rights demonstrators, including children.

MAY 15 . . . Polak, who had led my Jamestown team with seventeen home runs, finally hit his first four-bagger of the season, helping us beat the Durham Bulls 8-7. Although he would lead the team in hitting, he would hit only one other home run all season. No one could explain his power outage. Polak made the All-Star team, as he had in Jamestown, but that would be his last hurrah. Unhappy with the contract Detroit sent him at the end of the 1969 season and having two young sons at home, he quit. Walking away from the game was something very few players did; hardly anyone believed there was another occupation, at least one within reach, that could measure up to playing baseball for a living. Polak took up softball and before long was selected to play for the U.S. national team; in 2010 he was elected to the National Softball Hall of Fame in Oklahoma City.

MAY 17 . . . My hometown friend and former college teammate Danny Frisella, the ace of the Durham Bulls' staff, beat us 3-0 on a two-hitter. In the sixth inning I got the first hit of the game on a Texas Leaguer single that dropped in front of their charging right fielder. Danny gave me a quizzical look as I stood on first base, as if to say you're not supposed to break up your buddy's no-hitter with a cheap hit. In September the Mets called Danny up, and over the next few seasons he and Tug McGraw gave the Mets a potent bullpen. But on New Year's Day 1977, Danny was killed in a dune-buggy accident outside Phoenix, Arizona. As the buggy began to roll over, he tried to jump out and was crushed. At the time I was living in Ireland, where there was no baseball news, and didn't hear about it until six months later. It was hard to believe; while trout fishing together the year before, Danny had shown me pictures of his toddler son and his young wife, Pam, who was a cornerback in the first woman's professional football league. Pam was eight months pregnant with their second son when the accident occurred. His death has remained a reminder to me of how fragile life is.

MAY 18 . . . Having broken my slump, I was back hitting cleanup and got two hits, as we clipped the Burlington Senators 3–1. At the bowling alley after the game, Hook met a woman at least ten years his senior who invited him home. As he told it well the next day, they were making out hot and heavy on the sofa and just about to do it when she, noticing the time, shrieked, jumped up, and told him to put his pants on and leave quickly. "My husband just got off work and will be home any minute!" Hook had no idea that she was married and afterward would have nothing to do with her. Shifty, who usually didn't want to be distracted from baseball, changed his mind after meeting a shy girl-next-door type in the bowling alley. He fell in love the second he laid eyes on Marla. The players teased Shifty by calling her "Bushel Tits," such as "Hey, Shifty, going to lay some pipe in Bushel Tits tonight?"

MAY 20 . . . We left on a six-day road trip to Burlington, Greensboro, and Winston-Salem. I described the bus ride in a letter to my mother: *Four of us gathered in the back of the bus—We debated everything from evolution to whether the Ten Commandments could really be a divine revelation from God. We never agree, but it makes the bus trip pass quickly.* Another topic of debate on that road trip was whether marijuana was more harmful than alcohol. I argued, based solely on what I'd heard at Stanford, that marijuana was no worse than drinking. No one took my side. I don't think anyone on the team, including me, had yet tried grass or at least would admit to it.

In our first game against the Burlington Senators, Shelby Morton was on the mound for us. With a runner on first he made a quick pickoff move to first base just as I had removed my glove. I caught his hard throw barehanded. There was laughter in our dugout. Federoff hadn't realized that I had taken my glove off to knock some dirt from the fingers. All he saw was the barehanded catch; he gave me an earful when the inning was over and didn't listen to my explanation. A few innings later the sky darkened, and the ballpark announcer came on the PA, instructing everyone to quickly leave the stands—a tornado was approaching. Both teams took cover in the locker rooms underneath the concrete grandstand. We sat in the dark, listening to the howling wind and the din of the heavy downpour. When the lights came back on, I saw Richie Williams emerge from his cramped locker, where he'd taken refuge for added security. Bob Gilhooley and I were bummed because the game had been canceled and none of that night's stats would count, including both of our two hits.

Two weeks later, on May 22, while playing in Winston-Salem, I was about to head to the ballpark when Al Federoff called me aside. "I just got a telegram from Detroit from Don Lund [the farm director] who wants you to go straight back to Rocky Mount. Get your gear and get over to the bus station." Al gave me a number to call when I arrived and told me I was to meet with the mayor and the police chief. It was the longest, loneliest bus ride of my life. I couldn't stop thinking about the trouble I might be in. It must be the article, I realized, trying frantically to recall exactly what I had written. Damn! Why hadn't I had listened to Shifty's warning?

After getting back late and enduring a near-sleepless night, I arrived at city hall the next afternoon, exhausted. I was led into a windowless wood-paneled room where an intimidating collection of southern men—police chief, city attorney, city manager, and the president of the Rocky Mount Leafs—was gathered. I was twenty-two. The men in the room were all twice or three times my age. A stenographer took notes. I winced when the city attorney read the most incriminating lines from my article—"The police chief is a Klansman, and his brother is the area grand dragon." And then "Klan meetings are the only entertainment locals have." Beyond that, what I remember most vividly is the men's grave demeanor and how seriously they viewed my assertions. I apologized several times and told them that I had meant no harm, that I had written only what someone had told me. I promised not to write anything else about Rocky Mount. They said I would hear again from them in a few days.

Soon after leaving city hall, I wrote my parents,

Things look very bleak, as the chief of police is threatening a libel suit, the president of the ball club wants my dismissal, and the farm director [Don Lund] *is hot about the article. Their biggest concern is the possibility of a civil rights action against the police chief for being a Klansman. It was a really stupid thing to do. . . . I've written a formal letter of apology to the club officials and police department and now I just have to wait and see what develops. The city attorney wants copies of all the articles I've written this year. I should hear from them tomorrow. . . . I don't know who sent the articles to Rocky Mount or why. . . . As for Detroit, I got three hits in my last game, and still lead the club in home runs and RBI's. I sure hope that helps. Love, George*

MAY 25 . . . We lost both ends of a doubleheader to the Winston-Salem Red Sox, with their southpaw Ken Brett shutting us down in the nightcap, 1–0, on a one-hitter. Like me, Ken was born in New York but raised in

California. He was the second of four brothers to play pro ball, the best known being Hall of Famer George Brett. Ken was called up to the Red Sox at the end of the season in a close pennant race with the Tigers. He was just nineteen and would become the youngest pitcher ever to appear in a World Series. But, like so many others, he developed arm trouble, underwent several surgeries, and never regained his form. Often struggling on the mound, and playing for ten different big-league teams, he became one of the best-hitting pitchers of his era (a .262 lifetime batting average). After retirement Ken managed in the Minor Leagues, was a color commentator for the Mariners and the Angels, and ran a sporting-goods company with his brothers until he died of brain cancer, still in his fifties.

MAY 26 . . . We beat Asheville, 8-4, and I had three hits, including a home run, raising my batting average to .235, which put me above the team batting average. The *News Telegram* noted that Polak and I were "the hottest hitters on the club." I figured my streak couldn't have come at a better time. Yet over the next few games, with no explanation from Federoff, I was either benched or played right field, while Dave Bike and a few others auditioned at first base. Playing me in right field was puzzling, since I had been a sure-handed first baseman all season. I had never been a reliable outfielder. *I don't get it. Why am I in right field? . . . It would be nice if they'd tell me what this is all about.* In hindsight it's clear that Detroit was trying to find someone to replace me.

JUNE 5 . . . We lost a doubleheader to Kinston, 3-1 and 4-2. I ended the first game by swinging at a bad pitch on a 3-2 count with the bases loaded, "Jesus H. Christ on a goddamned crutch, that fuckin' pitch was in your eyes," steamed Federoff. "It would've been fuckin' ball four . . . would've tied the game." I rode the bench in the second game.

JUNE 7 . . . We survived a scary bus ride to Portsmouth, Virginia, at the start of a five-day road trip when our bussie, Harold, dozed off at the wheel. Afterward, ever-cautious Dave Bike stayed awake to keep an eye on him.

Some of us gathered in Bike's hotel room to watch the news. Israel and Egypt were fighting in the Sinai in what became known as the Six-Day War. I wrote in my journal, *What is the world coming to—Israel, Vietnam, guerrilla fighting in South America and Africa? Are we going to destroy ourselves?* I continued my rant in a letter to my brother, Walt, who was a political science major at Stanford: *Our foreign policy is a bad joke—the Bay of Pigs, CIA scandal, U2 incident, Vietnam. . . . We must develop our intellects . . . and time is running out.* I urged him to think about a career in politics. *The little you may do may make a difference. . . . Have to catch the bus to the ballpark. Love, George.*

We had lost five straight games by the time I was returned to first base. I was also back hitting in the cleanup spot but struggling at the plate. I had a lot of company, as our team was last in the league in hitting, with only Polak and Dave Bike near the .300 mark.

"**WHAT A NIGHT**!" ran the June 11, 1967, sports headline in the *News Telegram*. "Gmelch exploded for five hits including two triples and drove in five runs to increase his club leadership," reported the article. In the ballpark that night to watch her husband pitch had been Mamie Van Doren. She was one of the first actresses, along with Jayne Mansfield, to imitate the look of Marilyn Monroe, turning herself into a sex symbol. She'd had a much-publicized engagement to Angels pitcher Bo Belinsky before marrying Minor Leaguer Lee Meyers, who was fourteen years her junior. They divorced after the season ended. During the game we had our heads in the stands, trying to get a good look at her, wondering how Lee, who would win only three games all year, had managed to land a Hollywood star.

My big night gave me confidence that I might be out of the woods with the front office. But then the next two nights I was back riding the pine. *I can't figure this out*, I wrote in my journal. *Something is up. After going five for five, I've been on the bench, and they moved Bike* [one of our catchers] *to first base, as if to see if he can play my position.*

As we were leaving on the road trip to Peninsula, we learned that our ball club had been sold. Unknown to us, the Leafs had been struggling to break even all season. The president of the new ownership group, John Dickens, arrived in Peninsula and met with us. He said the new owners were determined to keep Minor League Baseball in Rocky Mount. Since we were under contract to Detroit, who paid our salaries, the fate of the local club didn't really matter much to us. Nevertheless, when Dickens returned to Rocky Mount, he assured *News Telegram* readers that he had found a "new spirit" in the Leafs and that "the boys are now smiling; tensions have eased and they are playing with more desire and fight." The whole thing was made up, didn't make much sense, and added to my skepticism about truth in sports reporting.

JUNE 14 . . . Playing at home against Raleigh, the lineup card posted on the dugout wall showed me back in the lineup but batting eighth, instead of my usual cleanup. It didn't make sense, as the Pirates were throwing a right-hander. I went hitless that night, and we lost 2–0. After the game the clubhouse manager told me that Federoff wanted to see me in his office. Unusually soft-spoken, Al told me in as gentle a way as humanly possible that Detroit was releasing me. He expressed regrets that things hadn't worked out, wished me luck, and told me to report to the general manager's office in the morning to sign the papers for my dismissal and get my plane ticket home. I was hardly able to decipher his words.

When I called home to tell my parents—the most difficult phone call I have ever made—I could hear the disappointment in my father's voice as he feebly tried to raise my spirits. He said he'd try to reach my brother, Walt, who was then driving cross-country on his way to Rocky Mount to watch me play. I was heartbroken. Baseball, even during my slumps, was who I was. As much as I liked my teammates' overblown notion that I was a "scholar" of sorts because of my penchant for libraries and attendance at Stanford, I really didn't have any identity other than baseball.

I recalled how Federoff had sat down next to me that day on the bench after BP and engaged in light banter. It was obvious that he knew this would be my last game in pro ball. The end of my career. The next morning when I talked to Joe Summrel, the general manager, he hinted that an agreement had been struck. The police chief would drop his threatened libel suit if Detroit removed me from Rocky Mount. Summrel had called a few other general managers to see if they were in need of a first baseman, but none were. If Detroit had big bonus money invested in me, or if I had been playing like a *prospect*, as I had in Daytona Beach, they might have reassigned me to another farm team. It didn't help that the farm director was already miffed that I had ignored his demand over the winter to stop writing newspaper articles about life in the Minor Leagues. I had continued to write because I thought they were pretty innocent pieces and, furthermore, that the Tigers had no right to tell me not to. As I left Rocky Mount, I wondered how long it would be before I would be completely forgotten, like so many of my teammates that had been released before.

That season the Leafs finished third in the league. Polak led the club in hitting at .293, after hitting just .205 the season before in Daytona. Shifty, who'd gotten off to a hot start, faded and finished at .253. Despite making the Carolina League All-Star team, Shifty was returned to Rocky Mount the following season. Hook had a breakout year, winning fifteen games, and that fall was placed on the forty-man Major League roster. The following spring he would stick with the big club throughout their World Series–winning 1968 season.[1] Larry Calton was released the following season. Bob Felber had been sent to Statesville but hadn't managed to hit any better there (.216); he was badly spiked in the hand and retired. Doc Olms, who had starred on the Daytona staff (9-4, 1.82 ERA), never regained his form after the umpires discovered his Vaseline ball, and he was let go the following season. After having been such a poor fielder at Jamestown two seasons earlier, earning me the nickname

I-beam, I had become a respectable first baseman with a .992 fielding percentage. It offered no consolation.

A year ago I acquired all the clippings of the 1967 season and read them through in a single day. Vivid memories of teammates and events came back to me. After forty-seven years, the season unfolded with clarity for the first time: the preseason hoopla, Federoff's great expectations for me based on my strong spring training, becoming cocaptain of the team, my slumps and redemptions as I regained my groove, experiencing Jim Crow, and finally the trouble over the Klan article. As I worked my way through the clippings, day by day, knowing I would be released, I grew increasingly upset. By the time I finished, I was in a deep funk—angry for having been so reckless in continuing to write articles after being told not to and then ignoring Shifty's warning. Around midnight I went out for a walk in my mist-shrouded San Francisco neighborhood, the low, mournful wail of a foghorn in the distance, trying to talk myself into feeling better; then came the moment when I realized that Rocky Mount was the reason I became an anthropologist. Returning to Stanford the fall of 1967, I changed my major from biology to anthropology. I had become far more interested in understanding people and culture.

Not long after reading the clippings, I felt compelled to uncover the truth about the police chief. I enlisted the help of the Southern Law Poverty Center, but they couldn't find any records earlier than 1970. I did, however, locate two people in Rocky Mount, including a local historian, who were in positions to know. They were cautious, neither confirming nor denying the chief's ties to the Klan. But one did say, "It wouldn't have surprised me," and then added that the local Klan chapter, dressed in their hoods and white robes, had held their meetings in our ballpark when we were playing on the road. Obviously with permission from someone in authority.

Reliving my Rocky Mount season also made me wonder what my black teammates had thought about the town and about Jim Crow. I had a chance to find out in 2013 when I attended the first-ever reunion of Detroit Tigers players from the 1960s and '70s.[2] During the four days we spent reminiscing together in Tiger Town, our old Florida spring-training site, I was surprised to discover that my white teammates remembered more than my black teammates about Rocky Mount's racial segregation. How could that be? As I talked to more players and very pointedly asked them for their memories of life in the Carolina League, it became apparent just how confined my black teammates' lives had been. They had lived with local families just a few blocks from the ballpark, taken their meals at home, and seldom ventured far. They had not gotten to know the town the same way I and most white players had. The same was true when we were on the road. "I knew it [segregation] was out there," explained Al Diggs from Philadelphia, "but I didn't see much of it because I never went nowhere." And for black players who were from the South, Rocky Mount was no different from the places they had come from. Unlike me, for them there were no surprises—and nothing to write home about.

Even today, usually around spring-training time, I wonder what would have become of my baseball career had I not written about the Klan.

11

EXILED

The Québec Provincial League

The day after my release I decided that I wasn't ready to call it quits. Shifty Gear urged me to telephone our former teammate Steve Oleschuk, who was playing in the independent Québec Provincial League, to see if he could hook me up with a team. He figured that the good numbers I'd put up in Daytona and hitting cleanup in Rocky Mount might get me an offer. There were no agents in those days, at least not for Minor Leaguers, so if I was going to catch on somewhere, I'd have to do it on my own.

Looking back, it seems ironic that at the close of the previous season, my best ever, I'd considered giving up baseball, and then one year later, after being released, I was trying to hang on any way I could. Walking away from the game was a lot easier than being booted out. In *Ball Four* Jim Bouton had a good line about this: "You spend a good piece of your life gripping a baseball and in the end it turns out that it was the other way around all the time." Bouton was so anxious to hang on that, unable to interest any team in signing him, he took a job as a batting-practice pitcher for the Braves' Triple A team in Richmond, Virginia. That, he later claimed, contributed to his financial difficulties and the breakup of his marriage. But he was still in baseball.

While I was waiting to hear from Oleschuk, I flew to New York to visit relatives. After a few days without any word, I made a plane reservation for San Francisco. Then, just eight hours before my scheduled flight, I got a call from the Drummondville Royals (Les Royaux) of the QPL with an offer. It was for $125 per week ($750 in today's money), the standard contract for players in the league and easily enough to live on. I accepted without hesitation. I would still be playing professional baseball, but of a lesser brand. Because the QPL teams were not affiliated with Major League clubs, there was no track leading to the big leagues and therefore little chance of upward mobility. This was the case, and still is, with all independent leagues. But going to Quebec would allow me to avoid the shame of returning to California a failure, just another pro-ball reject. Plus there was the attraction of getting to explore an entirely new place, French-speaking Canada.

The next day I took a Delaware and Hudson train to Montreal and then a bus 65 miles east to the town of Drummondville, on the St. Francis River. On the bus ride I listened to the conversations in French swirling around me and tried to guess the meaning of the French road signs and billboards. *I think this will be an adventure. I have never lived in another culture before. Maybe I will try to learn French.* The latter would have amused my high school French teacher, Miss Reinero, who gave me an F in the subject and informed me that I had no aptitude for languages.

Drummondville was on the main artery between Montreal and Quebec City (145 miles apart). The town had taken advantage of its key location to attract a host of industries, including Celanese, a large chemical company that employed five thousand. Drummondville's thirty-five thousand inhabitants were almost entirely Francophone. The ballpark, near the town center, boasted a large wooden, covered grandstand with an unusually high roof. A big sign at the entrance read *Bienvenue à tous les sportifs* (Welcome to all sports fans). The rest was a letdown. The infield was all skin and the stadium lights dim. It was the worst ballpark in the league. Several umpires had filed complaints with the league about its poor lighting, a hazard to hitters and pitchers.

I wrote in my first journal entry, *The ballpark is so bad that other teams have threatened to refuse to play here.*

JUNE 17 . . . The next day I joined the team for an away game against the Quebec City Indians. I played first base and batted sixth, wearing an unflattering baggy uniform. Most players paid to have their pants tailored. The club must have wondered about Oleschuk's scouting report and the wisdom of signing me, as I proceeded to strike out three times, chasing curveballs in the dirt. Striking out had more stigma in the sixties than it does today; it meant you were overmatched by the pitcher. Unlike today's hitters, we routinely choked up with two strikes and did whatever we could to make contact, to put the ball in play.[1]

On the back of my home uniform, above my number, was *Gatean Pharmacie*, one of the Royals' many sponsors. I thought advertising on the uniform was unbecoming of professional baseball. It reminded me of my teenage years playing in the San Mateo City League with *Bay View Federal Savings* emblazoned across my back. With the stitching already coming loose, I pulled the sponsor's nameplate from my jersey. Team captain Chuck Hughes noticed and called me aside. "Our sponsors help pay the bills," he told me, clearly annoyed, "including your salary. Sew it back on."

The next night, playing against the Thetford Mines Miners, my timing was better, and I banged out two sharp singles, which made me feel better about my decision to come to Quebec, and even better the following night after two extra-base hits against the Lachine Mets. Both were off Ray Daviault, who had pitched for Casey Stengel's New York Mets in their inaugural season. Daviault, who in New York was nicknamed "Frenchy" because of his Quebec origins, liked to regale his teammates with Casey stories, such as the time Stengel came to the mound after Ray had given up a towering home run. Ray told Casey that it had been a perfect pitch, to which he replied, "Son, perfect pitches don't travel that far." In frequent retellings over the years, his stories, like those of many veteran ballplayers, not only were finely honed but sometimes grew to mythical proportions. Daviault would soon be forced to retire with what was then called a "dead arm," which might have been anything from a torn rotator cuff to merely a fatigued and overworked pitching arm.

Lachine also had three players whose siblings were current well-known big leaguers: Chuck Foster, whose brother George played for the Cincinnati Reds; Chuck Klimchock, whose brother Lou played for the Cleveland Indians; and José Cepeda, my Daytona teammate and brother of Orlando, who played for the Giants. Lachine released José after he was caught stealing a stereo from a Montreal department store. The rumor in the clubhouse was that he needed money for a marijuana habit.

In our next game, against the Granby Cardinals, I hit my first home run. The Drummondville newspaper, *La Parole Journal*, called it one of the longest home runs ever hit in Granby, curiously adding that I was of German origin, as if to say Germans come naturally big and strong. I had never thought of myself as having an ethnicity, and I never mentioned my family's ancestry. In fact, while growing up in the postwar 1950s, I felt shame over my German heritage because of the Holocaust, even though my relatives had immigrated to America in the 1880s, long before there was even a Nazi Party in Germany.

Besides Drummondville, seven other teams filled out the Provincial League: the Québec City Indians, Plessisville Braves, Granby Cardinals, Sherbrooke Alouettes, Thetford Mines Miners, Coaticook Canadians, and the Lachine (Montreal) Mets. When we commuted to away games, we returned the same night because no town was more than ninety miles away. On the bus rides home, we always had two cases of free beer—provided by one of the team's sponsors, a marketing manager for Dow Brewery. Having beer on the bus was a common practice throughout the league, and quite unlike anything I'd seen in the United States, where alcohol on team buses was taboo.

Most of the QPL teams were in the region known as the eastern townships in southeastern Quebec, south of the St. Lawrence River and tight against the U.S. border, marked by gently rolling hills, picturesque back roads, and pretty villages. The region was originally sparsely settled by Quebecois as part of Nouvelle France (New France), and then during the American Revolution by Americans who, wishing to stay loyal to the British Crown, moved north. The loyalists mostly got displaced by Quebecois in the twentieth century. Although the region is predominantly French speaking, the influence of the loyalist settlers from New England can still be seen in the architecture of older buildings and in the names of a few towns, such as Sherbrooke and Thetford Mines. The eastern townships are today a popular tourist destination, especially for vacationing Montrealers.

Unlike the U.S. Minor Leagues, there was an enormous range in the size of the league's towns, from metropolitan Montreal, with 2.5 million people, to tiny Plessisville, with just 5,000. Their populations, however, didn't have much influence on the size of the crowds the teams drew, as most teams averaged about 1,500 spectators per game. The exception was Quebec City, which had the nicest stadium and the largest crowds, about 5,000 per game. Quebec City was everyone's favorite place to play and also a great place to visit, since it had a European flair, with the old city partially encircled by centuries-old walls. Quebec is the only fortified city in North America north of Mexico.

The most striking town visually, though, was Thetford Mines, hub of one of the world's largest asbestos-producing regions. Monstrous piles of slag—stony waste matter left over from asbestos refining—swallowed up parts of the town. Reputedly, Thetford had a baseball team because the mine owners considered sport a good way to pacify workers unhappy over labor conditions and making demands that the company do more to combat "the white death," as asbestosis was then known. The ball club's president and GM was Lou Lamoriello, who at that time was learning the front-office ropes. Later he would become the GM of the New Jersey Devils hockey team.

What Thetford Mines had in minerals, Plessisville had in trees. It claimed to be the "World's Maple Capital" and was known for its maple syrup. The Institut Quebecois de l'Érable (Quebec Maple Institute) is still headquartered there. In fact, the entire region was known as *érable,* French for "maple." Half of the Plessisville team was Hispanic, mostly from the Dominican Republic, but they also had many French Canadians. *On all the teams I've played on, there were three distinct groups—white, blacks, and Latins. But here in Quebec there's a fourth group, Francophone Canadians, and that means a third language spoken on the bus and clubhouse. Pretty neat.*

After a few weeks I decided that I'd really try to learn French. Not speaking the language was proving to be a big handicap. *I'm not really able to understand anything. Most locals speak only French, and the radio, TV, newspaper, and even the announcements at the ballpark and the national anthem are all in French.* The first words I learned were *le terrain* (field), *le jouer* (player), *l'arbitre* (umpire), *le gérant* (manager), and then names for the positions on a ball field: *le lanceur* (pitcher), *le receveur* (catcher), *le premier-but* (first baseman), *l'arrêt-court* (shortstop), and so on. Soon I picked up other French baseball terms, especially ones whose translations I thought were quaint, such as *le mauvais lancer* (wild pitch; the direct English translation is "bad pitcher"), *la balle rapide* (fastball), and my favorite, *le coup de circuit* (home run). In the sport pages of the local newspaper, *La Parole,* I could find my batting average under *la moyenne au baton.* My primary tutors were our trainer Jacques Desautels, teammate Claude Coté, and later a young woman named Monique Plouffe, who also taught me to say, *Voulez-vous coucher avec moi ce soir?* (Would you like to sleep with me tonight?).

It helped my ego that the Québec Provincial League, which had been in existence since 1934, was well known to serious baseball fans and historians for having once signed some prominent Major Leaguers. Max Lanier, Sal Maglie, and others had joined the league in the late 1940s after being blacklisted by MLB commissioner Happy Chandler, who wanted to punish them for jumping to the Mexican League in 1946. They had been lured to Mexico by large signing bonuses and generous salaries. When things didn't work out as promised and their salaries were cut, they returned to the States. But Chandler wouldn't let them back in. Banned from the Major Leagues for five years, some accepted offers to play in the QPL. Drummondville acquired former New York Giants Sal Maglie, Max Lanier, and Danny Gardella, and St. Louis Brown Tex Shirley.[2] The team also signed the Negro Leagues' star catcher Quincy "Big Train" Trouppe and future Major League All-Star Vic Pellott, who changed his name to Vic Power while in Quebec. He did so after noticing that the French-speaking fans laughed when his name was announced. Initially, he suspected the laughter was because he was black, but he soon learned that Pellott sounded similar to the Quebecois slang word *plotte*, for "vagina." So he switched to Power, which was close to his mother's maiden name, Pove. At home in Puerto Rico, some resented their local star going by the Anglo name Power, accusing him of selling out.

Power's flamboyant fielding and hitting style is often said to have contributed to the showboat image of the early Latino ballplayers in the big leagues.[3] Although Power became a six-time American League All-Star and the winner of several Gold Gloves, he is probably best remembered for a witty remark he made in a whites-only restaurant in the South. As the story goes, a waitress told him "the restaurant doesn't serve Negroes," whereupon Power told her not to worry, that he didn't eat Negroes and just wanted some rice and beans.

After MLB's ban against the Mexican League jumpers was lifted in 1949, most of the big leaguers returned to the United States. I asked local sportswriter Pierre Roux, who as a teenager had gone to every

Drummondville home game, what he remembered of the famous Major Leaguers. He told of how Sal Maglie, on the eve of the final playoff game in 1949 in which Drummondville was deadlocked with the Farnham Black Sox at four games apiece, went to the general manager and demanded an extra one thousand dollars or he would not pitch in the championship game. The GM gave him cash, and the next day Maglie beat the Black Sox 1-0.

The large salaries the QPL teams paid the big leaguers led to several clubs going broke and the league folding in 1956. When the league was reconstituted the following year, only Canadians were signed to save on salaries and travel expenses. Foreign players were allowed back into the league in 1961, but with a limit of three "imports" per team. In 1966 all restrictions on foreign players were dropped, and with that the caliber of play went up, as many American and Caribbean players were signed. When I arrived in 1967 the QPL compared favorably to a mid–Class A Minor League, with the major difference being that its players were mostly older guys finishing up their careers rather than younger ballplayers starting out. QPL pitchers, many being seasoned veterans, did not throw as hard as the youngsters in A-ball, but they had more pitches and were craftier.

After I spent a few nights in the Motel Cardin, teammates Norm Timmins and Bob Wolfarth invited me to share their apartment. A washed-out snapshot shows us wearing the off-the-field uniform of white American players: Ban Lon polo shirts, alpaca cardigans, chinos with pegged cuffs, and desert boots or loafers. Timmins was a freckled, redheaded second baseman from western New York, released by the Tigers organization with the all too common tag "good glove, no hit." In Drummondville too often even the glove failed him. Wolfarth, from Cleveland, Ohio, and a physical education teacher during the off-season, was a catcher. He had several permanently bent fingers from the trauma of years of foul tips slamming into his hands. He liked to call me Meat.

"Hey, Meat, what's up?" was a favorite greeting. *My roommates are quite likable, but they are silent-majority types who support the war and believe that it's necessary to stop the spread of communism. So we don't talk much about it.* The United States at the time was tearing apart over the war. Historians would later say the country was more divided than at any time since the Civil War. I was no longer just opposed to the war, but thought of my country as, I noted in my journal, *guilty of imperialistic aggression. We don't deserve to win the war. It's morally wrong.* To my roommates that thinking was treason. Timmins later enlisted in the Marine Corps and served as an infantry officer and platoon leader in Vietnam.

Our apartment was conveniently across the street from the Motel Cardin, where many of Les Royaux ate two meals a day on the "American plan"—which was all the food you could eat for twenty-five dollars a week. We ate our fill of steaks, shakes, and chocolate cake and gained a few pounds. But I was also developing a liking for French Canadian foods, such as crepes, meat pies (*tourtières*), blood sausage, and french fries (*patates frites*) with vinegar.

By the end of my second week in Quebec, I was fairly settled, hitting well, and liking my teammates. *People have been really nice to me, and, except for our terrible ballpark, I'm really enjoying being here.* It was a good thing because I received a letter from Audrey, mailed from Yugoslavia, saying that she was breaking off our relationship. *This can't be happening to me. We are so perfect for one another. How will I ever find someone like her?* Audrey had been hitching around Europe when she met and fell in love with a Czech linguist who, she said, spoke "nine languages and was a fantastic dancer." I could neither dance nor speak foreign languages, evident in my fumbling attempts at learning French. I was devastated. When I showed the "Dear John" letter to roommate Norm Timmins, he did his best to console me by saying Audrey must be a "moron" and that he was going to write and tell her so. I urged him not to. If I had been more astute, I would have seen the breakup coming, as Audrey had been writing less often and with fewer mentions of missing me. But I was often clueless when it came to reading the commitment of girlfriends. Unlike most young men today, I told my mother about our breakup and even sent her Audrey's letter—perhaps because Audrey had said some nice things about me, and oddly I still wanted my mother to think well of her or at least to think I had chosen wisely by falling in love with her.

Prior to our breakup I had been faithful to Audrey, ignoring the groupies that hung around after ball games at the Hotel Rocdor's nightclub. Now I let it be known that I was available. My first opportunity came soon when a director of the ball club, Mr. Bessette, who owned a funeral parlor, invited me to dinner to meet his twenty-year-old daughter, Francine. She had a pleasant personality and wasn't unattractive, and I enjoyed talking to her. But her feet were enormous; they looked larger than mine. Today, my attitude reminds me of a *Seinfeld* episode where Jerry dates a woman whose only flaw is having "man hands." I knew it was shallow to dismiss Francine over her feet, but I also suspected my teammates would have been all over me had I dated her: "Hey, Moonbeam, you into Bigfoot?" or "Hey, Moonbeam, I'll bet she never puts her foot in her mouth."

The following week I met Monique Plouffe at the Rocdor. Monique spoke little English, which forced me to speak what little French I knew. Although she was happy to help me improve my French, her real interest after ball games was mostly carnal. She loved having sex and was very open about it. The first night we went out, it wasn't long before Monique had removed all her clothes. She was always a great date because I never had to feel conflicted, wondering whether she'd be willing or whether I'd have to expend a lot of energy on seduction. She had the lure of the wrong kind of girl and for the rest of the season did wonders helping me take my mind off baseball, especially forgetting a bad night at the plate. My teammates reported that the groupies they met and bedded were much less sexually inhibited than the girls back home. They also thought the local girls generally had nicer bodies and were better looking, and as one teammate remarked, "You'll never see them in curlers. They're always made up." In the QPL the emphasis on a girl's looks was no different from the U.S. Minor Leagues.

Pitcher Steve Cushman's groupie girlfriend liked kinky sex and especially enjoyed doing it furtively in public places at night where there was a risk of being seen or caught. She was, he claimed, always looking for a new erotic adventure. She later married a Montreal mobster. In Quebec we all delighted in the opportunities for hooking up, well before the sexual revolution kicked into high gear in the United States. But most of Drummondville's groupies, like elsewhere in the league, were more interested in blacks and Hispanic players than in white guys. Very few blacks lived in the eastern townships at the time, so nonwhite ballplayers were viewed as exotic, and, a bonus, they could usually dance. White players typically weren't interested or couldn't dance very well. Fortunately for us, with too few blacks and Hispanics to go around, some girls looked in our direction. It was so different from Rocky Mount, and the South generally, where my black teammates wouldn't dare approach a white girl—it wouldn't be safe. Interracial mixing was illegal under "antimiscegenation laws" that prevailed in most southern states until 1967. In some places it was a felony. In Quebec, however, no one thought anything of white girls hanging out and sleeping with black or Hispanic ballplayers.

Thirty years later, while I was doing research on tourism on the Caribbean island of Barbados, I had one of those "aha" moments that explained what I had seen in Drummondville. I was living in a coastal village a few miles from the tourist belt. Every now and then, I'd see one of the local "beach bums" (gigolos) bring home a white tourist girl. I gave a ride to one who turned out to be from a town near Drummondville. I soon learned that the first foreign women to journey to Barbados looking to hook up with local boys, or what is called "romance tourism," were French Canadians. They had come down on the first charter flights from Montreal in the 1960s. As Ricky Hinds, a gigolo who was my neighbor and also a jet-ski operator, explained, "They have a feeling that black guys have bigger dicks than white guys. Some women look at me, and I can tell that fantasy enters their minds. . . . They think that being a black man you're going to give them that feeling, that explosion, they're looking for."[4] Ricky believed that "Canadian women are more horny . . . because their men are outdoors working and then spend a lot of time in bars drinking. Their women don't get enough [sex], so they come down here on holiday . . . and they want to screw your head silly."

Recreational sex and casual relationships were common among my Drummondville teammates. Even the married players consorted with groupies. Lachine pitcher Jack Fitzpatrick, who later became a psychoanalyst, said it had to do with all the professional and financial insecurities in baseball. "We lived with a high level of uncertainty. You could see its effects in the prevalence of rituals, alcohol, and sex. Sex and booze for us weren't just about orgasms and good feelings; it was how we dealt with the insecurity of being a ballplayer." Or maybe Fitz was off, and it really was just about sex. Whatever the underlying motivation for sleeping around, this wasn't something that you'd tell anyone about for fear of it getting back to one of the wives. Much like the unwritten rule that what you saw and heard in the clubhouse stayed in the clubhouse, so it was for nights out.

A few of the local girls married Hispanic and African American players. When I returned to Quebec in 2012, they were still living there and still with their French Canadian wives. Among them were Granby Cardinals outfielder John Mentis, who worked as a prison guard; Maddy Alston, a bank manager; and first baseman John Self, a golf-course groundskeeper.

One day in Drummondville I watched a French Canadian motorcycle gang roll by. I must have assumed that motorcycle gangs were uniquely

American. *I can't believe I saw all these tough guys wearing leather jackets and boots speaking beautiful French.* Of course, I had no way of judging how well they spoke French. I was becoming interested in understanding French and French Canadian culture, though. I had always been curious and also on the lookout for material for my next newspaper article about Minor League life. I recorded my invariably untutored and sometimes wild anthropological generalizations in my journal: *Quebecers are more inclined to live for today and not worry about tomorrow. . . . The teenagers here are not as ambitious as American teens. They're not in a hurry to get through school, and they seem to enjoy life more and not put off pleasure as much as American teens. Maybe that's why the girls are more promiscuous. . . . Adults are less time conscious, never in too much of a hurry to take time to help out others . . . but they all drive like crazy.*

During the 1967 season we drew seventeen hundred people per game, more than double the attendance in Jamestown, Daytona, or Rocky Mount. During the playoffs we averaged thirty-five hundred per game. The scarcity of other forms of entertainment probably helped fill the ballpark. The fans, primarily from Drummondville's working class, were enthusiastic and loyal supporters of the team; some even traveled to our road games—something I had not seen in U.S. Minor League towns. Many of those who followed the team gambled on the games. With wagers from twenty to one hundred dollars, they bet on the home team, and that gave them a financial stake in the outcome of the game and a stronger identification with the team. After a win gambler-fans at the Rocdor night club would sometimes buy us beers. Once, after Chuck Hughes hit a walk-off home run against Thetford Mines, a smartly dressed, middle-aged fan wearing dark glasses in the Rocdor told Chuck to order whatever meal and drinks he wanted for the evening; the tab was on him. He was a professional gambler.

QPL teams played a seventy-game schedule from late May to late August, followed by nearly a month of playoffs and a championship series.

Rather than playing every day as in the Minor Leagues, the schedule called for five games a week, including a Sunday doubleheader. That gave us three days off, which, coming from the grind of playing daily in the Minor Leagues, we relished. Many players used off days to catch up on sleep after later than usual nights out. But there were others who liked to get out and explore. Some days we drove to Expo—the highly successful World's Fair on the St. Lawrence River that celebrated Canada's centennial. *What I like best at Expo is watching all the different people—all sizes, shapes, and colors. I could watch them all day*, I wrote after one trip, reflecting my developing interest in anthropology. Other days we drove into downtown Montreal, where we would walk along the main drag, rue Sainte-Catherine, with its people, bars, restaurants, department stores, and other entertainments. *It's like living in Europe. This city is really alive. I could easily live here.* (Five years later I would get my first teaching job in Montreal, at McGill University.) We toured Molson's brewery and Seagram's distillery. On most trips to Montreal we tried to squeeze in a movie as well, since all those shown in Drummondville were in French without subtitles. Among our favorite flicks that season were *The Russians Are Coming* and *A Man and a Woman*.

Less often we'd drive around the surrounding countryside, stopping in some of the villages of the eastern townships. *As you approach the small towns, you can always see a tall church steeple from a distance. . . . [T]he Catholic Church is everything here. There is usually one main street. Sometimes it's not even paved, and some villages have lots of rickety, rundown houses. It doesn't seem like there's much to do. I wonder how these people amuse themselves. Maybe that's why the girls are horny.* Just a half hour from Drummondville was the small town of Asbestos, which boasted one of the world's largest open-pit mines, nearly a thousand feet deep, where they extracted the cancer-causing fibrous mineral. Sometimes we just hung around Drummondville and went horseback riding or raced go-carts. *The owner kicked us off the carts today for reckless driving. We kept*

crashing into one another, despite his pleas of "no bumpy, no bumpy." Jensen
fell out of his cart in a pileup and skinned his arm and leg and sprained his
hand. No one, of course, told the skipper how he did it.

JULY 18 . . . The coach of Celanese, a company fast-pitch softball team,
offered my teammates Claude Coté and Jim Ridley and me twenty-five
dollars each to play for his team in a big tournament. I accepted instantly,
"Sure, why not." That was my general attitude to any new opportunity.
In fact, I would have played for nothing. Expecting us to be big hitters,
the coach had us batting in the middle of the order in the first game. Big
mistake. Like Coté and Ridley, I discovered there was even less time to
react to a fast softball than to a baseball pitch because the pitching mound
is fifteen feet closer to the batter. At that distance the top flamethrowers
in softball pitched at speeds equivalent to 100 mph in baseball. To give
myself a few extra milliseconds to judge the oncoming pitch, I smudged
out the chalk line at the back of the batter's box and positioned myself
as far back as I could. It didn't help. The underhand pitches, which
Ridley said looked to be coming in upside down compared to baseball,
were on top of us in no time. We baseball players all had o'fers the first
game, as our Celanese team lost. We lost the next two games as well,
with we baseball ringers collecting only two scratch hits between us. I
can't imagine the Celanese manager ever again hired baseball players
for a softball tournament.

JULY 22 . . . I was playing left field in a game against the Lachine
Mets when I slid for a sinking line drive and missed it. The ball rolled to
the fence, and by the time I got there I could see the runner heading for
third and knew he would score the go-ahead run. Rather than pick up
the ball and throw it to the cutoff man, I raised my hand and motioned
that the ball had gone under the fence. It hadn't. While the umpire was
making his way to the outfield, I turned my back to the infield and stuffed
the ball under. The umpire arrived and was unconvinced; he asked me
if I had pushed the ball under. I said no. The hometown Mets and their

manager, former Dodger Tim Harkness, knew that it was impossible for the ball to simply roll under and protested vehemently. But with the ball sitting on the other side, the umpire had no choice but to rule it a ground-rule double. I had cheated to save a run (the run eventually scored anyway) and then lied about it to make it stand.

Most baseball people would say there is nothing wrong with trying to find a competitive edge, as long as you don't get caught. As former White Sox manager Ozzie Guillen put it, "If you don't get caught, you're a smart player. If you get caught, you're cheating." Cheating like this happens at all levels of pro ball—pitchers sometimes scuff or load up the ball, like Doc Olms's Vaseline ball; batters lean in to a pitch or pretend to have been nicked when they aren't; outfielders act as if they caught balls they had trapped. Trying to gain an advantage by cheating was, and still is, rationalized as "strategy," just part of the game. But when I came back into the dugout at the end of the inning, I could see that a few of my own teammates were not enthusiastic over what I had done. My coach looked the other way. The next time I came to the plate, Lachine's pitcher drilled me in the back.

On the bus ride home, ashamed and with a painful bruise as a reminder, I reflected on what I had done and concluded that, like other forms of cheating that we engaged in, such as occasionally peeking back at the catcher to see where he was setting up for a pitch, it was not in the spirit of fairness. And wasn't that—fairness—supposed to be a fundamental value of sport? Before I had never questioned these actions.[5] Nor had any of my coaches discouraged us as long as we could hide it from the umpires. In fact, some coaches did their best to cheat as well, such as trying to steal the signs of the opposing team and in the big leagues by sometimes instructing groundskeepers to doctor the base paths (for example, extra watering to slow fleet-footed base stealers) or gently sloping the foul line fair or foul (depending upon which club had good bunters) to suit or minimize the strengths of an opposing team.[6] Research has shown that athletes score significantly lower in "moral reasoning" than do nonathletes. And that team-sport athletes, as in baseball, are less likely to act morally than those in individual sports, like swimming and tennis. This, researchers suggest, is due to team pressures to conform and win. Worse still, the longer one remains in athletics, the more negatively affected is one's moral reasoning.[7]

JULY 24 . . . With none of the local media available in English, and still struggling with French, I knew little about what was happening in the outside world. But on this day a huge political scandal got everyone's attention. On an official visit to Quebec, France's president, Charles de Gaulle, gave a speech to a large crowd from the balcony of the Montreal City Hall. Leaning in to the microphone, in a slow and deliberate manner, he said, "*Vive le Quebec libre!*" (Long live free Quebec!). It was the slogan of a small minority of Quebecers who favored sovereignty and secession from Canada. De Gaulle's statement was not just a serious breach of diplomatic protocol; it emboldened the Quebec independence movement and encouraged separatist radicals, who later planted bombs and kidnapped and murdered the Canadian minister of justice, Pierre LaPorte. It seemed that everyone in Drummondville thought that de Gaulle had been outrageous, and their opinions inflamed my own—*He's lucky to get out of Canada with his life* . . .[8]

AUGUST 1 . . . When I arrived at the ballpark, I saw that Steve Cushman's locker was empty. Normally, a vacant locker was a sure sign of the player having been released, but that didn't make any sense in Cushman's case. He was our number-two starter and pitching well. No one had any clue to his whereabouts. A few days later we learned from his groupie girlfriend that Cushman had quit and left town in the middle of the night. He had been a loner, and no one knew him well enough to understand his reasons, nor did anyone, including his girlfriend, ever hear from him again.

Throwing BP that night, Claude Coté took a line drive in the gut that broke two of his ribs. In the sixties few teams, and certainly not Drummondville, had screens to protect the BP pitcher from smashes through the box. Later, during the game, our thirty-eight-year-old Dominican catcher, Walter James, was laid out after being struck in the throat by a foul tip. Catcher masks in 1967 didn't offer any throat protection. It wouldn't be until 1976 that a flap was added below the mask and became an everyday accessory for catchers and home-plate umpires.

We won the game that night, 6–5, against the Québec Indians in extra innings on a Mike Sawyer home run. Sawyer, a gifted two-sport athlete— baseball and hockey—was actually from Drummondville and a local hero. He had once been invited to the Philadelphia Phillies' spring-training camp in Clearwater, Florida, where it was said he had impressed the brass, but, not speaking English and having a difficult time adjusting, he had walked away and returned home. The story painted Sawyer as the French Canadian equivalent of homesick Hispanic rookies, who could only order ham and eggs for breakfast because they didn't know the English words for any other dishes.

Pierre Roux brought a new style of batting helmet to the ballpark for us to try out. Bright blue, it looked like a football helmet with a bill on the front. Batting helmets in those days did not have a flap that protected one's ear and temple. This one did, and I liked the idea of having my ear protected, especially hitting under Drummondville's anemic lights. I knew that in the Major Leagues the Phillies' Tony Gonzales had begun wearing a helmet with a premolded ear flap after he was beaned. But Pierre's experimental helmet felt confining and uncomfortable and, everyone agreed, looked "dorky." After that night none of us ever used it again.

AUGUST 12 . . . Playing in Lachine, I struck out twice and hit two dribblers against their big right-hander, Jack "Fitz" Fitzpatrick, as he got me to chase sharp-breaking sliders in the dirt. After the game Lachine's Steve Oleschuk, who'd brought me to the QPL, introduced me to Fitz, who in the off-season was a doctoral student in history at Cal-Berkeley. Steve thought we'd have a lot in common since "you both read books." Fitz was the first player I'd ever met who sported a mustache. That was daring. Even in the QPL most players still looked like clean-cut throwbacks to the Eisenhower era. It wasn't until the early 1970s that ballplayers would catch up with college kids in adopting facial hair and shaggier manes. I liked Fitz, and we soon became friends. After the season I visited him in Berkeley, where he and his wife and two-year-old daughter, Maia, were living in married student housing, on the flats, surrounded by abandoned factories and old warehouses. After cooking hamburgers on a hibachi grill, on a tiny strip of grass behind the apartment, Fitz put Maia to bed and then lit up a joint for all of us to share. Like most ballplayers in the late 1960s, and quite unlike most of my Stanford classmates, I had never smoked marijuana before. I was blown away by the sensations—everything said suddenly seemed so significant or funny, and the brownies and ice cream served for dessert were out of this world. The one downside was that the drive home across the bay seemed to take forever.

After Berkeley Fitz worked as a psychoanalyst at the Menninger Clinic and cofounded the *Psychohistory Review* before opening his own consulting business. When I reconnected with him during the research for this book, he was back playing baseball at age seventy-one in an over-thirty league in Topeka, Kansas. His teammates called him "Thunder Jack" and "Gramps." The local TV station did a news piece on the gray-bearded wonder. No longer effective on the mound, he had moved to first base and finished the 2012 season hitting over .300. Despite aching knees and shoulders, and the urging of his wife, Anne, to hang 'em up, Jack planned, he said, "to keep playing as long as my body will let me."

AUGUST 15 . . . We finished the season tied for third, good enough to make the playoffs and meet Granby in a best-of-five quarterfinal. *The fans are feverish. You can't buy yourself a beer because everyone wants to treat you. The stadium in Granby was packed last night with loud, enthusiastic fans from both Granby and Drummondville.* The sixties was a time when small-town fans could still worship and identify with local entities—like Minor League Baseball teams. For Provincial League fans, we were their big leaguers.

It's hard to believe this season is almost over. It's been a very long season, but I'll be sorry to see it end. Granby rallied in the eighth inning of the first game to beat us 5–3. I had three hits, including my tenth home run of the season. Our manager, Fred Bourbeau, who believed in an old superstition that seeing white horses would give the team luck, had driven around the countryside that day looking for white horses. He reported to us before the game that he had seen several and that we were going to win.

In the second game of the series, with my brother, Walt, and his pretty stewardess girlfriend in the stands visiting from California, I hit my eleventh home run, but we lost again, 7–5. And the next night, as we lost the third and final game, 8–6, I had two more homers, giving me five for the playoffs. Everyone figured that might be some kind of QPL record, but in the absence of good stats no one knew for sure.

Before leaving Drummondville for home, I was invited to play for a QPL All-Star team that was going to barnstorm in Cuba for several weeks (there were a number of Cubans in the QPL since they were not allowed to play in the United States). I was excited but then dejected when I learned that I couldn't go because of the U.S. travel ban to Cuba. *It's so stupid. What would be the harm of letting a few American ballplayers travel to Cuba? What would be the harm of letting a few Cubans play in the U.S.?* Later I heard that the All-Stars saw a good deal of the country and played one game in Havana before fifteen thousand fans with Fidel Castro in the crowd. I settled for watching a few Cuban Winter League games on television at home.[9]

Reflecting on the season as I flew home to California, I was glad that I had played in Quebec. I had regained my confidence by putting up good numbers, especially finishing second in the league in home runs with fourteen, nearly equal to the combined total of sixteen for the rest of the Drummondville team. I had also learned some French and something of French Canadian culture, and I had recovered from being dumped by Audrey. Yet it was clear there was little chance of being re-signed by a Major League organization. I wrote in my final journal entry of the season, *While I am still enjoying playing and like the status of being a professional, it's not leading anywhere. This is it. This is all there is ever going to be.*

LIGHTS OUT

Drummondville Les Royaux

I had planned to attend Tulane University in New Orleans in the fall as a visiting student, to be with Audrey. But after she left me, there was no reason to go. My heart set on trying out a new school and taking a break from Stanford, I opted instead for the University of California, Santa Barbara. I had a few friends there and liked that it was an oceanside campus. It was at UCSB in a four-hundred-student anthropology class called Magic, Religion, and Witchcraft that I saw a tall, dark-haired girl with high cheekbones and a porcelain complexion sitting in the row in front of me. Unable to take my eyes off her, I finally tapped her on the shoulder and asked if she would like to study together for the midterm. She said something pleasant but then streaked out of the auditorium as soon as class was over. I later learned that she had been pestered before. When I got back to my apartment, I described her to my roommate, Gary Geiger, who knew exactly who she was—Sharon Bohn. As I stood there he called and asked her out. I asked out someone else, and we joined them on a double date.

Sharon Bohn was just as stunning as I had remembered in class—sort of modelesque. She would later turn down a good modeling offer in Ireland despite my urging. I remember thinking, "Boy, if my teammates saw a snapshot of her, they'd give her a 10." Having a good looker as a girlfriend ranked right up there with your batting average or ERA as a measure of self-worth. Most of us didn't yet understand the notion that in choosing a partner, beauty eventually fades, but not the need for conversation.

That evening Sharon and I ended up being more interested in each other than in our dates. We were soon inseparable. I stayed at UCSB an extra trimester to be with her, before returning to Stanford. One day Audrey called me to say that perhaps she'd made a mistake and offered to come to California to visit and see what would happen. She had broken up with the Czech linguist. I still cared for her, but now, dating Sharon, I halfheartedly declined.

After I returned to Stanford that spring, Sharon came up to campus and then to meet my family; she made plans to join me in Drummondville that summer. At Stanford in the spring of 1968, antiwar activity had reached fever pitch. Student body president David Harris, whose campus speech the year before had stirred me, was jailed after becoming a nationally prominent draft resister; the campus erupted with demonstrations, occupations, arson fires, and street clashes with police. One fire, most likely set by student activists, destroyed the Naval ROTC building. The university president's office was also torched. Some of my brightest classmates, inspired by Marx, Fidel, Mao, and Che, believed in revolution, to bring an end to American imperialism.

It was during this time that I received a letter from my best childhood friend and college baseball teammate, Chris Nelson, saying he was in an infantry division at Fort Lewis, Washington, about to embark for Vietnam. He hated the army. In my return letter I sympathized and told him how immoral and wrongheaded I thought the war was. I added that, on my weekend job, I had joined longshoremen in writing peace symbols and antiwar messages on the army vehicles we loaded into the holds of ships leaving the Oakland waterfront for Vietnam. Chris misunderstood my thinking, which was that protest in any and all forms

19. Sharon Bohn, whom I met in an anthropology class at UCSB and later married. We would both become anthropologists. Photo by Edna Gmelch.

might help end the war sooner. I had failed terribly to see how my comments and actions—as a buddy who had cheated to avoid the draft and was happily playing baseball in Canada when not in college—would be interpreted as unsympathetic. Sometime later I received Chris's reply, mailed from South Vietnam. It was a single line, "I'll remember what you said when I lie dying in a rice paddy with a bullet in my head." He never wrote again, and although he escaped Vietnam unscathed, he rebuffed my attempts to see him for some time. The loss of his friendship was painful, a senseless personal consequence of a senseless war.

But worse was the death of another Bay Area teammate and College of San Mateo star, Charles Chase, who had been drafted by the Minnesota Twins and hit .269 as a rookie before being conscripted into the army. The Twins tried to help Chuck avoid the draft by getting him into a reserve unit, but it hadn't worked out in time. A thoughtful, quiet kid with a peculiar habit of always putting his baseball cap on backward and then turning the bill to the front, Chuck died soon after arriving in Vietnam—killed by friendly fire, or what the military called "misadventure," during action in Kontum. Years later, I sobbed when I found his name on the Vietnam Memorial wall.

The Royals had fired our skipper from the previous year, Fred Bourbeau, because of drinking. They hired my former college coach, John Noce, to replace him. I looked forward to playing under Noce, although I was a little unsure how his conservative and superdisciplined approach and heavy emphasis on fundamentals would go over among older ballplayers in the independent and laid-back Provincial League setting. The first test came when pitcher Bob Nauman wanted to wear black stirrup socks, the ones he had worn while in the Red Sox organization, instead of Drummondville's royal-blue ones. Noce thought wearing a different-colored sock was "bush." Nauman thought that the black stirrups would give him luck and that how he pitched was far more important than how he looked. Being the skipper, Noce got his way, and Nauman, after a fifteen-dollar fine for the first offense, pitched wearing blue socks. Despite his superstition, Nauman pitched well the entire season.

It looked as if we were going to have a good team. Noce had recruited some excellent West Coast ballplayers, including college stars Norm Angelini, Frank Pignataro, and Rich Jefferies. The new general manager, Pierre Roux, who had been a local sportswriter the previous season, had signed four good players from the Dominican Republic, the poorest country in baseball's Spanish-speaking world.

I found a cabin on the bank of the St. Francis River five miles out of town to rent with the new California ballplayers—Angelini, Pignataro, and Young. Angelini, a.k.a. "Stormin' Norman," was a fiercely competitive pitcher with an attitude. He became a favorite with Drummondville's fans, who nicknamed him "Papillon" (Butterfly), after the cocky way he walked, rocking from side to side. He threw hard, but his best pitch was a curveball that dropped off the table and would lead him to a league-leading 1.25 ERA and eventually to the big leagues with Kansas City. For twenty-year-old second baseman Frank "Pig" Pignataro, coming to Québec was like going to Europe for the first time. He'd never been out of California. Pig relished living in a foreign environment, hearing French spoken everywhere, and trying new foods, especially the crepes and *patates frites* with vinegar. Whenever he saw his name in the Drummondville paper, *La Parole*, he clipped the article and sent it home, even though his parents couldn't read French. Superstitious, Pig never washed his sanitary socks after a good game (for fear of washing away the luck), jumped over all chalk foul lines, and always touched third base on his way to the dugout. And no matter how cool the evening, he wore short sleeves on the field, believing that he couldn't hit well in long sleeves. The scouts had passed on Pig because of his small size, just five-foot-five, in spite of his having excelled at every level he had played. Prior to Drummondville he hit .375 in one of the best junior-college circuits in the country and was named Conference Player of the Year.

Our third roommate, Mike Young, was tall, slim, and so quiet that I never really got to know him. We called him "Coyote" because of a resemblance to the cartoon character Wile E. Coyote. Coyote liked the smell of leather and would often perch his baseball glove in front of his nose, not altogether different from our center fielder Rafael González, who kissed his bat after each base hit.

In the cabin next to us was Drummondville's new third baseman, Rich Jefferies; his eye-catching wife, Joan; and their two sons. One of them, Gregg Jefferies, then just an infant, would be playing for the New York Mets at age nineteen and go on to star for six Major League teams over a long career. In the Drummondville grandstand, Joan became more popular with the fans than her husband, Rich, who struggled all season on the field, finally being released. A stone's throw from our cabins in a large summer house lived skipper John Noce and his family, including their young son, Paul, who would also someday be a big leaguer—a shortstop for the Chicago Cubs.

The cabins had a good view of the river and were set among trees, making the area five to ten degrees cooler than town. The only downside was that the river was polluted from untreated sewage and effluent from upstream pulp mills. Drummondville, despite having thirty-five thousand people, lacked a sewage treatment plant. When I returned for a visit in 2012, however, the paper mills were closed, and strict environmental controls had cleaned up the river to the point where locals proudly claimed that you could drink straight from it.

After getting settled into our cabin, the four of us bought a seven-year-old white Vauxhall for two hundred dollars. It got us around until Stormin' Norman skidded on a wet street and crashed on the way home from a nightclub. Not having his license with him, and having had too much to drink, he made Pig get into the driver's seat. The police had the car towed away, and we never saw it again.

JUNE 1 . . . Not having had any spring training, I was rusty and struggled at the plate during the first week. *I hate disappointing Noce and the fans who seem to be expecting a lot from me. In the newspaper there is a nice picture of me under the headline "LE PUISSANT FRAPPEUR"* [The powerful hitter]. *They predict that I am going to have a good season.* But it took eight painful games before I found my stroke.

Playing the Québec City Indians that night, I crushed a belt-high heater to dead center. Certain it was going out, I wasn't running particularly hard when it hit the top of the center-field wall and bounced back into the field. Switching gears into a full sprint, I missed tagging first. The first baseman noticed, called for the ball, and stepped on the bag, whereupon the umpire called me out, erasing my base hit. Even though we won 7–6, I was down the rest of the evening over the loss of five points from my batting average.

JUNE 5 . . . Entering the Motel Cardin restaurant for lunch, I caught a French headline through the scratched window of the newspaper box: "ROBERT F. KENNEDY ASSASSIN." Duke, the owner of the place, translated for me, which is how I learned that the candidate I hoped would win the Democratic nomination for president—the candidate whom many believed would get us out of Vietnam—had been fatally shot. When it came time for Kennedy's funeral, MLB's commissioner, William Eckert, and many team owners chose not to cancel their games, even though a few players threatened to boycott rather than fail to honor Kennedy's memory. Nor were games canceled on President Johnson's designated national day of mourning. There was widespread criticism of MLB. Typical was the *Philadelphia Bulletin*'s Sandy Grady, who opined, "It was the weekend they buried Robert F. Kennedy, the brightest and best hope of youth, a man who loved athletics and the people who played them—and baseball made $1 million. Remember those values, kids." To me it was no wonder that on American campuses, young people were disillusioned with professional sports.

Just two months earlier Martin Luther King Jr. had been murdered, sparking race riots in many cities. And casualties of Americans in Vietnam, like Chuck Chase, were mounting. Images flashed across America's television screens of riots, smoldering cities, and napalmed Asian villages. It was too much. America was becoming unglued. And there was the haunting prospect of nuclear destruction. It was a confusing time for all Americans, but especially for the young, as our world seemed dangerously fragile and without good prospects for righting itself. *I am so glad to be living in Canada*, I wrote. *Everything here seems so much safer and saner. I almost don't care if I ever go back to the U.S.* One of my Stanford classmates became so pessimistic about the country's future that he dropped out of school, saying studying was a waste of time when the world was descending into chaos.

JUNE 18 . . . During the off-season the Drummondville City Council had made a few improvements to the ballpark. But it was still the worst ballpark in the league. The Royals' ownership group threatened to leave the city unless further improvements were made and a full-time groundskeeper hired. Several umpires filed new complaints with the league over the poor stadium lights. I wrote a letter about the ballpark conditions on behalf of the team. It was translated into French and published in *La Parole Journal*. In part, the original English read:

> We address this letter to you, Drummondville fans, so that you may understand our difficulties playing in Municipal Stadium. We have played baseball throughout the U.S., Canada, and Latin America and have never seen or played in a worse baseball facility. . . . The Stadium lights are only 25 candlepower, half the minimum required for Class A baseball. They are so poor that they pose a danger to hitters. . . . [I]t's a miracle that no one has been seriously hurt. The condition of the infield is no better than that of the lights. The poor conditions in the infield deny you the pleasure of watching a good brand of baseball. (June 28, 1968)

The city council did not respond, and two weeks later, in a game against the Granby Cardinals, their batter Reggie Grenald was badly beaned. He lost sight of the pitch in the bright streetlights behind center field. The thud of the ball striking his head was sickening. Blood flowed from Grenald's right ear as he lay motionless in the batter's box. Unlike in football, violent collisions are rare in baseball; blood is rarely spilled on a baseball field. Grenald was taken by ambulance to the hospital for observation, having a severe concussion. The chance of another serious injury was not unlikely, since pitchers in the 1960s often worked the inside corners of the plate.[1] Our general manager asked the city if it would turn off the problematic streetlights during games or erect a screen. Still no response.

A week after the beaning, and annoyed over the city's inaction on the streetlights, I suggested to roommates Pig, Coyote, and Stormin Norman that we take care of the lights ourselves with a .22-caliber rifle that I had brought to Quebec for target practice. Pig bowed out of the plan, but Norm and Coyote agreed, even though as pitchers they had little to gain personally by knocking out the lights. We fetched the rifle and drove into town. It was around two in the morning when we parked directly under the streetlights and with four or five shots knocked them out. It was easy. Too easy.

On the way back to our cabin, we began to wonder if we had taken out the correct lights, since there was another one close by. Foolishly, we turned around and headed back to the ballpark. Just as we pulled up under the remaining light, two police cars closed in; three officers jumped out, hands on their pistols. We tried to hide the rifle, which wasn't easy in the backseat of a Vauxhall. We were taken to the station and booked. I asked to see the officer in charge to explain why we had done it, that it wasn't mindless vandalism. They brought me upstairs, where, while drawing a diagram of the ballpark, the lights, and connecting dots, I tried to explain in my limited French and perhaps with some exaggeration that we had shot out the lights "to protect the lives of innocent ballplayers." I could hear Norm yelling downstairs. He had talked back, claiming that he had certain rights being an "American citizen." That didn't go down well, and one cop spit on him.

After a few hours of detention, we were issued a court summons and released. Until the streetlights were replaced a few weeks later, left-handed batters no longer had to fear losing track of a pitch. We could see the ball so much better that the first game after the lights were out was a slugfest in which we beat Québec City 13–12. Word about shooting out the lights spread around the league. As I was getting into the batter's box, Sherbrooke's catcher needled, "Hey, Sharpshooter, lights out." Another player, mimicking a thick French accent, said, "Hey, Sharpshooter, how goes it with *les gendarmes?*" Sharon addressed her next letter, "Dear Sharpshooter." She told her mother about the incident, which made her wonder about the kind of guy her daughter was engaged to marry.

The team's attorney met with the city officials and was able to get the criminal charges dropped. Norm, Coyote, and I were, however, ordered to pay for the replacement lights. Our GM said he'd pass a hat in the stands to raise money, but he never did. Some months after the season ended, I received a bill for six hundred dollars for two mercury-vapor lamps and labor. We didn't pay the bill, and five years later when Sharon and I drove from San Francisco to Montreal to take up my first teaching job at McGill University, I feared my name would be on a list and that the Canadian immigration would not let me cross the border and I might lose my job.

As bad as Drummondville's ballpark was, or the other bad ballparks I had played in, none were as decrepit as Minor League parks are typically portrayed in films like *Bull Durham*, *The Rookie*, *Chasing Dreams*, and *Long Gone*. It always disappoints me that Minor League Baseball is depicted as bush league, with ballplayers playing under awful conditions and traveling in beat-up buses. Is it for comic effect? Or are the filmmakers worried that viewers wouldn't otherwise grasp the difference between the Majors and the Minors?

We often went to movies on our trips to Montreal. Those good enough to make it into my journal that season were *In the Heat of Night* and *Bonnie and Clyde*, but we were easy to please. The only film I recall not liking was *Dr. Doolittle*, a musical about a vet who can speak to animals and embarks on an epic search for a Great Pink Sea Snail. My movie mates gave me a hard time afterward for having suggested it. Sometimes I seemed to invite ridicule. On one trip to Montreal I wore a pair of bright-yellow pants that I had bought supercheap in a clearance sale. Most of my wardrobe was and still is purchased on clearance. I couldn't tell how bright the pants were in the muted light of the clothing store, and, having spent nine dollars, I was determined to get some use out of them. On the street in Montreal the yellow fabric attracted the attention of a gay man who hit on me. Like the incident in the Miami hotel, it provided good material for joking in the clubhouse the next day, as Chuck Hughes mimicked the guy and my startled and awkward reaction.

Now engaged to Sharon, I had not gone out with Monique, my groupie partner from the previous season, although there were times when I was tempted. As much as I enjoyed the company of my teammates, I missed the companionship of girls. Letters to Sharon reflected my loneliness: *I wish you would hurry up and get here. The Drummondville I enjoyed so much last year is a drag without you. I'm just killing time until you come.* This was, of course, the pre-Internet era, and international telephone calls were very expensive; our only way of communicating was through letters. We wrote to each other almost every day. A lot of mushy stuff typical of young lovers, including some cornball expressions like *I love you more than home runs.* In truth, that would depend upon how many home runs we are talking about. I closed every letter with *j't'aime beaucoup*. Sharon wrote back with equally sentimental passages, such as *I miss you terribly, but I force myself to concentrate on our future plans and about what I'll wear when I first see you, about whether or not you'll think I'm pretty.* Who could have ever guessed that she would bloom into an ardent feminist and years later direct Union College's first Women's Studies Program, becoming, as a male colleague liked to jest, the college's "chief ball buster"?

Finally, on June 10, 1968, I received a long-awaited telegram: "George, will arrive Thursday. Air Canada flight 565 at 2:10 PM. Miss you. Sharon." After Sharon arrived I left Pig, Norm, and Coyote to move into a white clapboard cottage nearby, on the riverbank. Sharon's religious mother, apparently more concerned about her daughter living in sin than being with a "sharpshooter," asked us to move up our wedding date so that we would be married shortly after the season ended and before starting graduate school together at UCSB.

Sharon's arrival coincided with my falling into a slump. In the clubhouse after several hitless nights, Noce accused me of being worn down by "banging" my girlfriend all night and told me to get my priorities straight. But as Casey Stengel once said, it wasn't the sex that wore out players but being out all hours chasing after it. And that wasn't my situation.

On my off days Sharon and I explored the surrounding countryside by car and then ventured farther afield, traveling to the Laurentian Mountains north of Montreal and beyond. At the ballpark Sharon became friendly with the other players' wives and girlfriends, including Pauline Noce, the coach's wife. In the Minor Leagues the wives of players kept their distance from the wife of the coach, who had control over their husbands' careers. But in the QPL, as in all independent leagues, teams were not part of a larger organization, so there was less to fear that unwise remarks or a clash of personalities would have repercussions for a player's career.

JUNE 16 . . . With no game that night one of the team's directors let us take out his water-ski boat on the St. Francis River. The polluted water made me ill, and the team sent me to a doctor. It was my second exposure to Canadian health care, and I came away impressed. *The doctor even showed up at the ballpark later to check on me, but maybe because he is a baseball fan.* My first encounter with the national health system had occurred on my flight to Quebec when, because of a severe head cold, my ears would not clear when we landed in Montreal. The pain was intense. Air Canada took me to a doctor, who gave me relief and medication. I was puzzled that there was no bill, no cost to me. While I was being treated Air Canada had passed my bags through customs and checked on the bus schedule for Drummondville. *I don't think I'd get this kind of treatment in the U.S. When I landed in Chicago* [earlier to change planes, where my ears also hadn't cleared] *United Airlines didn't offer me any assistance at all.* The medical care was one of several things that I began to really like about living in Canada.

JUNE 27 . . . We lost to the Granby Cardinals, 5–4, on a bases-loaded double by their thirty-seven-year-old player-manager, Nick Testa. I remembered the name from the roster of my hometown Giants when they first moved to San Francisco in 1958. Nick may have had the shortest Major League career in history, catching one inning and being the on-deck batter when the game ended, thus never having an at bat. He spent most of that season in the Giants' bullpen. After that he bounced around the baseball world, playing in Colombia, Nicaragua, Panama, Italy, Mexico, and Japan before landing in the Québec Provincial League in 1965. Despite his age the well-muscled Testa was a feared .300 hitter. In the off-season Nick taught physical education at Lehman College in New York. In the mid-1990s I saw Nick again at Yankee Stadium. Then in his midsixties, he was the Yankees' regular batting-practice pitcher.

JUNE 28 . . . Pig cranked his first home run of the season and then got the silent treatment. Everybody was in on it. Even Noce in the third base coach's box turned his back on Pig as he rounded third. When Pig reached the dugout, we all ignored him and avoided eye contact. It was an impressive effort by the entire bench to remain straight-faced. Pig's reaction, finally, was "Hey, guys, come on. This is my first home run, and it's not an inside-the-park job. Give me a break. I don't get many of these."

Pig's home run wasn't enough to prevent us from losing our fifth consecutive game. We had played sloppily, and in the clubhouse after the game Noce was pissed. He called an early practice for the next morning and instituted a 1:00 a.m. curfew. *Noce acts like the world has come to an end. Sometimes he takes this game way, way too seriously for me. In his life baseball is always number one. Everything else comes second. My devotion to baseball never seems to meet his standards. He even complained about my reading on the bus, and I'm not even reading that much.*

I had shared Noce's zeal for the game when I played for him in college. But now five years older and in my fourth season of pro ball, I was no longer fanatical. Noce hated it whenever I mentioned politics. He was from an era that was not just more conservative but frowned upon athletes taking a stand on controversial matters of politics and social justice. Noce supported the U.S. Olympic Committee's decision to send home sprinters John Carlos and Tommie Smith for their Black Power salute on the medal stand at the Olympics in Mexico City. I admired Carlos and Smith for having the guts to do it. Actors and musicians had already awakened to the amazing platform they had and begun to use it. Why not athletes too? But to Noce and many of my teammates, sports and politics should not mix.

Noce's curfew and early-morning workout didn't have the desired effect, as we lost our next four games. *Our college phenoms who don't have any pro experience are not producing, and Perez has been a bust.* Dominican pitcher Simon Perez had been acquired from the Sherbrooke Alouettes in a trade. The previous season the tall, all-elbows-and-knees Perez was a lights-out fireballer, winning twelve games. But when he arrived in Drummondville, he had a dead arm, a fact his old club kept secret prior to the trade. Now forced to rely on junk, Perez had a losing record and a hefty ERA. He won only four games all season. Nonetheless, he had an affable personality and a one-hundred-watt smile, and because he spoke the best English of all the Dominicans, he was a valued member of the team and good for its chemistry. These same qualities also endeared him to the groupies who hung around the ballpark and went to the Rocdor nightclub after games.

We snapped out of our losing streak at eight and then won six of our next seven games, using the same personnel and same batting order. Nothing had changed other than some timely hits, a few good pitching performances, and a little luck. I almost single-handedly blew the first win, however. We were leading the Plessisville Braves at home, 2–1, with two outs in the ninth and a runner on. The batter hit a comebacker to our pitcher, who fielded the ball cleanly and tossed it to me, striding toward first base. Somehow, I missed stepping on the bag, and the runner was called safe. Noce was livid and came storming out of the dugout to demonstrate for all to see how easy it was to make a putout by stomping on the bag. With the game now entirely on my back, I was sweating bullets until the next batter struck out. The next day during batting practice, Noce made me step on the first base bag several dozen times, saying that in all his years of coaching, that was the first time he'd ever had anyone practice "stepping on the fucking base."

I was hitting a respectable .273 but was no longer the team's big home run hitter like the year before. *I have been unseated by Hector Soto, the player I had recommended to* [general manager] *Pierre.* Hector, who like Simon Perez was from the Dominican Republic, had been my teammate at Daytona Beach, where he had led the team in home runs. Hector was tall and handsome, with a bright gold cap on one of his front teeth that glittered when he smiled. He was a dead-red fastball hitter. In my mind's eye I can still see him clearly in the batter's box, standing erect, hands low and close to his body, then curling back as the pitcher wound up. Hector had all five tools but never lived up to his potential. He had been released by several organizations, each time after putting up decent numbers, including a .310 average in the Appalachian Rookie League his first season. For reasons no one understood, Hector didn't always hustle, or, as we would say, he "jaked it." It was hard to understand because, coming from a poor family in the Dominican Republic and without much education, Hector didn't have much to fall back on. He couldn't go home and hope Daddy would find him a job. Some said Hector was just a malingerer, as though loafing was in his genes.[2]

JULY 4 . . . We were leading Québec City by one run in the eighth when their big slugger Fred Hopke, a six-foot-three, 240-pound first baseman who'd had seven good years in AAA, came to the plate with the tying run on second and first base open. Noce went to the mound and told Angelini to walk him. Norm thought he could get Hopke out and tried to blow one by him. Hopke went deep to win the game. Noce was furious and called for an early workout the next day, punishing everyone. In the clubhouse after the game, Angelini was nowhere to be found. Fearful that Norm might do something foolish in his distressed state, Noce sent our GM to look for him. Pierre found Norm wandering in the old city, talking to himself.

We were on the bus driving toward Montreal to play the Lachine Mets. Third baseman Rich Jefferies and I were sitting together with a good view out the front window when a blue sedan pulled onto the highway from a side road and collided full-on with a fast-moving car. Quebec drivers were known for speeding; many routinely exceeded the provincial speed limit of 70 mph (112 km), which had only recently been introduced. Our bus slowed as we passed the crash; the bussie shouted not to look, but most of us did. Bodies had been ejected from both vehicles, and one car was badly crushed. Mangled and contorted bodies lay on the pavement. It was horrifying, and it was the second crash I had seen through a bus window on a road trip. Both involved young people, and both resulted in fatalities. In this crash three died. Rich was shaken. He called his wife, Joan, as soon as we reached Lachine and told her not to come to the game. He didn't want her driving on Quebec's bloody highways ever again, especially with their two young boys. *The driving here is crazy. It's scary. Over one weekend fifteen people died in road accidents. That's fifteen people in a population of just four million. No wonder insurance for eighteen-year-olds is $800 a year.*

AUGUST 1 . . . With a three-day break in our schedule, Sharon and I drove to La Tuque (150 miles) in northern Québec and then talked our way onto a logging train into the interior, hoping to see the Cree Indians that we'd heard about from a Drummondville neighbor. A Catholic missionary put us up in his rectory. The Indians were living in canvas-wall tents and subsisting largely by hunting and gathering. *They live just like they did 100 years ago,* I misreported in a letter to my parents, failing to understand the degree to which the Cree had been changed by their contact with the outside world. The trip was an adventure, an attempt by two fledgling anthropology students to learn something about Indians. Norm and Coyote said it was a "weird way" to spend one's break.

AUGUST 10 . . . We were playing at Granby when the umpires blew two calls, each costing us a run. In a letter home I described what ensued after a third bad call:

> In the seventh inning I hit a hanging curveball a mile down the right field line. It was clearly fair as it left the park and only then did it hook foul. But the umpire, maybe out of spite over the rough time we had given him over the previous bad calls, called my home run foul. It caused a ruckus. . . . I was thrown out of the game. Our trainer turned off the hot water in the umpires' locker room and took their soap and towels. Some Drummondville fans went to the parking lot and let the air out of the tires of the umpires' car. When the umps came out of the stadium, some fans were still there. They cursed the umps and beat on the hood of their car.[3]

Even though I had lost a home run and been ejected, which also resulted in a twenty-five-dollar fine from the league, it was strange seeing fans get that upset over a fairly unimportant ball game. We had witnessed similar behavior in Plessisville, where angry fans not only deflated the umps' tires but had been so threatening that the police were called to provide them with safe escort from the stadium. I wondered why the fans cared more about the outcome of the game than we players did. Claude Coté, a French Canadian longtime QPL veteran, told me there had been heavy betting on the game and that the irate fans were probably those who blamed their losses on the umpires' bad calls. In a 1937 incident enraged fans at Trois Rivieres swarmed the field and not only attacked the umpires but beat up the team, according to Merritt Clifton's history of the QPL.[4] When our fans were upset they would sometimes swear in English, and since it was not their native tongue they could say some pretty amazing things. One petite young woman screamed at Angelini, "Fuck you. . . . You do be cocksucker," probably with little clue as to its crudity.

The ball club made money selling fifty-fifty raffle tickets in the grandstand (it was rumored that the club actually kept 70 percent instead of 50 percent). The shapely wife of our trainer, Jacques Desautels, sold far more than anyone else by showing a lot of cleavage and letting her customers get a long look as they paid for their tickets.

AUGUST 15 . . . We closed out the season with a 4–1 win over Thetford Mines, finishing in second place. We then lost in the first round of the playoffs to the powerhouse Granby Cardinals, who went on to win the league championship. I finished the season hitting .252, with nine home runs and forty RBIs, all numbers down from the previous year. After the season Norm signed with the Kansas City Royals and within three years was with the big club as a left-handed closer. Despite putting up decent numbers, he was sent down to Triple A Omaha and then traded to the Atlanta Braves. Never making it back to the big leagues, he spent the rest of his career in AAA with the Denver Bears. He retired in Denver and, like many of my baseball teammates, went on to work in sales, everything from beer to Keebler Cookies. When I spoke to Norm in 2012, the first time since our Drummondville days, the first thing he said upon answering the phone, having seen my name on his caller ID, was, "Sharpshooter, I didn't pull the trigger."

Pig, despite having a good year at the plate and in the field, turned down an offer to return to Drummondville so as not to be separated from his fiancée, Sue, whose job would not let her join him in Quebec. He coached college and high school baseball for a while, became a high school principal, and then left education to work in insurance. He rose through the ranks to become a vice president of State Farm Insurance. Today, he regrets not having played another year in Drummondville and says that if he could do his brief pro career over, he would drink less beer and get more sleep.

Coyote signed with the Chicago Cubs and played a few years of A-ball. After being released he became a coach and physical education teacher in Ventura, California. John Noce returned to Drummondville the following year (1969) and led the Royals to the league championship. He would later manage the Nettuno Baseball Club in the professional Italian Baseball League.

Sharon and I married two weeks after the season ended and then immediately set off for UCSB to begin graduate school. I didn't return to Drummondville for the 1969 season, as I chose instead to participate in an anthropology field school in Mexico.[5] But there, living in a highland Tlaxcalan village, I had vivid dreams about playing baseball again. I decided that I would play one final season the following year. While I was enthusiastic about my new field of anthropology, I wasn't quite ready to abandon playing ball. Or maybe it was that I didn't yet want to give up my identity as a professional ballplayer. Sharon didn't object but said that she might have plans of her own for the following summer and not join me in Drummondville.

The next spring, the day after taking my comprehensive exams in the Anthropology Department at UCSB, I returned to Drummondville. I was eager to play again, but now part of my motivation was to write something on the anthropology of baseball. An editor at the *Atlantic Monthly* had liked an article I'd written called "Baseball Magic," about superstitions and rituals among ballplayers, which had been published in the social science magazine *Transactions*, and suggested I write a piece on the culture of baseball.[6]

When I arrived in Drummondville in the spring of 1970, I immediately set to work collecting data—interviewing teammates and recording my observations in field notes. But it was a futile exercise because I was still too inexperienced as an anthropologist and too close to my subject—the culture of baseball—to see it clearly. Forty-five years later, however, those field notes have been useful in writing this memoir. As my research floundered, I was also struggling at the plate and losing my joy for playing the game. *It was probably a mistake coming back. I have hung on too long.* Although I still felt fortunate being paid to play the game that was the dream of so many young men, a few weeks into the season I left Drummondville and baseball for good.

Although I didn't know it at the time, it was soon to be lights out for the QPL as well. At the end of that 1970 season, the league disbanded, unable to compete for fans with the new big-league Montreal Expos. Expo games were televised and could be seen live by commuting on the newly built expressways that gave Quebecers easy access to Montreal's Jarry Park. When the QPL folded most of its players never played professional baseball again. The best baseball towns in the league—Québec City, Sherbrooke, Trois Rivieres, and Thetford Mines—became new franchises in the AA Eastern League. The Eastern League's Quebec experiment lasted only a few years, as by 1977 all the Quebec-based teams had relocated to U.S. cities. Today the Expos are gone as well, having moved to Washington DC. Only Quebec City has professional baseball—a team called Les Capitales in the independent Can Am League.

From Drummondville I traveled to Ireland to join Sharon, who was doing fieldwork in a small fishing village on the southwestern coast. For the rest of that summer, I often felt depressed around four o'clock each day, unable to understand why. Then one day I realized that for four of the past five years that had been the time I was at the ballpark each day getting ready to play. Like my teammates who had been released, I was, at just twenty-four, having to adjust to retirement from my chosen vocation and childhood passion decades before workers in most professions ever contemplate stepping down. It helped that my last experience in baseball was in Quebec, where I grew tired of playing ball, rather than in Rocky Mount, with all the disappointment and anger over having been summarily fired. At least in Quebec I was able to leave the game on my own terms. And while I left baseball with regrets over my many mistakes, I was mindful of the rich experiences it had afforded me and the many new places it had taken me. Unlike some of my teammates, my life had not peaked but rather was taking a new direction.

One unfortunate consequence of leaving baseball was that my father and I had much less to talk about. He had always followed my career closely, reading the local newspapers from each town where I played, and had been intensely proud of my being a ballplayer, bragging to others about my baseball accomplishments. As my brother, Walt, sometimes reminded me, "Dad is living his dream through you." Until my release in Rocky Mount he had faith that I would make it to the big leagues, although he never revealed his confidence in front of me. That, he believed, could give me a "big head." Given the clash between my father's conservative, probusiness, staunchly Republican politics and his commitment to the American suburban, consumerist way of life and my emergent antiwar, antimaterialist, and leftist sympathies, baseball was where we found common ground. My father would never find the same satisfaction in my future academic achievements. Of the books that I went on to write, the only ones he showed real interest in were two on baseball, *In the Ballpark* and *Inside Pitch*. We would never again be as close as we were during my baseball days. I wish it hadn't been so.

EPILOGUE

Let me say a few words about the research behind this memoir and what I learned about memory and myself along the way. At the outset I had assumed that memory together with journals, letters, and notes taken for my newspaper articles would provide all the material I would need. But as I started tracking down former teammates to bounce some of my recollections off them, I was instantly struck by the discrepancies in our memories. Some of them recalled events and details about our shared experiences that I had completely forgotten, and vice versa. There were even a few happenings I was absolutely certain about that on closer inspection turned out to be wrong. One occurred during a conversation with Gene Lamont in the dugout before a game between the Oakland A's and the visiting Detroit Tigers. I asked Gene what he remembered of our stay at the Pendleton apartments in Daytona Beach, where for part of the season I thought he had been one of my four roommates. Gene said that not only had he not lived at the Pendleton, but he wasn't even on the Daytona team that season. I was incredulous and at first argued that he must be wrong. In Lamont I discovered how fallible my own memory could be.

Former Kinston Eagles first baseman Ted Bashore, who after baseball became a psychologist, cautioned me, "Keep in mind that memory is *productive*, not *reproductive*. It is never a literal rendering of the past." I heeded Ted's advice and began to treat memories, mine and others', as data in need of verification. Verification meant checking my recollections against the "written record" of newspaper accounts, journal entries and letters, and the memories of teammates. So my initial informal contacts with a few old teammates soon evolved into full-blown tape-recorded interviews. For each team I played on, I was able to interview about a half-dozen former teammates and for Jamestown, Daytona, and Drummondville the managers as well. The other managers were no longer living. And once I had finished a draft, I sent the chapter to each of them for checking and clarifications.

I learned that what we remember is not always related to its importance. Often teammates recalled only trivial details about events that I thought were significant. And sometimes really big things in our baseball lives had disappeared from remembrance altogether.

I tried to enhance my own recollections by returning to Tiger Town and the towns where I had played. Revisiting the old ballparks, in particular, brought back many otherwise inaccessible memories—the smells of horsehide, pine tar, and rosin; the sound of metal spikes clacking on a cement runway.[1] Best of all, at night I dreamed that I was playing again and hitting better than ever. I was a star and mildly disappointed when I awoke that it was only a dream.

While acknowledging the fallibility of memory, I believe the account of Minor League life presented in this work is the most accurate that I can render. Having said that, I surely got a few dates wrong, and some details of games may be somewhat off where the news coverage was lacking or my journal entries are sketchy. But otherwise I have done my best to tell a truthful and exact story.

I did not anticipate that the greatest pleasure in working on this memoir would be reconnecting with former teammates, managers, and girlfriends. The first was pitcher Les Cain, who traveled across the bay from Richmond to my home in San Francisco. He came just for lunch, but was still sitting on my living room sofa nine hours later with no sign of tiring when, exhausted, I had to beg off. In March 2013 seven of my teammates were among more than seventy-five former Detroit Tiger Major and Minor Leaguers who returned to Tiger Town for a reunion.[2] As far as anyone knew it was the first reunion of its kind in pro ball. Not the usual one-day golf outing for big leaguers but four days of socializing over food and activities and bringing together both Minor and Major Leaguers, including the likes of Al Kaline and Willie Horton. I felt a deep connection with my former teammates, much deeper than anything I've felt at a school reunion. The first few seasons of pro ball create strong and lasting bonds. In a difficult environment we had depended upon each other for companionship and support. As rookies most of us had never before lived away from home. We had to adjust not only to new places and multicultural teammates, but also to the absence of families and girlfriends. We faced enormous pressures to succeed, "to put up good numbers." And we all had shared and devoted our lives to the same dream of making it in pro ball and getting to the big leagues. In an e-mail inviting us to the reunion, former Tiger John "Duke" Young spoke to the bonds formed between teammates,

> As I roll into senior citizenship, I find that the years I played pro ball were probably the most significant in my life. Not a day passes when I don't recall the snakes in the Winter Haven shower, the bus trips from Montgomery to Charlotte, the night Tim Hosley woke up the dead with a walk-off homer that landed in the cemetery behind Patterson Field. Many memories, but none as precious as my teammates. We are part of a special fraternity, part of the Tigers Family. . . . I want to see those fellows that played such an important role in my life.

In conversations with old teammates I discovered that the mental images we had of one another were fixed in time, unchanged from nearly a half century ago. What I found especially surprising was that most of our images of each other came from the ball field. Among position players they were of hitting. Almost always we were able to recall each other's stance and swing. For those who were pitchers, it was windups and delivery. This was probably because our attention at the ballpark, when not scanning the stands for pretty girls, was focused where the action takes place—the batter at the plate and the pitcher on the mound. Conversely, we had few or only vague memories of one another fielding or in off-the-field activities, unless it was a good prank.

Many of my teammates still think of themselves as *ballplayers*, despite being in their sixties and having spent decades in other careers. Even for those who had played only briefly in the low Minors, having been a professional baseball player was a singular achievement of which they are still proud. For many, nothing in their lives since leaving the game has measured up to the glory and excitement of playing pro ball. Not everyone had hung on to their past to the same degree, however. There were some like Dave Bike, Bob Felber, and Rudy Burson who, though still ardent baseball fans, no longer give much thought to their earlier careers. And there are others like Jon Warden, Larry Calton, and Shifty Gear for whom baseball remains a huge presence in their lives. Larry Calton talks about baseball daily—past and present—on a sports talk radio show in West Plains, Missouri. When at home Shifty spends a lot of time in a basement den, a shrine to his playing days, stuffed to the gills with baseball memorabilia—old caps, uniforms, bats, and even postcards of the hotels we stayed in on the road. In an e-mail inviting me to visit him in Ontario, Canada, Shifty wrote:

All you have to do is come in my basement, where I write now, and our pro pictures are all around you, and in the corner are four of my bats with GEAR in block letters. . . . I think baseball and the experiences we had together built our character for our later lives. . . . I am still playing ball today against 25 year olds. I don't want to grow up, baseball brings back my youth even though I'm 67 years old. So I never get away from the past. . . . Take it easy for now, Shifty.

20. Bob Gear, photograph taken for his 2008 induction into the St. Catharines Sports Hall of Fame in Ontario, Canada. Photo courtesy of Bill Potrecz.

While a handful, like Shifty and Jack Fitzpatrick, still play baseball in senior leagues, most have turned to golf and play it frequently and well. The hand-eye coordination and skills developed in baseball carry over. Golf is also an arena where old ballplayers can satisfy their competitive juices and feel good about themselves.

I was fascinated by what teammates had done with their lives. I knew beforehand that Jim Leyland managed the Detroit Tigers, that Gene Lamont was his bench coach, and that Dave Bike was the basketball coach at Sacred Heart University. But I had no idea about the others: Dennis Grossini an administrator in the federal prison system, Jon Warden teaching high school and then returning to baseball as a humorist and top draw on MLB's lecture circuit, Larry Calton reaching the big time in both MLB and the NBA as a sports color commentator, Les Cain a Laundromat entrepreneur, Jack Fitzpatrick a psychoanalyst and consultant, Shifty Gear an overseer in a paper factory, Frank Pignataro a vice president for State Farm Insurance, and Polak, Norm Angelini, Rudy Burson, Dick Drago, Bob Felber, and George Korince all salesmen of one type or another (see the appendix).

While most had done well, I was a bit surprised that teammates who had enjoyed Major League careers had not led more glamorous lives after baseball. But then, given the relatively small salaries paid to Major Leaguers in the sixties and early seventies, most didn't have the funds to set themselves up in lucrative businesses, or make investments, as is typical among today's big leaguers. But after interviewing Jim Leyland and Gene Lamont and recounting their colorful baseball lives to my anthropologist wife, Sharon, she suggested that I title my memoir "Minor Leaguer: A Minor Life." She was only half joking. But learning more about the postbaseball careers of my other teammates, including those with more than a few years in the Majors, gave me a greater appreciation for the life and career that anthropology and academia have provided me. But if you were to ask me if I would trade all that for a career in the big leagues, I would be hard-pressed to answer. I'd be tempted. Leyland hinted that he would swap all his big-league managerial success for a single season as a big-league player. At least being an anthropologist gave me the opportunity to spend time with big-league teams and get a taste of what that life would have been.

The sad aspect of my research was learning of teammates who had died young, some of them quite young: "Harvard Bob" Welz, forty, of a heart attack; Tom Hamm, forty-five, hit by a cement truck while jogging on vacation in Florida; George Kalafatis, fifty, of a stroke; Norm McRae, fifty-five, of cancer; and my close friend Danny Frisella, thirty-one, in an Arizona dune-buggy accident. They reminded me of how unpredictable life is and made me thankful that I've made it this far.

Audrey, in an e-mail from New Zealand, where she has lived and worked as an artist since the 1980s, asked me what I had learned about myself from mining my baseball past and reconnecting with her and my teammates. As she put it, "How does the new image of you differ from the authorized version that you held before undertaking your project?" She suggested there might be many revelations because in repressing my baseball past for so many decades, I had never examined that period of my life. Indeed, I learned a lot. One question I began to ask in my interviews with teammates at the end of our conversations was what they remembered of me and what kind of person I had been way back then. It was usually easy for them to answer because we hadn't seen each other in the intervening years, and therefore they had no new memories or shared experiences that might cloud the distant past. Most described me as being "different" from the norm, particularly an intense curiosity about things. Several remembered me jotting notes to myself. Margie Emmons (Felber's Daytona Beach girlfriend) said, "You always looked at things from a different perspective. For you baseball wasn't everything; it wasn't all that mattered." "You were always looking for a new adventure," said Arkansan Shelby Morton. I also discovered that I had been a better ballplayer than I remembered.

But not all was so upbeat. The biggest downer was the discovery of how reckless and lacking in judgment I had been and for which I had paid dearly in being released. What was I thinking in posting the phony team rosters in Tiger Town and sending a fake telegram to Nick Ross about his fiancée dumping him?! Worse were shooting out the streetlights in Drummondville and writing the newspaper article linking the Rocky Mount police chief with the Ku Klux Klan. At first glance the latter may seem a righteous deed, but given the small readership of my hometown newspaper my article would have no real benefit. Such behavior stemmed from immaturity and a failure to grasp the possible consequences of my actions. Reading my journals after so many years sometimes made me cringe with embarrassment over things I had done or said, such as telling my manager Gail Henley that if given the opportunity, I would abandon the Minor Leagues to play in Japan. I wondered why my mother, who read portions of my journal during my playing days, never cautioned me. My parents generally took a laissez-faire approach to child rearing.

After I gave a baseball talk in 2001 celebrating the centennial of Minor League Baseball at the Smithsonian's Museum of American History, their sports history curator asked if I would donate my journals to the museum's archive, saying it was rare for ballplayers to have kept one. My first reaction was, "Sure, I'd be honored to have my writings at the Smithsonian." Later, though, after rereading my journals and seeing how juvenile my actions often were, I changed my mind.

Falling in love with girls who were early feminists and also had little regard for baseball, and then allowing myself to be influenced by their critiques, I think, also reflected this lack of judgment, at least in terms of my baseball acumen and prospects. Only one girlfriend, Monique in Drummondville, really enjoyed coming to the ballpark and watching me play (although that might have been in anticipation of postgame entertainment). Ironically, my pursuit of these young women, all of whom were quite pretty, was likely related to the excessive emphasis I, like my teammates, placed on physical attractiveness.

I found plenty of evidence in my journals of being impatient, such as expecting immediate success on the ball field, and when it didn't happen doubting that I had the ability to go far in baseball. After my first days in Duluth, and taking a few o'fers, for example, I concluded that I didn't have a future in baseball. And when mired in a slump, I often began thinking about alternative careers. It may be that I was never confident that I had the tools to make it to the big leagues, or maybe it was just immaturity.

An epiphany for me during the research was that I had not squandered my youth trying to become a big leaguer. I always suspected that I would have been better off finishing my education without delay. But reconnecting with old teammates, it was easy to see that the experiences and skills we acquired in pro ball carried over into new careers and lives. We learned what career counselors call *transferable skills*. Traveling half the season and being at the ballpark for eight hours every day with a diverse bunch of guys fostered "people skills." As Shelby Morton said to me, "You're together so much, you had to learn to get along." Interacting with Latino teammates, I got to expand on the Spanish that I learned in college classrooms, and by playing in Quebec for two seasons—and dating Monique, who spoke little English—I learned French. Well, sort of.

What is more important, baseball taught us how to deal with failure—hitless nights, slumps, losing streaks, subpar seasons, injuries, and demotions. In everyday life, whether academic or business, people rarely deal with the level of failure so commonplace in pro ball. Most hitters fail three out of every four times at bat. Championship teams typically lose one-third of their games. We learned from baseball that one game doesn't mean much; what counts is what happens over the long haul, over the course of the season. Baseball taught us how to deal with pressure, and it required concentration and focus. We learned discipline and that you have to work hard to survive, to stay in the lineup, and hopefully to move up to the next level.

Finally, I rediscovered the greatness of baseball and why as a youth I had worshipped it. By the end of my research I came to believe that my four years in pro ball had actually been good preparation for the academic career I later pursued, and for life generally. While the journey back occasionally became personal, it was an understanding of the life and culture of baseball that I was after, and that has become a permanent interest. I now teach a course on the anthropology of sport in which baseball is a component, and every now and then I request a media credential and go back to the ballpark to talk to players to keep up with how things are changing.

During a spring-training game at Hi Corbett Field in Tucson, I had a chance encounter with Gail Henley, my manager in Jamestown and Daytona. I saw him sitting in the wooden grandstand, a dozen rows up from home plate, and went up to him and said, "Hello, Gail Henley! Do you remember who I am?" He looked up, squinting in the sun, and said, "Yeah, you were my first baseman." It took him longer to remember the name. We sat together during the game, eating hot dogs and reminiscing about old times. I confessed that I concocted the phony telegram to Nick Ross about his engagement being off and that the water balloon that hit the pedestrian below the Miami Colonial Hotel was dropped from my room. I asked Gail what kind of a ballplayer he remembered me as. I was taken aback when he gave me a detailed scouting report of all five tools: "Pretty good power, average arm, not a bad glove, a bit slow afoot . . ." In a later conversation I asked him how he had been able to do that. His reply was something like, "When you watch your players night after night and are always writing reports to the front office on them, you don't forget what tools they have and don't have."

At the end of the game, just before we were about to part, I blurted out the big question that had nagged at me all these years: Had I been a real prospect? Could I have made it to the big leagues had I not screwed up in Rocky Mount? Gail hesitated before answering. "No," he said softly, "you were good, but you weren't the complete package. You were probably lucky to get out of baseball when you did and finish school." I felt a pang, disbelief, and some defensiveness. I wanted to say, "But Gail, what about my being awarded a Louisville Slugger bat contract and signing a Spalding shoe and glove contract? Weren't they only for prospects? And what about the big numbers I put up in Daytona and your telling me that if I kept it up, I might even be a September call-up?" But I didn't. There was no reason to argue. Later I felt an odd sense of relief. Gail's assessment put an end to my fantasies about the profession I had lost. Still, I would love to turn back the clock and do it all over again, knowing what I know today.

APPENDIX

What They Did after Baseball

Norm Angelini signed with the Kansas City Royals after the 1968 season in Drummondville. He spent parts of 1972 and 1973 with the big club as a reliever, posting a 2.70 ERA, and then nine seasons pitching in Triple A, the last four with the Denver Bears in the Pacific Coast League. He settled in Denver and has worked there ever since in sales for Sysco and Keebler Cookies.

Audrey (a pseudonym) earned a PhD in anthropology and taught at a large American university before dropping out and moving to New Zealand in the 1980s, where she is an accomplished artist, teaches yoga, and is an avid walker and kayaker. She and her husband live off the grid in a remote area. "I am lucky to live in a country like New Zealand where God is nature, and everyone loves the out of doors. We'd all be happier if we could spend two hours alone in a wild place every day," wrote Audrey in an e-mail.

Dave Bike left baseball after his eighth season in the Tigers' farm system—having reached Triple A—to accept a basketball coaching job at Seattle University. He recently retired, after his thirty-sixth season as the head coach of Sacred Heart University, in his hometown of Bridgeport, Connecticut. He led his team to a Division II national championship in 1986 and was inducted into the New England Basketball Hall of Fame in 2003.

Rudy Burson's baseball career ended after an automobile accident in which he was hit at a stoplight by a drunk driver. After baseball Rudy worked in sales for thirty-two years, first for a steel company, then a concrete pipe company, and finally a heavy equipment dealer. Now retired, he lives in Fort Wayne, Indiana, where he enjoys watching baseball, fishing, and cycling.

Les Cain was called up to the Tigers in 1968. He was in Detroit's rotation off and on for four seasons until injured when being forced to pitch with a sore arm by his manager, Billy Martin. It caused permanent damage and ended his career. Les sued the Tigers, and in the first-ever workmen's compensation victory for a professional baseball player, the organization was ordered to pay Les $111 a month for the rest of his life. He returned to the Bay Area, where he opened a Laundromat, worked in a bank, and drove a bus.

Larry Calton was released by the Tigers organization in 1969 and then signed with the Pirates and briefly played for their AA club before being let go again. He went into radio and TV broadcasting, eventually becoming the play-by-play announcer for the Minnesota Twins and later radio and TV play-by-play for the NBA San Antonio Spurs. Over the years he hosted sports talk shows in Los Angeles, San Francisco, Cleveland, and Kentucky before moving back home to the Missouri Ozarks. Mostly retired, he now plays golf and broadcasts the AA Springfield Cardinals home games and college football and basketball.

Claire (a pseudonym), after struggling to make it as an artist in Greenwich Village and missing life in the countryside, packed all her belongings into two steamer trunks and returned home to western New York. There she married, settled on a large farm, had three children, and lost her husband to cancer. Now remarried, she and her partner raise free-range cattle on a four-hundred-acre farm in New York.

Bernie DeViveiros died in 1994 at the age of ninety-three after working in professional baseball most of his life, including nineteen years as a player—a big-league shortstop for the Chicago White Sox in 1924 and Detroit Tigers in 1927—and twenty-five years as a scout and instructor. He taught sliding, bunting, and infield technique at every level from kids to the Majors. A strong and vocal advocate of the bent-leg slide, he would say, "[Over the years] I have saved five hundred thousand broken legs."

Dick Drago had a thirteen-year career in the big leagues with the Royals, Red Sox, Angels, Orioles, and Mariners. After retiring he worked in sales and marketing before starting an all-natural pest-control business (for fleas) and then, after selling that business, started another, recycling toner cartridges for laser printers. Now living in Tampa, Florida, he still does Red Sox fantasy camps and charity events for the MLB Players Alumni Association.

Al Federoff managed in the Minor Leagues for nine years before leaving baseball in 1969 to start a photography business in Detroit. Al retired to Gilbert, Arizona, where he died in 2011 at age eighty-seven, just a few months after the death of his wife.

Bob Felber retired in 1968 after being spiked in the hand and struck on the elbow by a pitch. Three years later he tried to come back as a pitcher, "but after a few weeks in spring training I packed it in . . . My curveball was flat, didn't have much movement on my fastball, and I was now twenty-four." He returned home to Baltimore, took up fast-pitch softball, and went to work for Brooks Robinson Sporting Goods. He later switched to Shasta Beverages, where he became vice president of sales. Like so many former players, he is an avid golfer.

Jack Fitzpatrick, after earning a PhD in history at the University of California, Berkeley, worked as a psychoanalyst for the Menninger Foundation and later, with his wife, Anne, founded the Family Business Resource Center in Topeka, Kansas. Now seventy-one, he still plays baseball in several over-thirty leagues.

Bob Gear was released by the Tigers in 1968 and then briefly caught on with the Minnesota Twins organization. After being released again, he signed with the Los Angeles Wildcats in the short-lived Global Baseball League and later played for Drummondville in the QPL. Out of professional baseball at twenty-four, he went to work for Domtar Fine Papers in St. Catharines, Ontario, and began playing for local teams, which he still does at age sixty-eight. About Shifty's passion for the game, his wife, Carol, said, "You have to understand that baseball is something deep, deep inside him. He loves it beyond anything else. When we got engaged, he refused to consider a summer wedding or honeymoon because he didn't want to miss any games." Today Shifty golfs five days a week and travels to Buffalo, New York, to play baseball in a serious over-thirty league, where his new nickname is "Gearso." "Every year," said Shifty, "I say this will be my last as a player, but then when spring arrives I can't resist getting back out there."

Bob Gilhooley, after being released from the AAA Iowa Cubs in 1970, became a lawyer and then a widely respected agent for SFX Sports Group, whose clients included Pedro Martinez, Larry Walker, and Vladimir Guerrero. In the 1990s he was named one of the top-twenty-five power brokers in baseball by *Baseball America.*

Sharon Bohn Gmelch earned her PhD in anthropology at UCSB and is currently professor of anthropology at the University of San Francisco and Roger Thayer Stone Professor of Anthropology at Union College. She is the author of eight books. After holding out for forty years, she finally became a baseball fan when her hometown San Francisco Giants won the World Series in 2010 and then again in 2012 and 2014.

Dennis Grossini, a sixth-round pick and bonus baby in the 1965 draft, never recovered from an arm injury and shoulder surgery during his second season. Released in 1969, he never pitched another inning of baseball, finished at age twenty-four. He earned a master's degree in education and became a schoolteacher in a medium-security federal prison. Dennis worked for the Federal Bureau of Prisons for twenty-six years, retiring as an associate warden at age fifty-one. In retirement he fills his time with cycling, skiing, running marathons, and golf. Looking back on his baseball career, he says, "Even though it was full of disappointments—all stemming from my injury— having been an athlete has always set me above others as I was considered for positions or promotion [in the Federal Bureau of Prisons]. How I wish I could do it all over again without the arm problems."

Tom Hamm was let go by the Tigers in 1967 after putting up good numbers in Statesville. He graduated from Georgetown University. Around 1995 Tom was hit and killed by a cement truck in Florida while out jogging on vacation.

Gail Henley worked in pro ball for sixty-two years, including one season (1954) playing center field for the Pittsburgh Pirates. He spent twelve years managing in the Minors and then forty years scouting for the Dodgers and the Devil Rays, not retiring until age eighty-two. He lives in La Verne, California. Two of his sons, Dan and Bill, played in the Minor Leagues. About his playing career he wrote in an e-mail, "We all think that maybe we could have taken a better path, but I consider myself fortunate to have stayed in baseball for sixty-two years. I enjoyed the life, but if I were to do it over again, I would be nicer to the people who made the decisions in the early part of my playing career."

Chuck Hughes died of a heart attack at age forty-five. After the Québec Provincial League folded in 1970, Chuck stayed on in Drummondville for ten years, coaching baseball and conducting clinics. His son, Chuck Hughes III, is a celebrity chef and television personality in Montréal.

Rich Jefferies taught middle school and was an assistant baseball coach at Serra High School, in San Mateo, California, until retirement. His son Gregg had a fourteen-year Major League career.

Jerry Klein worked in the Tigers organization as one of its all-time most colorful clubbies until he died of a heart attack in 1973. At the first-ever Detroit Tiger's "Family Reunion" in 2013, many former players told Jerry Klein stories, like the time he was told to pick up general manager Jim Campbell at the Tampa airport. It was raining hard when Jerry arrived, and Campbell, struggling with three bags, got soaked. When he finally got into the car, he said, "Jerry, why the hell didn't you get out and help me?" Jerry replied matter-of-factly, in his usual gruff way, "No point in both of us getting wet."

George Korince, after spending parts of two seasons with the Tigers before his twenty-first birthday, was out of baseball in 1970 at age twenty-six. He returned to his native Ontario, where he worked for an industrial cleaning firm, and then General Motors until he retired. He is now living in Fort Myers, Florida.

Gene Lamont, Detroit's first-round pick in the 1965 amateur draft, was called up to the Tigers in 1970 and hit a home run in his first at bat. Gene stuck around for five years as a backup catcher with a lifetime batting average of .233. After nine years managing in the Minor Leagues in the Kansas City Royals organization, he became the third base coach for the 1986 Pirates, managed by his former teammate Jim Leyland. He later became the manager of the Chicago White Sox (1992–95) and the Pittsburgh Pirates (1997–2000). He is currently bench coach for the Detroit Tigers. He lives in Sarasota, Florida, in the off-season.

Jim Leyland, after six seasons as a Minor League catcher, never hitting higher than .241, became a manager in the Tigers' farm system. In 1982 Chicago White Sox manager Tony LaRussa hired Jim as his third base coach; a few years later Leyland became the manager of the Pittsburgh Pirates, where he won three straight division titles. He led the Florida Marlins to a World Series championship in 1997 and took the Detroit Tigers to the World Series in 2006 and 2012. He has won the Manager of the Year Award in both the National and the American Leagues. Considered one of the best managers in baseball, he retired at the end of the 2013 season. He once said that he'd have given up all his managerial successes for one year as an everyday player in the big leagues.

Norm McRae was twenty-two years old when he was called up to the Detroit Tigers in September 1969. He stuck with the big club in 1970 but then was traded to the Washington Senators, where he played for two more seasons. After his release from Washington, Norm pitched ten years in the Mexican League for the Chihuahua Goldens, once pitching a sixteen-inning complete game. He later became a coach for Los Dorados, another Mexican League team, where he married the daughter of the team owner. Norm died in 2003 from cancer at age fifty-five.

Shelby Morton, a hard thrower and possessing one of the best curveballs around, saw his playing career end in 1968 after an off-season construction accident. After baseball he became an industrial engineering manager for Monro Shocks, retiring in 2003. He now lives in Paragould, Arkansas, and works with handicapped adults. He likes to remember that as a teenager, he never lost a game over a three-year span in Pony and Colt Leagues.

John Noce, after the QPL folded in 1970, managed in the professional Italian Baseball League and was the assistant coach for the Italian national team in three Olympics (1984, '92, and '96). He was the head baseball coach at the College of San Mateo for thirty years, retiring in 1992, and soon after was elected to the American Baseball Coaches Hall of Fame. He conducted baseball clinics in Holland, Romania, Austria, and Lithuania for MLBi. Three of his boys worked in pro ball, two as players (Paul Noce played for the Chicago Cubs) and one as a coach. Now eighty-one, Noce lives in Aptos, California, and still travels to Italy to consult for the Nettuno baseball club.

Steve Oleschuk became a scout after the QPL folded in 1970. He has scouted for the Pirates, Diamondbacks, Padres, and Angels and now lives in Montreal.

Julio Perez, a .240 career hitter, was released in his second season and settled in Buffalo rather than return to Cuba.

Frank Pignataro, after his rookie season in the QPL, married, returned to college, and became a teacher and baseball coach and soon a school principal. Disgruntled over the policies of a new school superintendent, Pig left education to work as a State Farm Insurance agent in Fairfield, California, rising through the ranks to become a vice president. Now retired, he divides his time between Fairfield and Truckee, California, and plays golf.

Jim Ridley taught physical education at a Toronto, Ontario, high school until he died from lung cancer in his midfifties.

Carl Solarek quit the Tigers organization in 1970 after having reached Double A. "I was married and had two boys and had given myself five years to make it to the big leagues. Many times I look back and think, 'What if? What if I had played just one more year? What if?'" After baseball Carl worked as a sales manager for two Philadelphia breweries and coached baseball at Alvernia University, where his son was a Division II All-American. Carl took up major fast-pitch softball and within a few years was selected to play for the U.S. national team. He was inducted into the National Softball Hall of Fame in 2010. Now retired, he lives in Leesport, Pennsylvania.

Norm Timmins, after Drummondville, served as a platoon commander in the Marine Corps during the Vietnam War. He later earned accounting and law degrees at the University of North Dakota. Today he is a financial adviser with Wells Fargo and lives in San Diego, California.

Jon Warden spent the 1968 season with the World Series champion Detroit Tigers, ending with a 4–1 record. He was just twenty-one. After the season Hook was selected in the expansion draft by the Kansas City Royals; in his first spring training with the Royals he injured his shoulder (torn rotator cuff) and never fully recovered after it was treated with cortisone shots and drugs that merely masked the pain. He would never pitch in the big leagues again. Once out of baseball Hook worked in sporting goods, finished college with a degree in education, and became a high school teacher and baseball coach. He has been a regular at the Tigers Fantasy Camp, where he dons the robe and performs the duties of a judge in a kangaroo court. His popularity among the campers elevated him to becoming a regular at the Hall of Fame

Fantasy Camp in Cooperstown, New York. Warden also stays busy with speaking engagements through the MLB Alumni Association. He relishes the opportunity it gives him to see old teammates.

Bob Welz quit in the middle of the 1969 season in Rocky Mount, packing his belongings and driving off in a huff in the middle of the night after a heated argument with Al Federoff in which Welz accused the Detroit Tigers of wooing away young players from college and baseball scholarships with the promise of professional baseball and then releasing most of them a year or two later, ruining their lives. Welz returned to Boston, never married, and worked in the liquor business until he died of a heart attack around age forty.

NOTES

INTRODUCTION

1. The *Burlingame (CA) Advance-Star.*

1. AMBITION FOR THE GAME

1. The West Coast, where a favorable climate enabled a much longer playing season, was actually better known for producing position players.

2. BREAKING IN

1. All quotations from my journal and letters are italicized.
2. When the park reopened in 1966, the game would be played on Astroturf, a newly invented plastic carpet laid directly on a concrete base. It would enrage purists, but owners would never have to worry about rainouts.

3. WEARING KALINE'S PANTS

1. In 1997 the stadium was renamed Russell Diethrick Park, after our general manager.
2. By 2013 the league had doubled in size to twelve teams, with clubs in five additional states, from Maryland to Vermont.
3. The Auburn electric chair was invented by a dentist who had watched a drunk man accidentally shock himself to death in 1881.
4. The Doubleday story was fabricated by Albert Spalding and the 1905 Mills Commission, which sought to convince the American public that baseball, unlike the English game of cricket that was challenging baseball's popularity, was uniquely American.

5. Despite this, Auburn's current New York–Penn League team is called the Doubledays, proving that old myths die hard, especially when they still have marketing value. Besides, some American baseball fans still believe Abner Doubleday invented the game, including former MLB commissioner Bud Selig. In response, the *New York Times* said that the idea of Doubleday inventing baseball had been "so thoroughly debunked" that it ranked as one of the "great American myths, alongside George Washington's cherry tree, Paul Bunyan and Johnny Appleseed" (http://latimesblogs.latimes.com/sports_blog/2011/03/bud-selig-baseball-abner-doubleday.html).

4. A LITTLE WILDNESS

1. Promotions became increasingly common in Minor League parks in the 1960s as owners tried to counteract declining attendance.
2. In the 1980s the inglorious feat of striking out four times in a game became known as the "golden sombrero," that is, a "hat trick" plus one.

5. SPRING TRAINING

1. On the Atlantic coast were the Orioles (Miami), Yankees (Fort Lauderdale), Senators (Pompano Beach), Braves (West Palm), Dodgers (Vero Beach), and Astros (Cocoa Beach). Inland in central Florida were the Twins (Orlando), Red Sox (Winter Haven), and Tigers (Lakeland). And on the Gulf Coast were the Reds (Tampa), Cardinals (St. Petersburg), and Mets (St. Petersburg).
2. This heritage was commemorated by Detroit's Lakeland team in the Florida State League changing its name from the Tigers to the Flying Tigers.
3. Down the coast at Vero Beach the Dodgers would take over an abandoned naval air station and convert it into their training facility—Dodgertown.
4. When I returned to Tiger Town in 2012, I discovered that the two entrance roads to the stadium had been named after two Tiger outfielders, Willie Horton (Horton Way) and Al Kaline (Kaline Drive), who were my contemporaries at Tiger Town. The clubhouse had been named after our clubbie, George Popovich, whose son Paul later played for the Chicago Cubs.
5. Short-sheeting is remaking and folding the top sheet in half so that when the victim gets in, he is trapped in the fold, unable to extend his legs.

8. DOUBLE PASSAGE

1. That was eclipsed twenty years later by Rickey Henderson's 130 steals.

9. SOUTHERN EXPOSURE

1. With the Rocky Mount Leafs in the Eastern Division were the Wilson Tobs, Tidewater (Portsmouth) Tides, Raleigh Pirates, Kinston Eagles, and Peninsula Grays; the Western division comprised the Durham Bulls, Asheville Tourists, Winston-Salem Red Sox, Greensboro Yankees, Burlington Senators, and Lynchburg White Sox.

2. There are no records for how many times it's been done in the Minor Leagues.

10. WHEN THE CHEERING STOPS

1. Of all the clubs in the Carolina League, Peninsula had the most players, fifteen (38 percent), who would make it to the big leagues. The average for the league as a whole was 24 percent. Rocky Mount had just six players, or 15 percent. The Tigers' Double A Montgomery Rebels, the next level above Rocky Mount, saw 57 percent of their players make it, and at the Triple A level—the Toledo Mud Hens—80 percent of the players would make it or already had big-league experience.

2. See George Gmelch, "Raised by Tigers: As Autumn Settles on the Boys of Summer an Anthropologist Touches Base," *Natural History* (September 2013): 15–19.

11. EXILED

1. The average number of strikeouts per team per game in the Major Leagues in the period 1960-69 was 5.70, compared to 7.5 for the 2013 season. Also contributing to the higher number of strikeouts is that hitters today are more likely to look for a particular pitch and not swing when they don't get it. Therefore, they more often go deep in the count, making them more vulnerable to striking out.

2. Drummondville's most famous athlete-ballplayer, however, was hockey player Maurice "the Rocket" Richard, one of the best National Hockey League players ever. Like several other NHL players, Richard played baseball in the Provincial League during the off-season, just as some cricketers in Australia turned to baseball in their off-season as a way to stay in shape. Richard was just an average outfielder for Drummondville, whereas during his eighteen seasons with the Montréal Canadiens (1942-60) he played for eight Stanley Cup championships and was the all-time scorer in the NHL until Gordie Howe eclipsed his mark.

3. Power's black skin and Latin heritage delayed his being called up to the New York Yankees, the team that had signed him in 1951. Even after he put up huge numbers in the AAA American Association (hitting .331 in 1952 and .349 the following year), the Yankees did not invite him to spring training. Yankee owners felt his exuberant playing style and personality weren't suited to the conservative image they wanted in their first black player on the team. The Yankees buried Power in the Minor League for several seasons before trading him to the Philadelphia Athletics.

4. George Gmelch, *Behind the Smile: The Working Lives of Caribbean Tourism* (Bloomington: Indiana University Press, 2003), 129.

5. Sports sociologists refer to these actions as "normative cheating."

6. It may be that "rule bending" in baseball traces deep to American roots, a time that was less bound by hardened strictures.

7. See M. Kavussanu, "Morality in Sport," in *Social Psychology in Sport*, edited by S. Jowett and D. Lavallee (Champaign IL: Human Kinetics, 2007), 265–77.

8. In a weird twist of fate, years later I would leave Montreal and McGill University in part because of changes in Quebec, and on campus, brought on by the proindependence separatist movement. At the time (mid-1970s) many English-speaking workers in Montreal also departed, with most migrating to Ontario. A demagogic English Canadian media played a role by propagating fear of the "evil" separatists.

9. Playing in Quebec and then the anticipation of going to Cuba had piqued an interest in seeing how baseball was played in other places, which decades later would lead me to edit a book on the international pastime called *Baseball without Borders: The International Pastime* (Lincoln: University of Nebraska Press, 2006).

12. LIGHTS OUT

1. Today they mostly pitch on the outside part of the plate because they grew up pitching to hitters swinging aluminum bats whose large sweet spot makes it easier to hit a pitch on the fists.

2. The following season (1969), Noce removed him from right field in the middle of an inning after Hector misplayed a base hit and didn't run hard to track it down. Noce had him traded to the Granby Cardinals for Shifty Gear. With Granby, Hector wound up among the league leaders in batting average, while Shifty hit just .235 for Drummondville. Despite losing a good

bat, Noce never regretted his decision, saying, "I'd rather have a team where everyone plays hard."

3. One night when a drunken fan came onto the field to protest a bad call, the plate umpire retaliated by hitting the trespasser over the head with his mask, knocking him flat.

4. Merritt Clifton, *Disorganized Baseball*, vol. 1, *The Quebec Provincial League* (Richford VT: Samisdat Press, 1982).

5. I was one of a dozen students on a National Science Foundation–funded field-training program. Each of us lived in a different village while doing full-time field research.

6. George Gmelch, "Baseball Magic," *Transactions* 8, no. 8 (1971): 39–43.

EPILOGUE

1. Psychologists call this improved recall of specific episodes or information when the subject returns to the place or scene "environmental context-dependent memory."

2. See Gmelch, "Raised by Tigers."